David Foster Wallace

Fiction and Form

# David Foster Wallace

## Fiction and Form

David Hering

Bloomsbury Academic
An imprint of Bloomsbury Publishing Inc

B L O O M S B U R Y
NEW YORK • LONDON • OXFORD • NEW DELHI • SYDNEY

**Bloomsbury Academic**
An imprint of Bloomsbury Publishing Inc

| | |
|---|---|
| 1385 Broadway | 50 Bedford Square |
| New York | London |
| NY 10018 | WC1B 3DP |
| USA | UK |

www.bloomsbury.com

**BLOOMSBURY and the Diana logo are trademarks of Bloomsbury Publishing Plc**

First published 2016

© David Hering, 2016

All rights reserved. No part of this publication may be reproduced or transmitted in any form or by any means, electronic or mechanical, including photocopying, recording, or any information storage or retrieval system, without prior permission in writing from the publishers.

No responsibility for loss caused to any individual or organization acting on or refraining from action as a result of the material in this publication can be accepted by Bloomsbury or the author.

**Library of Congress Cataloging-in-Publication Data**
Names: Hering, David, author.
Title: David Foster Wallace : fiction and form / David Hering.
Description: New York : Bloomsbury Academic, 2016. |
Includes bibliographical references and index.
Identifiers: LCCN 2016009041 (print) | LCCN 2016019858 (ebook) |
ISBN 9781628920550 (hardback) | ISBN 9781628920581 (ePDF) |
ISBN 9781628920574 (ePub)
Subjects: LCSH: Wallace, David Foster–Criticism and interpretation. |
Wallace, David Foster–Technique. | BISAC: LITERARY CRITICISM /
American / General.
Classification: LCC PS3573.A425635 Z695 2016 (print) |
LCC PS3573.A425635 (ebook) | DDC 813/.54–dc23
LC record available at https://lccn.loc.gov/2016009041

ISBN: HB: 978-1-6289-2055-0
ePub: 978-1-6289-2057-4
ePDF: 978-1-6289-2058-1

Cover design: Daniel Benneworth-Gray

Typeset by Integra Software Service Pvt. Ltd.

*For Jill and Ian Hering*

# Contents

| | |
|---|---|
| Acknowledgements | viii |
| Introduction | 1 |
| 1 Vocality: 'A Flickering Hand, Dead and Cold': Reading Wallace's Ghosts | 15 |
| 2 Spatiality: 'In the Middle of the Middle of Nowhere': Regionalism and Institutions | 41 |
| 3 Visuality: 'Seeing by Mirror-Light': Wallace on Reflection | 79 |
| 4 Finality: 'Not Even Close to Complete': The Many Forms of *The Pale King* | 123 |
| Notes | 163 |
| Works Cited | 185 |
| Index | 199 |

# Acknowledgements

This book is the result of several years of research, revision and conversation, and I want to take this opportunity to thank the organizations and individuals who have helped to make this monograph what it is. The archive research that is such an important component of this book was made possible by the award of four academic bursaries: a 2013–2014 Harry Ransom Centre Research Fellowship in the Humanities (Andrew W. Mellon Foundation Research Fellowship Endowment), a research grant from the British Association of American Studies and, from the University of Liverpool, a Price Memorial Scholarship and bursary from the Research Development Initiative Fund. I want to offer my thanks to Paul Baines, Ian Bell, Tom Staley and Marcus Walsh for their support in regard to this funding. I would also like to thank D.T. Max for his support of my candidacy for the Harry Ransom Centre Fellowship and for several invaluable discussions over the chronology of Wallace's drafts. The reproduction of the archive materials within this book was made possible by the generosity of the David Foster Wallace Literary Trust and the Harry Ransom Centre.

David Seed, Nick Davis and Brian Jarvis offered some very useful advice about this project when it was in its nascent stages, and I am grateful to them for that. Certain elements of the second chapter of this book were workshopped as part of the inaugural Post45 UK symposium at University of Notre Dame, London in June 2015 and I thank all participants for their generous insight and feedback. In particular I would like to thank Amy Hungerford, Merve Emre and Jak Peake for their comments on the terminology and structure of the chapter. The other chapters of this book were road-tested in various forms at a number of conferences and symposia, most notably the Infinite Wallace conference at the Sorbonne-Nouvelle and École Normale Supérieure in Paris in September 2014, the second annual David Foster Wallace conference at Illinois State University in May 2015 and the conference on Wallace's short fiction at the University of Bristol in July 2015. At these events and others I was able to participate in an ongoing and constructive dialogue with many other scholars of Wallace and contemporary literature, and this sharpened and improved a number of aspects of this book. In particular I would like to thank Marshall Boswell, Stephen Burn, Greg Carlisle, Ralph Clare, Clare Hayes-Brady, Mary Holland, JT Jackson, Lee Konstantinou, Dave Laird, Bill Lattanzi, Nick Maniatis, Pia Masiero, Tony McMahon, Mike Miley, Josh Roiland and Tom Tracey for their advice and conversation during this time. I offer my thanks to Steven Moore for his generosity in discussing Wallace's various drafts of *Infinite Jest* and for sharing his apparently limitless knowledge of literature old and new during the composition of the book. I also want to thank my departmental colleagues at Liverpool, particularly Matthew Bradley, Alex Broadhead, Lucienne Loh, Greg Lynall, Sandeep Parmar and Will Slocombe, for their ever-illuminating conversations about literature and the essential ability to have a good laugh, and long-time fellow travellers William Corner, David Franklin, Jonathan Hall, Paul Hagan, Richard Hughes, Louis Johnson, Jamie Navarro and Paul Yates for the companionship and for our endless discussions on creativity, politics, structure and form in literature, music, cinema and seemingly everything else.

I want to specifically thank two individuals for their sustained support and companionship during the book's gestation. Matt Bucher offered endless advice and information pertaining to Wallace and contemporary fiction in general during my visits to the United States and latterly via email. I have had countless enjoyable and enlightening conversations with him during the writing of this book, and I look forward to many more. Adam Kelly read substantial sections of this book and offered both friendly conversation and rigorous scholarly advice, and I am in no doubt that the book is better for his input. We have had an ongoing conversation about Wallace's work and the value of contemporary fiction that is now entering its seventh year, and long may it continue.

Haaris Naqvi and Mary Al-Sayed at Bloomsbury offered friendly and immensely useful advice on the manuscript and editing process throughout composition, and I am very grateful to them for guiding me through the process with ease and good humour. Relatedly, I would also like to thank the anonymous peer-reviewers who gave invaluable feedback on the proposal and manuscript and helped me to think about certain structural questions I had not previously considered.

Finally, I must offer thanks to those people without whom, for multiple reasons, this book would not exist. To my parents, Jill Hering and the late Ian Hering, to whom this book is dedicated, who made me realize what I could achieve and in so many ways continue to inspire me to learn and understand. To my brother, Jonathan Hering, with whom I have had so many wonderful conversations about making and understanding art and whose dedication to his own art is endlessly inspiring. And finally to Claire, whose love, kindness and support makes anything and everything possible; I cannot thank her enough.

# Introduction

## The Situation of Wallace Studies

In the second decade of the twenty-first century, critical discussion of the writing of David Foster Wallace has reached an extraordinary level of suffusion. We are experiencing a period of sustained critical fecundity: three international academic conferences took place in 2015 alone, with at least three monographs released in 2016 alongside the continuing publication of numerous essays and articles on Wallace across academic journals, newspapers and online periodicals. This is the latest stage in a substantial diffusion of criticism that has attended Wallace's writing since his death in 2008. During his life, the foundational works of Wallace scholarship were fairly limited in number.[1] After Wallace's suicide, critique of his work expanded dramatically, with the following seven-year period seeing the publication of seven edited collections and numerous scholarly articles, as well as Wallace's incorporation into a number of large-scale studies of contemporary fiction and culture.[2] Outside the academy, large-scale social media events such as 2009's *Infinite Summer*, an online reading group dedicated to *Infinite Jest*, increased the visibility and readership of Wallace's most celebrated and daunting work, and pointed to the ongoing importance of an online community of readers to public visibility of Wallace's writing.[3]

Earlier foundational scholars such as Marshall Boswell, Stephen J. Burn and Tom LeClair necessarily make the case for Wallace's canonicity as part of their criticism, stressing the importance of intertextual and theoretically inflected readings of the fiction and locating his work under the sign of modernism and postmodernism.[4] Adam Kelly characterizes this wave of scholarship as 'reaching its peak' in 2009 ('Death'), suggesting that the study of Wallace is now diverging, 'reaching a point of critical mass at which it should no longer be necessary to argue for Wallace's place in the literary canon by attempting to encapsulate his various ideas with reference to a single key text or set of unchanging principles' (Kelly, 'Novel' 4).[5] Accordingly, the edited collections *Consider David Foster Wallace* (2010), *The Legacy of David Foster Wallace* (2012), *A Companion to David Foster Wallace Studies* (2013) and *David Foster Wallace and the Long Thing* (2014) contain essays that alternate between single-text analysis and more diverse appraisals of Wallace's cultural engagement, while the publication of *Fate, Time and Language* (2010), *Gesturing Toward Reality* (2014) and *Freedom and the Self* (2015), which perform philosophically inflected readings of the fiction and non-fiction, take as read the understanding that Wallace's writing is a worthy object of interdisciplinary academic study.[6] In a further development, Philip Coleman's *Critical Insights: David Foster Wallace* (2015) and Stephen J. Burn and Mary Holland's forthcoming *Approaches to Teaching the Works of David Foster Wallace* provide a pedagogical context for the work, focusing on the process of teaching Wallace in the classroom. The publication of D.T. Max's biography *Every Love Story Is a Ghost Story* in 2012 and the appearance of characters based on Wallace in a number of contemporary novels (Jeffrey Eugenides' *The Marriage Plot*, Richard Powers' *Generosity*, Jonathan Lethem's *Chronic City* and Jonathan Franzen's *Freedom*) have also led to the presence of a new iteration: Wallace as textual subject.[7] Relatedly, 2015 sees the release of James Ponsoldt's film *The End of the Tour*, which dramatizes David Lipsky's *Rolling Stone* interview with Wallace from 1996 and, significantly, affords audiences the opportunity to engage with Wallace as public persona without reading his work.

In keeping with Kelly's contention that the period after 2009 sees a more ethically inflected response to the writing ('Death'), a number of critiques of Wallace's own political position have also started to appear in recent years. After the revelation in Max's biography that Wallace voted for Reagan and Ross Perot (Max 259), and following Wallace's admission in 2006 that he is a 'fairly traditional, conservative kind of writer' ('Interview with Ostap Karmodi'), critics remarked on areas of conservatism in his writing, incorporating analysis of Wallace's essay on John McCain and his valorization of the federal institution in his final, unfinished novel *The Pale King*.[8] However, while this bears out Kelly's speculation that the post-2009 wave of Wallace scholarship will be characterized by a focus on 'Wallace's literary ethics' and a related 'growing awareness that Wallace's non-fiction need not simply be read in the shadow of his fiction' ('Death'), I would argue that academic analysis of Wallace criticism after 2010 must also take into account another factor: the availability of Wallace's papers to the general public in the Harry Ransom Centre at the University of Texas in Austin, an occasion of serious importance to the analysis in this book.

If the period 2009–2015 is largely characterized by the edited collection, 2016 sees the emergence of the second wave of single-author Wallace monographs, led by Clare Hayes-Brady's *The Unspeakable Failures of David Foster Wallace*, Adam S. Miller's *The Gospel According to David Foster Wallace* and this book. The first two monographs, unreleased at time of writing, respectively address philosophical processes of communication and prayer as response to boredom and distraction in Wallace's writing. The questions that must attend the publication phase of these monographs, including this one, should necessarily concern the purpose and value of the long-form study in the wake of the numerous preceding career-spanning edited collections and the first wave of monographs.

## Fiction and Form: A Monograph and its Purpose

My answer to this enquiry, as regards this book, is twofold. Firstly, to address in essay form the extraordinary narrative density of Wallace's fiction across his career necessarily requires a certain circumscription of example. A monograph allows something different; a degree of granularity in analysis that is of serious value to an evaluation of Wallace's extensively detailed, often encyclopaedic narratives. Secondly, I believe that the monograph form is the most appropriate mode in which to substantially address the extraordinary body of work to be found in Wallace's archive of drafts, letters and personal library of books. As the recent proliferation of references in conference papers and certain journal articles suggests, the sheer amount and quality of material in the archive is of serious import to Wallace scholars worldwide, and should essentially be considered, in its volume and complexity, as another 'text' in itself. To comprehensively address and catalogue the developing form of the fiction, from manuscript to publication, requires the kind of scope that a monograph affords.

Accordingly, the following chapters analyse and describe a history of key formal and structural motifs that are of sustained importance to Wallace's fiction. In each of the first three chapters I take a significant formal motif that recurs across the whole body of the work and perform a chronological process of twinned close and contextual analysis that tracks the development of this motif across the fiction from the early works to *The Pale King*, which novel's unfinished structure is the basis of the fourth and final chapter. When tracking these motifs I read the archive material alongside the published novels and collections, mapping an intertwined formal process: a palimpsest compositional history of the fiction read alongside and against the work in its final, published form. The dividends of this analysis are significant, as this process affords us an unprecedented twinned 'depth' and 'breadth': the most complete close analysis of Wallace's composition yet, with an imbricated discussion of certain specific critical and cultural contexts that inform and shape his formal methodology.

## Chapters and Contexts

The analysis of Wallace's fiction in this book is structured around four substantial chapters grouped under the headings 'Vocality', 'Spatiality', 'Visuality' and 'Finality', the latter referring to the unfinished state of Wallace's third novel *The Pale King*. I have elected to use this long-form chapter structure because, like the monograph form itself, it affords a particular degree of analysis. While a shorter, article-length chapter can explore a particular facet of the work, the long chapter format affords me the opportunity to read the formal motif through the entire body of fiction with a strong level of detail. With this analytical scope, I can trace formal developments in Wallace's work at both macro- and micro-level, drawing out accordance and conflict in form, and construct a map of the fiction as a developing system.

In Chapter 1, 'Vocality', I analyse the structural position of the narrating voice in Wallace's fiction. I begin with this chapter because it provides a useful overture to the analysis in the rest of the book, and initiates discussion of the questions of dialogism and authorial presence that will also appear in subsequent chapters. I read Wallace's interest with ghostly voices and malignant 'possession' as a formal dramatization of his anxiety over the post-structural effacement of the author on the authorial voice. I argue that while this post-Barthesian anxiety is initially twinned with a desire to perform a Bloomian *misprision* of his literary forebears, it gradually torques into a formal process of *self*-refinement that is represented by the developing materiality of Wallace's own vexed authorial presence in his fiction. Finally, I read this doubled formal anxiety over voice as implemented within a broader, career-length investment in transference from monologic to dialogic narrative. This focus upon monologism and dialogism underpins much of the analysis in the subsequent chapters.

In Chapter 2, 'Spatiality', I analyse Wallace's formal approach to landscape and architecture and the increasingly convoluted and recursive formal 'shapes' that underpin his fiction narratives. I read this pervasive spatial preoccupation within the context of region (specifically the region of the Midwest, with which Wallace has a problematic and, I argue, 'performative' relationship) and with matters of 'institutionality'. In mapping Wallace's deeply ambivalent spatial response to institutionality, which was of course a matter of serious significance for a writer who spent much of his life either learning or teaching in educational institutions, I read the fiction as expressing an increasing anxiety over the alternately dialogic, symbiotic and parasitic relationship between the region and the institution. I argue that this anxiety is informed by both Wallace's unstable regional identity and his implication within what Mark McGurl has called the 'Program Era', suggesting that while in many ways his fiction is an exemplary product of a culture of institutionalized literary production, Wallace also expresses his anxiety over this inheritance through a structural dramatization of spatial encroachment and entrapment.

In Chapter 3, 'Visuality', I propose that a comprehensive and coherent formal model of visuality in Wallace's fiction can be described by reading the work under the broader sign of 'reflection'. I argue that this model should be read not only in reference to Wallace's much-analysed critique of television but also to other modes of visual art, namely painting and cinema. I suggest that to read the televisual and the cinematic as equivalent entities is a mistake, and that Wallace's response to televisual culture is not predicated on the same formal basis as his engagement with cinema. I frame my reading of Wallace's career-long engagement with visual art and reflection within the formal model of *mise-en-abyme*, which appears repeatedly as a motif in the fiction and offers an invaluable way in which to read Wallace's anxiety over matters of self-reflexivity and the attendant dangers of narcissism. Finally, I suggest that out of these models of reflection Wallace attempts to stage a dialogic process of *refraction*, enacted here as a moment of transfiguration and 'seeing-through' of the reflective surface and engaging with the reader outside the text.

Finally, I devote the whole of Chapter 4 to an analysis of the problematic form of Wallace's third, unfinished novel *The Pale King*. This chapter is divided into two sections. In the first, I create a chronological map of the novel's composition with extensive recourse to Wallace's drafts in order to fully understand how its form develops and changes over the decade-long period of its composition. I argue that through reading the drafts closely, and by dividing the novel's form into three distinct compositional periods, we can achieve a more comprehensive understanding of *The Pale King*'s relationship to those works of Wallace's fiction that both precede it and are composed alongside, and sometimes as part of, this novel. This mapping of the novel's composition allows me to conduct a precise and extensive analysis of how *The Pale King* responds to the aforementioned contexts of vocality, spatiality and visuality: this analysis makes up the second half of this final chapter.

While the prevailing focus of these chapters is the fiction, it would be imprecise to ignore the relationship between Wallace's novels and short stories and the extensive amount of non-fiction he produced during his career. As the book progresses, I read Wallace's non-fiction persona as increasingly implemented across his career within his formal struggles over voice, regional and institutional identity, and visual perception. When appropriate, I draw from relevant pieces of non-fiction to provide a broader picture of the increasingly problematically intertwined personae of fiction writer and non-fiction essayist.

## Monologism and Dialogism

As indicated above, I believe that many of Wallace's formal motifs across the fiction are underpinned by a recurrent oscillation between narrative models of monologism and dialogism. Mikhail Bakhtin famously defines dialogism as 'the characteristic epistemological mode of a world dominated by heteroglossia', whereby 'everything means, is understood, as a part of a greater whole – there is a constant interaction between meanings, all of which have the potential of conditioning others'. The dialogic imperative seeks to ensure that no one is 'deluded into thinking there is one language' (*Dialogic* 246).[9] The implementation of this imperative is most immediately apparent in Wallace's sustained use of dialogue in his fiction. Kelly has offered a useful model of how sequences of dialogue across the three novels can be understood within an increasingly dialogic and sociopolitically inclined framework, arguing that Wallace 'utilized the novel as what Bakhtin would call a heteroglossic space in which those discourses could productively collide' (Kelly, 'Novel' 17). Kelly concludes that 'there is no bottom line in Wallace's novels, no master discourse' (17). However, while I broadly concur with Kelly's developmental model, I simultaneously read monologism and dialogism in Wallace's fiction as occurring within an ongoing process of oscillation that is based around the continual risk of a master discourse engendered by the degree of Wallace's authorial presence. In this sense, the model I describe in Wallace's fiction is both dialogic and *dialectic*, as it continually presupposes a greater degree of dialogical engagement towards some (crucially undefined) future communicative end.

While Wallace's work becomes more explicitly politically engaged throughout his career, I believe that the risk of monologism in his fiction is not tied to the totalitarian meta-language of a prevailing political authority to the same degree as Bakhtin's analysis, which was of course responding in part to the matter of totalitarianism. Instead, Wallace's monologic bête noir is *self*-consciousness: the risk of a monologic master discourse is generated primarily by his own presence. To this end, I read the oscillation between monologism and dialogism in Wallace's fiction as a continual modification and clarification of the mode of authorial presence, an ongoing attempt to establish an author persona that interacts dialogically with the text. This process is threatened by Wallace's increasing fame, and his emergence into the public sphere as a writer with a particular and idiosyncratic register. As the unitary persona 'David Foster Wallace' becomes ever more defined, and with it the implicit collapsing together of author and style, the possibility of the monologic text increases. Wallace associated this problematic persona with the immobilized figure of 'the statue' (Max 240). I argue that Wallace's response is to dramatize the emergence of his public persona as part of the restless oscillation between monologism and dialogism in his fiction, but that this response brings its own self-reflexive problems, specifically in the convoluted and paralytic amalgamation of Wallace-personae in *The Pale King*.

This process of monologic-dialogic oscillation is not only dramatized in degrees of direct authorial visibility in the text. It also occurs, as I will demonstrate in the second, third and fourth chapters of this book, at the level of spatial and visual form. In these chapters, I argue that Wallace makes increasing recourse to spatial models of centripetal and centrifugal motion to dramatize the oscillation between monologic and dialogic tendencies: in this way, the work resembles Bakhtin's heteroglossic model, defined as 'as close a conceptualization as is possible of that locus where centripetal and centrifugal forces collide' (Bakhtin, *Dialogic* 428).[10,11]

## Reading Wallace Genetically: The Archival Turn

In 2009, the Harry Ransom Centre at the University of Texas in Austin acquired Wallace's papers and library, which became available for public reading in September 2010. The archive, which is substantial, contains drafts of all Wallace's fiction and non-fiction and is described by Molly Schwartzburg, then Cline Curator of Literature at the centre, as having a 'consistently high' research value (Schwartzburg 247). I visited the archive twice for the purposes of this project, and during these visits I read all the archival manuscripts and letters pertaining to Wallace's fiction, as well as some relevant non-fiction drafts and the marginal notations in a substantial number of books in Wallace's personal library. Thanks to the attentive curatorial work of the archivists at the centre, the papers are relatively 'tidy', but the content itself is extremely dense and Wallace's handwriting frequently borders on illegible. As a result, the archive contains much information about the formal development of Wallace's fiction that is essentially hidden in plain sight. For example, a handwritten manuscript page that appears identical to the published version will contain short deleted sentences and miniscule notes that provide a key to understanding the relationship between the draft and the final text. Similarly, an apparently throwaway note in the margins of one of Wallace's books might actually describe the structure of an essay or short story, even if the content of the story is irrelevant to the content of the book.

It is therefore unsurprising that there has been substantial interest in the archive from scholars of Wallace and contemporary literature, and Schwartzburg notes in 2012 that interest in Wallace's papers outstripped any other topic on the centre's website (243). This interest has resulted in what might be referred to as an 'archival turn' in Wallace studies, as a significant number of conference papers and journal articles now cite material from the archive. This was perhaps at its most pronounced in the 'Infinite Wallace' conference in Paris in September 2014, when it was suggested that this recourse to the archival materials might now be considered an authentic new 'wave' of Wallace scholarship.[12] When archive material is used, as it is substantially in the book to follow, I think that it is important to ask two corresponding questions: what is its value to our understanding of Wallace, and what is its relevance to the research project at hand? Before beginning the analysis proper, I want to answer these questions with recourse to the history and terminology of 'genetic criticism'.

In her analysis of the archive, Schwartzburg makes the following observation about the polyvocal nature of Wallace's drafts:

> A large percentage of the papers show Wallace composing texts he expected to become public in some form, while many of the library's annotations appear to have been intended only for Wallace himself. But even within these more 'private' texts, Wallace was in conversation – sometimes with the book he was reading and sometimes with an earlier version of himself. (256)

It is precisely this dialogic and developmental sense of composition that underpins my analysis in the chapters to follow. Wallace's drafts are extraordinarily 'noisy', incorporating regular paratextual metacommentary upon their own compositional processes and bearing out Wallace's admission in 1999 that 'I am a Five Draft man' ('Interview with Stacy Schmeidel'). During composition, Wallace was also in frequent contact with friends, fellow writers and publishers about his work, as borne out by the large collection of correspondence that is also held in the archive, and to which I make substantial reference in this book. Furthermore, the historical development of the drafts is generally easy to trace, as Wallace frequently dates even the most minor handwritten pieces of paper (in the more confusing papers for *The Pale King*, the slack is taken up by the records of floppy disks, which helpfully have a record of 'date created' and 'last date modified'). This chronological detail allows the close reader to plot the emergence of what Paul Bowman refers to as the 'foretext'; the 'documentary mass [...] transcribed, selected, and arranged in such a way that it can be of use for criticism' (634), and in the case of the pre-*The Pale King* fiction in particular the foretext emerges from the 'documentary mass' via this dialogic process of self-criticism and amendment.[13]

I read this dialogic dimension of Wallace's composition as a kind of shadow process of the formal emphasis upon dialogism in the fiction itself. For this study, then, much of the value of the archive material lies in constructing a narrative of how earlier forms or registers are tried, rejected and torqued throughout Wallace's career. This methodology creates a genetic 'map' of Wallace's composition. Furthermore, the process of revision *itself* is heavily implemented within the contexts of authorial presence and institutionality I describe above. Hannah Sullivan reads the presence of the extensively revised text as indicative of modernist inheritance:

> [A]ssociation of revision and literary value is the legacy of high modernism and the print culture that nourished it. Modernist writers revised overtly, passionately, and at many points in the lifespan of their texts. They used revision, an action that implies retrospection, not for stylistic tidying-up but to *make it new* through large-scale transformations of length, structure, perspective, and genre. (2, emphasis original)

While Wallace is obviously not a high modernist, Sullivan suggests that the association of revision with value lives on in the institutional context of a younger generation:

> In the second half of the twentieth century, as modernism was institutionalized and writers became college professors, passionate correction began to seem not abnormal or excessive, but a *necessary* precondition of good writing. (238, emphasis original)

The result is a generation who 'began *ab ovo* to flag up or advertise their own practice of postcompositional change' (240). Sullivan aligns this directly with the 'program era', citing the emphasis placed by Mark McGurl on 'the value of craft as represented by the practice of multiple revision' (*Program* 244): it is worth noting that Wallace describes his five-draft process as emerging as a response to essay deadlines at Amherst College ('Interview with Stacy Schmeidel'). I am interested in how this process of revision as precondition of good writing is formally enacted within the development of the fiction itself. For example, my analysis of 'Westward the Course of Empire Takes Its Way' continually returns to the matter of the degree to which compositional process and authorial presence is revealed or hidden. I read this through an imbricated analysis of an early draft of the story, where Wallace's metafictional battle with John Barth was less disguised, and the published version of the story where Wallace more subtly masks his anxiety of influence. This combinatory analysis of the evolving foretext and the text itself affords a view of Wallace's fiction which analyses both the compositional evolution of his form and his connected responses, both overt and covert, to his literary and cultural inheritance.

The matter of the archive material that pertains to *The Pale King* is obviously different, as problems of composition overshadow the publication itself. Essentially, the foretext is also the text, so we do not have a final 'clean' text against which to compare and track Wallace's compositional process. My response to this problem is to move towards a clarification of *The Pale King*'s history by creating a map of the novel's composition from its inception proper in 1997 to its abandonment in 2007. I believe that this is particularly important as it obviates a critical tendency to read the drafts of the novel as a general mass from which to pick and choose associated points of narrative interest. While this can occasionally be illuminating, it can also be inexact: the danger of this method is that several elements of the novel's drafts can be aligned without an understanding of their order of emergence, which can lead to analysis based in a kind of creative conjecture rather than an understanding of how the form of the novel develops historically.[14] I outline in Chapter 4 how, through reading all the materials that pertain to the novel, the composition of *The Pale King* can be subdivided broadly into three stages: 1997–2001, 2001–2005 and 2005–2007. By creating this history of the novel's progress, I am able to not only analyse the development of Wallace's drafts while minimizing risk of inexactitude, but also untangle the notoriously convoluted compositional relationship between *The Pale King* and the two short story collections that emerged during its composition, *Brief Interviews with Hideous Men* and *Oblivion*. Furthermore, through this isolation of distinct periods of the novel's composition, I propose that we are better placed to understand how the major elements of the text, in particular the increasingly problematic presence of 'David Wallace' as character or narrator, relate developmentally to Wallace's earlier formal approaches to the cultural contexts I describe in Chapters 1–3.

It is, of course, germane to mention here the potential problems of intentionalism that attend genetic criticism. Bowman puts it succinctly when he describes the danger of allowing critical agenda to shape a reading of the materials:

There are some disarmingly honest suggestions that the foretext must be selected and shaped by the critical intent of the analyst, and this is surely true, but it could reduce genetic criticism to the forensic function of providing persuasive evidence and documentation, unless the critic is endowed with a courageous degree of open-mindedness […] there is a real risk of a kind of 'dunking-for-apples' approach to the whole procedure, a reader's intuition is tested, perhaps contested, more often confirmed, by dragging up evidence from the scriptural corpus, and the foretext is defined in terms of how apt it is to perform those desired functions. (634)

In response to this important caveat I would argue that by creating a genetic chronology of the entire body of Wallace's fiction, rather than one or two discrete works, and by making use of dialogic marginalia and letters to publishers and fellow writers to understand how Wallace conversed with himself and others during the drafting process, I can avoid making any overly untoward assumptions or leaps of critical faith in my analysis. Moreover, the cultural contexts to which I analyse Wallace's response in this book are in a sense always already overtly manifest in the work. Therefore, I do not have to perform an overly speculative analysis to draw out matters of anxiety over authorial presence, or ambivalence over the role of the institution. Ultimately, then, through the mapping and analysis of Wallace's fiction, we can detect a series of structural dialogues continually taking place: between the draft and the published text, between Wallace, his authorial personae and his contemporaries, and between the text and its reader. In the analysis to come, I will demonstrate how those dialogic structures, which carry the possibilities of both communication and monologism, are fundamental to an understanding of the form of Wallace's fiction.

1

# Vocality

## 'A Flickering Hand, Dead and Cold': Reading Wallace's Ghosts

David Foster Wallace, establishing the importance of 'mediated data' to his writing, explains that his use of form is intended to disrupt the reader's 'passive spectation', reminding the reader that 'this process is a relationship between the writer's consciousness and her own'. He argues that 'this might be my best response to [the] claim that my stuff's not "realistic" […] the classical Realist form is soothing, familiar and anaesthetic; it drops us right into spectation' ('Interview with Larry McCaffery' 33–4). In this instance, Wallace is referring to distortion of linearity and perspective, and by extension the reader's awareness of the presence of the 'writer's consciousness', but this disavowal of realism also extends beyond structural disruption and into jarring non-realist occurrences at the level of story. These eruptions range from the bodily (the gargantuan Norman Bombardini in *The Broom of the System*, Tom Sternberg's inward-facing eye in 'Westward the Course of Empire Takes Its Way', the levitating Shane Drinion in *The Pale King*) to the geographical (*Broom*'s Great Ohio Desert, the hyper-real endless Midwest of 'Westward', *Infinite Jest*'s Great Concavity/Convexity). However, both the structural foregrounding of the 'writer's consciousness' and the non-realist story event are synthesized through another formal motif developed by Wallace across his fiction: the figure of the ghost.

To read the function of the multifaceted ghost-figures in Wallace's fiction is to participate in an often problematic developmental relationship between writer and reader that operates in terms of what Wallace refers to, in conversation with McCaffery, as 'a living transaction between humans' (41). The synthesis of the supernatural and narrative self-reflexivity is, of course, not peculiar to contemporary literature. Terry Castle's argument, respecting certain iterations of modernist literature, that '[we have come] increasingly to believe, as if through a kind of epistemological recoil, in the spectral nature of our own thoughts – to figure imaginative activity itself, paradoxically, as a kind of ghost-seeing' (29) and Yeats' belief that ghosts 'have bodies as plastic as their minds that flow so readily into the mould of ours' ('Swedenborg' 35) remind us of the importance of this synthesis to late Victorian and modernist literatures. However, the epistemological modernist association of the dead and the creative imagination, which was informed in part by the pseudo-scientism of the séance and spirit mediumship of the era,[1] can also be read as a precursor to postmodern ontological preoccupations with the pastiche of pre-existing 'dead' styles and the resurrection of 'used-upness' (Barth, *Friday* 64) as a replenishment of literature.[2] In his engagement with postmodern enquiries, Wallace's fiction retains the motif of the ghostly 'apparition' as a way of explicitly disrupting narrative authority.

Wallace, who wrote his first major works in the 1980s, was continually faced with the ramifications of theoretical discourse upon the form of the novel itself. The question of authorial effacement haunted the academic environments within which Wallace thrived, as the integration of post-structuralist theory into academy syllabi, most famously Roland Barthes' seminal '"The Death of the Author"', interrogated the ontology of the author's presence in the text. In his 1988 essay 'Fictional Futures and the Conspicuously Young', Wallace claims that 'the climate for the "next" generation of American writers [...] is aswirl with what seems like long-overdue appreciation for the weird achievements of such aliens as [...] Barthes', arguing that 'the idea that literary language is any kind of neutral medium for the transfer [...] from artist to audience [...] has been cast into rich and serious question' (*Both* 63–4).

Four years later, Wallace makes a more vexed pronouncement on the post-Barthesian author figure in a 1992 review of H.L. Hix's *Morte D'Author*, glossing the post-structuralist effacement of the author as an attack on 'a post-Platonic prejudice in favour of presence over absence and speech over writing' (*Supposedly* 140) before offering a tantalizingly brief rebuttal in the final lines of the review on behalf of 'those of us civilians who know in our gut that writing is an act of communication between one human being and another' (144). In this implicit alignment with 'civilians', Wallace seeks, perhaps disingenuously, to position himself outside the 'ghastly jargon' (144) of the academy. In this sense, he belongs to the generation identified by Judith Ryan as 'troubled by the implications of theory for contemporary life' (208), but it is clear that he remains familiar with and influenced by the question of authorial effacement. The following year, he concedes to Larry McCaffery that 'once I'm done with the thing, I'm basically dead, and probably the text's dead; it becomes simply language, and language lives not just in but "through" the reader' (40).[3]

I believe that this oscillatory position is continually dramatized within Wallace's fiction through a fixation on the author's dialogic relationship with the reader, which is enacted through dramatized instances of 'possession' and ghostliness that implicitly refer to the absence or presence of the dead, among whom can be found the 'spectral' figure of the author. In staging this dramatization, Wallace practises what Benjamin Widiss describes as 'a continual rehearsal of Barthes' claims, but never an affirmation of them' (5). Widiss argues that the critical assumption of the steady effacement of authorial presence that developed as a response to modernism, an assumption that finds its apotheosis in Barthes' essay, is inaccurate, suggesting that 'only the most radically chance-driven works... prove so eager to shed all authorial design' (6). Widiss reads Barthes' author/scriptor binary as a false dichotomy, desiring instead to more subtly 'read the troping of a pervasive textual praxis of solicitation when it is not represented as explicit importuning' (17). Wallace's fiction, I would suggest, practises this implicit 'solicitation' but diverges from Widiss' rejection of post-structural authorial effacement in its recognition of Barthes' essay as a necessary moment of importance in literary history.

In Wallace's fiction, authorial presence is often implicitly amplified as a way of commenting upon its effacement, with specific recourse to motifs of vocality and dialogue. This is staged by Wallace through a reification of Barthes' question 'Who is speaking thus?' (*Image Music Text* 142), his fiction populated with multiple and competing indiscernible voices which originate from powerful absent and often ghostly figures. Over time, Wallace imbricates these presences with increasingly visible iterations of the revenant author figure, and an attendant focus on the importance of *dialogue* with both character and reader. I read this as a process of developing materiality, with Wallace performing a vexed dramatization of Barthes' claims before obtaining a situation in the later fiction whereby the 'revenant' author, who has undergone his theoretical 'death', returns as a modified, and sometimes explicitly curatorial, textual presence. I do not read the revenant author as a direct 'revival' of the pre-Barthesian author figure, but rather a 'ghostly' return of the dead author, one aware of his existential contingency upon readerly presence and interpretation and committed to a dialogic engagement with those readers.[4]

As part of this process, I read Wallace as entering into a connected dialogue with two further models of authorial anxiety: Harold Bloom's ghostly inflected model of *apophrades* and Mikhail Bakhtin's concept of dialogism and polyphony. *Apophrades*, whereby 'the mighty dead return, but they return in our colours, and speaking in our voices, at least in part, at least in moments, moments that testify to our persistence, and not to their own' is a form of misprision whereby the 'very strongest' poets achieve 'a style that captures and oddly retains priority over their precursors, so that the tyranny of time almost is overturned, and one can believe, for startled moments, that they are being *imitated by their ancestors*' (Bloom 141, emphasis original). However, as Charles Harris has acutely argued, 'the strong precursors Wallace was driven to overtake [also] include himself' (120), and I believe this is borne out by the steadily increased presence of an implied author figure across Wallace's fiction.[5]

This presence is also implemented in accordance with an understanding of dialogism as described by Mikhail Bakhtin, who is name-checked by Wallace in 'Fictional Futures' in the same list in which he includes Barthes. Marshall Boswell reads Wallace's approach to the death of the author directly via the *Morte D'Author* review, in which Wallace praises the way that Hix 'amends Derrida by way of Wittgenstein' (Boswell, *Understanding* 171). While I agree that this can be a useful approach to the early fiction, I believe that reading Wallace in relation to Bakhtin provides a sustained career-length model by which to map the problems of authorial monologism staged by the motifs of possession and ghostliness in the fiction. In his famous analysis of Dostoevsky's polyphonic method, Bakhtin analyses the manner in which the 'monologic plane of the novel' is destroyed by the character as 'fully autonomous carrier of his own individual world' (Bakhtin, *Problems* 5). Bakhtin praises Dostoevsky's narratives as 'a whole formed by the interaction of several consciousnesses, none of which entirely becomes an object for the other' (18), resulting in 'free people, capable of standing *alongside* their creator' (6, emphasis original). In concluding this chapter, I argue that Bakhtin's concept of polyphony and dialogism offers an important model through which to read Wallace's spectral response to the effacement, and possible return, of the author figure.

## Tracing Possession, Ghosts and Materiality in the Fiction

The narrative of Wallace's debut *The Broom of the System* does not make explicit recourse to the supernatural, but the novel retains a preoccupation with uncanny occurrences and the prescriptive authority of unseen forces. *Broom*'s plot is driven by the disappearance of a linchpin family figure: Lenore Beadsman's great-grandmother, also named Lenore, whose whereabouts are not conclusively addressed, but who exerts control over events from her unknown hiding place. The linguistic influence of 'Gramma', a student of Wittgenstein, on Lenore manifests as extreme ontological uncertainty, evidenced by her conversation with psychiatrist Dr Jay:

> Suppose Gramma tells me really convincingly that all that really exists of my life is what can be said about it? [...] that there's nothing going on with me that isn't either told or tellable, and if so, what's the difference, why live at all? (*Broom* 119)

Lenore's appeal is complicated by the fact that Dr Jay himself is under the control of Gramma, his apparently disinterested responses informed by the same authority that has initiated Lenore's existential crisis. The novel is littered with numerous minor examples of narrative or linguistic possession connected to Gramma's absent influence. For example, Lenore's lover Rick Vigorous is open about his desire to control her, explicitly stating, 'I am possessive. I want to own her, sometimes' (72). Rick's possessiveness, however, is inflected by Gramma's disappearance: he knows that his controlling nature 'does not sit well with a girl thoroughly frightened of the possibility that she does not own herself' (72). Rick's desire to possess Lenore subsequently manifests itself covertly and metafictionally in his own pseudonymous short stories (191). Furthermore, the sudden 'parroting' vocal articulacy of Lenore's cockatiel Vlad the Impaler, which is interpreted by Reverend Sykes as 'the voice of the Lord' (275), is actually due to his ingestion of the pineal supplement partially masterminded by Gramma (148–9). Gramma, the earliest iteration of a figure I will term the 'absent possessor', is also a site of generational anxiety, as it is possible to locate behind Gramma the presence of another absent possessor: Wittgenstein himself, whose influence on Wallace's writing was profound.[6] However, despite Gramma's substantial level of narrative control, her own voice does not directly appear in the novel.

A number of stories in Wallace's first short story collection *Girl with Curious Hair* develop the motifs of possession from his first novel. This process involves a deliberate transposition of the 'parroting' found in the plot of *Broom* to the narrative registers of the stories themselves. *Girl with Curious Hair* can usefully, if a little reductively, be read as Wallace's parroting of the register of several preceding and contemporary writers. Wallace imitates and parodies the narratives of Bret Easton Ellis ('Girl with Curious Hair'), Robert Coover ('Lyndon'), William Gass ('John Billy'), Philip Roth ('Say Never') and finally John Barth ('Westward the Course of Empire Takes Its Way').[7] While this technique can come across as more than a little obnoxious (Wallace himself later referred to it rather dismissively as 'formal stunt-pilotry' ['Interview with Larry McCaffery' 25]), the sequence of stories describe a slow convergence whereby the implicit mimicry of existing authorial styles builds towards a climactic 'breaking out' of the implied author in the death-of-metafiction fable 'Westward the Course of

Empire Takes Its Way.' This concluding story, operating as an 'Armageddon explosion' for the form, engenders a new approach to authorial presence in Wallace's writing (41). It is therefore possible to see *Girl with Curious Hair* as an iteration of Bloom's *apophrades* whereby Wallace deliberately tries to force his predecessors (as well as his contemporaries) to speak in his own voice: a methodology more aggressive than Bloom's 'holding open' of the work to the predecessor, and nakedly, deliberately artificial in its mimicry.

If Wallace's register throughout the collection often acts as a kind of low-level 'possession' of certain contemporary writers, the leitmotifs of ontological anxiety from *The Broom of the System* appear in a rather more restless and explicitly metafictional form. In 'Here and There', Bruce, who wants to be the 'first really great poet of technology' (*Girl* 155), articulates the basis of his anxiety about his identity thus:

> I begin to feel as though my thoughts and voice here are in some way the creative products of something outside of me, not in my control, and yet that this shaping, determining influence outside me is still me. I feel a division which the outside voice posits as the labor pain of a nascent emotional conscience. I am invested with an urge to 'write it all out', to confront the past and present as a community of signs, but this requires a special distance I seem to have left behind. For a few days I exercise instead […] my aunt is happy; she says I look healthy. I take the cotton bud out of my ear. (*Girl* 165–6)

This is an important passage, as it refers back to the kind of control anxiety experienced by Lenore but couches it in terms more explicitly concerned with writing. Indeed, the pointed addition of certain lines about 'fiction therapy' during the drafting of 'Here and There' (Box 1.1, Bonnie Nadell) suggests that Wallace wanted to further foreground an association between the sense of being externally controlled or possessed, and the question of 'writing out' as a possible solution, albeit one that is temporarily superseded by an un-self-conscious activity like exercise. Notably, the possessive force here is identified directly with the self ('still me'), rather than an external character, suggesting an immobilizing alignment of the possessor and the possessed. Accordingly, the story ends with Bruce paralysed with self-doubt while fixing a stove.

While 'Here and There' ends with a line that describes tentative resolve and acceptance ('Then welcome' [172]), Wallace's original ending to the story is somewhat different:

> 'Which brings things to a close, then'
> 'So to speak'. (Box 15.1)[8]

The final line here can be read alternately as in dialogue with the one that precedes it or as a monologic non-sequiter whereby Bruce prepares to articulate himself regardless of the 'close' of the story, and that the paralysing conversation with himself will continue despite the attempts of others to resolve his anxious predicament. The revised and published version of 'Here and There' suggests that the anxiety felt by Bruce can only be met by an unconditional act of dialogic communication (a 'welcome'), and that by affording another the final word Bruce's authority is subsumed into a dialogical narrative. If the original ending recalls the verge-of-annunciation climax of *Broom* ('I'm a man of my' [*Broom* 467]), the published version suggests that an acceptance of the authority of another's voice can resolve anxiety about loss of control to others.

However, the implication that one must subsume one's own voice within a larger dialogue in order to ameliorate anxiety remains ambiguously phrased here, oscillating between the possibility of a harmonious amalgamation of voices or subjugation to a larger narrative authority and loss of one's voice, which Bruce fears. Elsewhere in the collection this oscillation results in a less harmonious outcome. While Bruce's agitated episode is bookended by him inserting and removing a cotton bud from his ear, Edilyn, the female protagonist of 'My Appearance' wears an unpleasantly organic-sounding 'pork-colored earplug' (*Girl* 185) for the duration of her appearance on David Letterman's talk show in order to receive instructions from backstage on how to answer the host's questions. The possessing figure is dramatized here explicitly albeit in a consensual framework, with Edilyn agreeing to have her husband Rudy and his friend Ron guide her performance on the show. While Edilyn's ad-libs to Letterman represent a degree of autonomy from her husband's instructions, after the show her ear feels 'violated' by the plug (198) and her ironic and delusional suggestion that 'I am a woman who speaks her mind' (201) leads to an implied marital split with Rudy. While it is possible to see the breakdown of Edilyn's marriage as a moment of emancipation (her disentangling of her husband's voice from her own resulting in a more substantial kind of separation), her belief that the break with Rudy was a 'mistake' (201) suggests that autonomy was not her objective.

The dramatization of the surrender of one's personality and voice to another is substantially developed in 'Westward the Course of Empire Takes Its Way', as illustrated in the following passage, where the narrator relays protagonist Mark Nechtr's anxieties about his emotions:

> […] it's like he's denied access to them. He doesn't ever feel in possession of his emotions […] Except when he shoots, he very rarely feels anything at all. (*Girl* 303)

Mark's anxieties involve a loss of possession of the modes of expression, a loss partially resolvable through the performance of an action ('he shoots'). The rough equivocation of 'writing out' in 'Here and There' and 'shooting' (implicitly equated with writing) in 'Westward' locates the regaining of one's own expression in a metafictional action – the writing of the self. However, Mark's narrative is apparently 'written out' on the page by another, heterodiegetic narrator, an unnamed member of his creative writing workshop. If Mark's mode of expression seems, then, to actually be directed by an absent possessor, the climactic retelling of Mark's own short story further contests the site of narration and ownership of the narrative, making the positions of both character and narrator unclear (264). This is achieved via some deliberately ambiguous metaleptic shifts in narration: when towards the end of 'Westward' the mysterious narrator begins to relate Mark's own metafictional story, a story Mark feels is 'not his own' (355), the register becomes extremely uneven, moving between a third-person retelling of the content (356) and context of Mark's story, and an apparently unmediated telling of the story itself (363), which relates a power struggle between a jailed 'archer, named Dave' (356) and his violent and apparently omniscient counterfeiter cellmate 'whose name is Mark' (361).

This convoluted amalgamation of character, implied author and narrator is substantially more complex than the possessor–possessee relationship in *Broom*, confounding the more simplistic directional flow of preceding depictions of possession or lack of autonomy in Wallace's fiction. For the first time, it also makes the process suggestive of the presence of Wallace himself ('Dave') in the text. 'Westward' itself is, of course, Wallace's explicit rewriting of *another* metafictional story, John Barth's 'Lost in the Funhouse'. Mark Nechtr's name recalls the title of Barth's story 'Ambrose his Mark', while the MFA teacher, a stand-in for Barth himself, is named Ambrose. The mysterious Magda, who may or may not be (or may simultaneously be *and* not be) Ambrose in disguise is named after the object of young Ambrose's desire in 'Lost in the Funhouse'. This subversive rewriting of a story by Wallace's 'patriarch for my patricide' ('Interview with Larry McCaffery' 48) associates the dramatization of loss of voice, or possession by an unseen force, with the anxiety of influence. Here the process of anxiety is transfigured, via the story's funhouse-like hall of mirrors, into a multivalent process where possessor figures (Barth, Mark the counterfeiter, Wallace's implied presence) form an amalgamated chain of possession and counter-possession whereby each appears to infect or influence the other's narrative position. While Wallace's first name is invoked, and his authorial presence thus implied, it is deferred within a system whereby the narrative is not pervasively, palpably controlled by any single agent. While Boswell reads 'Westward' as Wallace enacting a *clinamen* of Barth's story (*Understanding* 103), I believe that the amalgamated chain of influence, counter-influence and metafictional mimicry described above ultimately brings the climax of the story closer to a multidirectional parodic form of *apophrades*.[9] Accordingly, while it may be tempting to assign 'Westward's final monologue to Wallace's own voice breaking through and speaking directly to the reader, it would be more accurate to say that it is delivered in the first person by a narrator of uncertain diegetic status, an unidentified composite voice engendered by the preceding 'Armageddon-explosion' ('Interview with Larry McCaffery' 41) of metafictional narrators and authors.

*Infinite Jest* takes the motifs of possession, metafiction and authorial presence and marries them to a diegetic environment that is explicitly supernatural, marking the beginning of a sustained interaction with the motif of the undead narrator in Wallace's work. This is a systematic development of the earlier models of possession, autonomy-anxiety and metaleptic narrative fluidity, and is continually linked, ever more explicitly, to the figure of the author. The return of the dead in *Infinite Jest*, specifically the return of a dead father figure who is also a cinematic *auteur*, stages even more directly than 'Westward' a dramatization of the anxiety of influence.[10] In doing so, it also creates a site of anxiety over narrative authority, as Wallace builds one of the novel's key sequences around a ghostly figure identifiable with what Brian Richardson terms the 'permeable narrator': 'the uncanny and inextricable intrusion of the voice of another within the narrator's consciousness' (Richardson 95).[11]

The principal supernatural event in *Infinite Jest*, the appearance of the 'wraith' of Dr James Incandenza to Don Gately, takes place towards the end of the novel, but is foreshadowed in a number of earlier scenes. In a flashback, James Incandenza's father makes the materialist suggestion that in order to achieve success at tennis his son must become 'a machine in the ghost' (*Jest* 160), an inversion of Gilbert Ryle's critique of Cartesian dualism. Stephen Burn, in an analysis of *Infinite Jest* and neuroscience, argues that 'materialism is a monistic thesis that does away with appeals to *soul* or *spirit* in its insistence that mind is simply an emergent phenomenon of the biological matter of the brain' (Burn, *Guide* 50, emphasis original).[12] This philosophical position is ironized when James later appears in the narrative *as* a spirit, the inversion of Ryle's famous quote reified through the implantation into James' cranium of a 'gyroscopic balance sensor and *mise-en-scene* appropriation card and priapistic entertainment cartridge' (31): there is, we can presume, a machine in Incandenza's ghost. The pedagogical doctrine of materialism, which is taught at Enfield Tennis Academy and which ultimately leads, it is implied, to Hal Incandenza's disintegration ('I'm not a machine', he protests during his mental and physical breakdown [12]) results in a form of self-taught social isolation. The narrator of *Girl with Curious Hair*'s 'Everything is Green' feels despair when he looks at his emotionally unresponsive lover and feels that 'there is all of me going into you and nothing of you is coming back any more' (230), but *Infinite Jest* performs a disturbing escalation of this monadic 'sealing up' of the self, a process that becomes expressly associated with questions of supernatural, generational and authorial anxiety.

In a conversation between Hal and Orin Incandenza, a discussion of superstition leads to the implication that 'primitive' beliefs lurk beneath the surface of the materialist mindset. Hal invokes his anthropological knowledge of Canadian tribespeople:

> The Ahts of Vancouver used to cut virgin's throats and pour the blood very carefully into the orifices of the embalmed bodies of their ancestors [...] apparently the Ahts tried to fill up the ancestors' bodies completely with virgin-blood to preserve the privacy of their own mental states. The apposite Aht dictum here being quote 'The Sated ghost cannot see secret things.' The Discursive OED postulates that this is one of the earlier on-record prophylactics against schizophrenia. (243–4)

This passage is significant in its development of the 'ghostly' influence wielded by Gramma in *Broom* and the fears of loss of psychological authority explored in *Girl with Curious Hair* (note also the homophonic connection between 'Aht' and 'Art'). Firstly, the absent possessor figure is configured as a literal ghost – a revenant spirit from beyond the grave. Secondly, the revenant is associated here with *mental* intrusion, which according to the Ahts is something to be feared, hence the contemporary association with mental illness. Finally, the spirit is associated with the figure of the *ancestor*. This composite figure, a ghost of the ancestor who permeates or possesses your own mind, is a significant advancement of the ideas about loss of authority explored in Wallace's earlier fiction while remaining tied to the anxiety of influence, of the ancestor controlling your brain. This is a literalizing and reversal of Bloom's return of the dead: in *apophrades* the voice of the dead appears, almost inexplicably, to have been generated through the work of the living, who have superseded their place in the canon. In the narrative of *Infinite Jest* the dead literally return, with the express intention of possessing the brain of their descendants. It is possible to see, in this fear of possession and the grotesque image of the 'stopping up' of the corpse, a narrative echo of the plugging up of the body in *Girl with Curious Hair*: Bruce's reaction to his anxiety over lack of autonomy is to plug the point of entry to his head, and Edilyn's receiving of the earplug is commensurate with a loss of self-articulation.

The passage also initiates two plot developments that lead to overtly supernatural events later in the novel. A reference to the Quebecois belief in the mobility of the soul after death (*Jest* 244) is directly enacted when Lucien Antitoi, a Canadian 'of the Quebec subgenus' (304), is murdered and 'sheds his body's suit' before being 'catapulted home' to Canada (488–9). Relatedly, James Incandenza is buried in 'Quebec's L'Islet County' (65), and despite being interred in a 'brass casket' (presumably a measure to prevent the theft of the master cartridge of 'Infinite Jest') it is implied that the 'annual hyperfloration cycles' (65) may have affected the integrity of the coffin to the extent that Incandenza's 'wraith' is able to escape and, like Antitoi, return home.

While Lucien Antitoi's ghostly journey initiates the idea of the supernatural into the world of the novel (it could be suggested that it is his spirit's 'call to arms' [489] that summons Incandenza's wraith from his coffin), the appearance of James Incandenza's wraith to the hospitalized Don Gately is a concretization of the tropes of possession, inheritance and authorship that have obliquely haunted Wallace's fiction since his first novel. Tom LeClair initially associates the wraith with the author himself ('Wallace enters his narrative' as a tall, lexically gifted, and etymology-conscious 'wraith') before conceding that 'the "wraith" sounds like a combination of Hal and his father' (LeClair, 'Prodigious' 32). However, LeClair concludes that the wraith sounds like this because Wallace is himself a 'prodigious collaboration' of those characters (33). In fact, the wraith implicitly identifies itself to Gately as a manifestation of James Incandenza, but LeClair's article remains valuable for its foregrounding of the conundrum of authorial presence posed by the wraith's manifestation.[13] Elsewhere, LeClair associates the living James Incandenza with Pynchon (33), another connection of the revenant figure with the literary ancestor.[14]

If the wraith is therefore a site of authorial confusion, the manner in which it communicates with the supine and effectively dumb Gately stages an advancement of the absent possessor figure from Wallace's earlier fiction. The climax of 'Westward the Course of Empire Takes Its Way' suggests an end to the more comprehensible directional flow of possession via the introduction of an amalgamated set of possessing and counter-possessing narrative voices, but the wraith-Gately interface appears to simplify the originary flow of the possession by having both possessor and possessee present in the same room. However, the *manner* of the possession itself is complex. The wraith converses with Gately through his own 'brain-voice' (831), implanting thoughts into Gately's own consciousness, including words that are not in his vocabulary but which nevertheless appear as part of his own thought process. This results in a narrative register that is virtually impossible to disentangle, as it is unclear to what extent the wraith is inflecting Gately's 'brain-voice'. For the first time in Wallace's fiction, we see the kind of 'permeable narrator' described by Richardson, whereby the dead directly influence the linguistic choices of the living, but here the possession is framed, however problematically, in terms of *dialogue*.[15]

The confounding status of the wraith's voice problematizes the possibility of an undisrupted narrative plane. The wraith itself takes a pragmatic approach, telling Gately that he should stop concerning himself about whether he is dreaming or not and 'just capitalize on its presence' (*Jest* 830). This sentiment, with its pointed use of the world 'capitalize', is delivered by a spirit who was in life a failed communicator. This speaks to Wallace's disillusion, concurrent with *Infinite Jest*'s composition, with the capitalistically inflected ironizing of avant-garde art of which much of James Incandenza's work is taken to be representative. Therefore, this complex iteration of *apophrades* ultimately involves Wallace bringing back the dead and having them parrot their (flawed) sentiments in his own narrative register, while in a radical ironizing of the process the sentiments of the ghost could also be attributed to some of Wallace's own contemporaries (the return of the living who embody dead sentiments) criticized in 'E Unibus Pluram' for being 'reverently ironic' (*Supposedly* 76, emphasis original).[16]

While one might be wary of LeClair's direct association of the wraith with Wallace, it is important to note that while he associates the *living* James Incandenza with Pynchon he does not extend that association to his ghostly presence. The wraith, as with the amalgamated narrative voice at the end of 'Westward', seems then to represent an amorphous, 'flickering' accretion of sentiments, some of which appear to have specifically been modified *through the process of death itself*. As well as occupying the brains of the living, wraiths move at 'the speed of quanta' (*Jest* 831), which appears to have infused Incandenza's wraith with a new empathetic facility. Wallace suggests to McCaffery that for living humans 'true empathy's impossible' (22), but the wraith permeates the barriers of consciousness, appearing at one point to literally feel Gately's pain (839). The 'dialogue' between Gately and the wraith, with its associated amalgamation of narrative contradictions and irresolution, presents a significant empathetic change in the mode of possession in Wallace's fiction and a move, albeit a problematic one, towards a more dialogic narrative model.

## Companion Ghosts

In *Infinite Jest* the absent possessor, who has until now occupied an ambivalent and occasionally malignant role, becomes present in insubstantial ghostly form, and engages in direct conversation with the mind it possesses. The 'apparition' of this figure and the newly dialogic nature of the relationship result in the establishment of what I term the 'companion ghost' in Wallace's fiction. The companion ghost carries some traits of the absent possessor (thus Gately's initial confusion over whether the wraith represents God or his disease [833]), but through its manifestation to the possessee and its tendency to directly entwine its consciousness with theirs, it engenders something akin to empathetic conversation. This figure still bears the traces of both ancestor and author, but makes plain its desire for *interaction*, rather than a kind of remote orchestration. In *Infinite Jest*, this interaction is marked by a degree of uncertainty over the authority and agency of the wraith, who intrudes uninvited into Gately's consciousness in an act of 'lexical rape' (832), with the brief appearance of a second wraith, apparently a representation of the still-living ETA guru Lyle, invasively licking sweat off Gately's forehead (933).[17] However, the mode of interaction here is more benevolent than the consciousness-controlling possessor figures of the earlier fiction. The wraith's lengthy speech about the importance of the voices of 'figurants' in his methodology of 'radical realism' transfigures the possessor from a monologic figure to one at least focused on a polyphonic approach to narrative in which all character voices can be heard together.

The figure of the companion ghost is developed radically in *Oblivion* but in the intervening collection, *Brief Interviews with Hideous Men*, Wallace performs a form of entr'acte which focuses on the granular development of metafictional tropes from 'Westward', but is nevertheless essential to the maturation of the possessor figure. The collection develops the conversational possessor–possessee relationship from *Infinite Jest* via the juxtaposition of the brief interviews with the explicitly metafictional story 'Octet' which, it is implied, should be read as an inversion of the format of the brief interviews themselves via the narrator's suggestion that the quizzes are 'supposed to compose a certain sort of "*interrogation*" of the person reading them, somehow' (*Brief* 123, emphasis original). Through the writer's intrusion into the story in 'Pop Quiz 9' of a supposed octet, it is also insinuated that the position of the metafictional 'Octet' to the brief interviews is roughly proportionate: that is, associatively related, but not *within*.

The notorious structure of the brief interviews involves the subsumption of the female interviewer's voice and its replacement with 'Q', the opinions espoused by the hideous men being so inherently monologic that a reciprocal dialogue cannot be obtained. In Interview #28, a particularly poisonous example, two academically affiliated men turn dialogic terminology to monologic ends in a conversation with each other about feminism to which the interviewer is a virtually mute witness: 'Q' appears only three times in nearly eight pages of dialogue (*Brief* 192-9). Conversely, in 'Octet', which structurally resembles the interviews in its 'Q&A' format, the narrator, a 'fiction writer', ultimately throws himself on the mercy of the reader. Unlike the occluded amalgamation of fictional and implied authorial voices in 'Westward', 'Octet' offers in its appeal to the reader something close to a reciprocal form of metafiction.[18] While the conversation between Gately and the wraith in *Infinite Jest* occurs between intradiegetic characters, here the ghostly presence is inverted and becomes extradiegetic, mapped on to the *reader*, who is given possession over the narrative's success. The importance of this appeal to the reader is reflected in Wallace's changing of the ending of 'Octet' during the writing process, where the original final line ('Q: Self Evident') was ultimately replaced by 'So decide' (Box 1.7, Steven Moore).

'Good Old Neon' from *Oblivion* appears at first to be a confessional monologue spoken to an unidentified partner, before a casual reference to the narrator Neal's suicide ('it gets a lot more interesting when I get to the part where I kill myself' [143]) reveals that the speaker is a ghost. It also appears that Neal's ghost can take physical form when he reveals that he's 'sitting here in this car' (152). 'Good Old Neon' is a development of both the wraith-Gately interface in *Infinite Jest* and the figure of the companion ghost, itself an inflection of and progression from the earlier absent possessor. There are several striking similarities between Neal and the wraith: both can move outside of linear time, with Neal's explanation that dying 'takes forever' (180) mirroring the wraith's observation that death involves 'everything outside you getting really slow' (*Jest* 883). Both have also experienced epiphanies regarding their own sense of solipsism when watching the show *Cheers* (*Jest* 835; *Oblivion* 168–9).[19] The embrace of communication in the post-corporeal iterations of Neal and the wraith are also drawn in stark contrast to the careers they pursued before their deaths. Neal worked in advertising, an industry repeatedly linked by Wallace to metatextually 'heaping scorn on pretensions to [...] virtues of authority and sincerity' (*Supposedly* 61), while Incandenza's avant-garde film-making career became blighted by 'metacinematic-parody' (*Jest* 703).[20] In this respect, their newfound incorporeal ability to be able to converse with or enter the consciousness of another mirrors both the metafictional 'Armageddon-explosion' that occurs at the climax of 'Westward' where the amalgamation of voices turn outward towards 'you', and the transference of power to the reader by the 'fiction writer' at the end of 'Octet'.

While the base similarities between Neal and the Wraith are striking, the degrees of 'possession' in 'Good Old Neon' are substantially more convoluted than in previous scenarios. Neal's assertion that ghosts can 'be in anyone's room' (178), as well as Wallace's note on his drafts of 'Good Old Neon' that '[ghosts talk] to us all the time, but we think their voices are our own thoughts' (Box 24.2) indicate a multiplication of the potential sites of possession, moving away from earlier scenarios where possession takes place between two individuals and suggesting, finally, that a conversation between the dead and living can occur in multiple consciousnesses simultaneously. This model is implemented in 'Good Old Neon' twofold. Firstly, the reader is manoeuvred into the listening position occupied by Don Gately, so that rather than being a witness to the dead-living conversation, they are implanted *within* it through the process of reading, resulting, as in 'Octet', in a radical and uncapped extradiegetic proliferation of listeners (a number that will continue to expand every time someone reads 'Good Old Neon'). Secondly, this proliferation is mirrored intradiegetically by the sudden outward shift in narrative focus at the climax of the story, where Neal frames the instantaneity of 'this whole seemingly endless back-and-forth between us' within the miniscule details of the lives of five supporting characters before entering, wraith-like, into the empathetic consciousness of 'David Wallace', who has a 'totally unorganizable set of inner thoughts, feelings, memories and impressions' (180). This sudden narrative shift, with all its metaleptic and metafictional possibilities, represents a significant broadening out of the modes of character-to-character possession thus far and deploys a character with the same name as the author. While Neal's narrative is a monologue, unlike the possessor–possessee dialogue in *Infinite Jest*, the marriage of that earlier interdimensional dialogue with the form of 'Octet's empathetic appeal to the reader results in a mode that, while retaining the motifs of possession in Wallace's fiction, ultimately results in a metafictionally inflected, extradiegetically directed relationship between narrator and reader that is not based in a monologically motivated power relationship.

Neal is endowed with a number of the characteristics that separate the companion ghost from the absent possessor: direct manifestation to the listener, a narrative register concerned with interaction rather than remote orchestration, and a less monologically invasive, more empathetic position. The explicit positioning of Neal as a contemporary of 'David Wallace' is also a development in the process of *apophrades* that shadows Wallace's possessive or ghostly figures. While *Infinite Jest* sees Wallace performing a conflation of the return of the dead with the voices of both his literary ancestors *and* his irony-bound contemporaries, 'Good Old Neon' places the revenant in direct proximity to an iteration of Wallace himself, an alignment compounded by 'David Wallace's' sense of himself as a 'pathetically self-conscious outline or ghost of a person' (181). It appears, then, in accordance with Harris' belief that Wallace wished to 'overtake [...] himself' (120) that the anxiety of influence in Wallace's work has caught up with him, the fiction now less concerned with the process of overcoming external influence and more with internal refinement.[21] What begins to take place in the metafictionally inflected 'Octet', before finding a more established form in 'Good Old Neon', can be described as Wallace performing a mediation of his own prior style, an interrogation of and escape from the voice which, until this point, he has possessed.

## The Dialogism (or Otherwise) of Possession

In 'Joseph Frank's Dostoevsky', Wallace argues that Mikhail Bakhtin's praise for Dostoevsky's polyphony, a method that 'supposedly allowed him to refrain from injecting his own values into his novels' should be framed as 'the natural result of a Soviet critic's trying to discuss an author whose "reactionary" views the State wanted forgotten' (*Lobster* 269). This footnoted observation, putatively a critique of the methodology of Dostoevsky biographer Joseph Frank, also speaks indirectly to Wallace's own approach to monologism and polyphony, his use of absent possessors and companion ghosts, and ultimately his own authorial presence in the text.

The situation of one consciousness as object for another, aligned with monologism in Bakhtin's formulation, can also act as description of the process of possession dramatized within Wallace's earlier works. The possessor–possessee relationship between Lenore and Gramma works on this principle, with Lenore's mode of expression, and even her name, appropriated and directed by her absent great-grandmother. However, while Gramma is the controlling consciousness of *Broom*, the novel therefore taking the *process* of monologism as subject, Adam Kelly suggests that the narrative of *Broom* itself is ultimately monologic, as it merely performs 'a *gesture* toward an open system and a readerly dialogue' that is ultimately subjugated to 'the desire to control meaning and the reader's agency' (Kelly, 'Novel' 10, emphasis mine). Kelly describes an example of fallacious ambiguity apparent in the final line of the novel ('I'm a man of my' [*Broom* 467]), whereby a sentence that is apparently left open for the reader to complete has in fact only one plausible outcome: the reader is essentially directed into providing the only word ('word') that will work syntactically. Kelly reads *Infinite Jest* as a move towards a less monologic approach to dialogue, using the example of the lengthy Marathe-Steeply interface to illustrate how Wallace has progressed to 'a dialogic context in which both sides of the argument can be offered to the reader, without a clear authorial conclusion drawn' (Kelly, 'Novel' 12).

While I concur with the argument that 'the desire to control meaning and the reader's agency' is a quality that is gradually refined out of Wallace's work, I believe that this development from monologism to dialogism is achieved not only through the development of the kind of peer-to-peer dialogue that Kelly identifies, and indeed that Bakhtin so praises in Dostoevsky, but also through a gradual revelatory process based around the changing modes of possession (both physical and metaphysical) in Wallace's fiction. In the transition from the absent possessor to the companion ghost, Wallace addresses the question of his own monologic tendencies before finding a solution that allows him to dramatize and separate out those same tendencies. Essential to this process is Wallace's acknowledgement in 'Joseph Frank's Dostoevsky' of the nature of Bakhtin's analysis: that the advocacy of polyphony is also inherently bound up with an author or critic's own position in relation to their work. This process can be observed most directly in the transition between the modes of possession employed in *Infinite Jest*, 'Octet' and 'Good Old Neon', as these texts all feature the materialization of the companion ghost: a visual apparition of the dead.

The dialogic process between the wraith and Don Gately is not founded upon an equilateral power relationship. While the wraith professes to be able to empathize totally, the terms of their conversation are founded on the wraith's decision to invasively enter Gately's 'brain voice' and it is unclear what degree of control the wraith has over Gately's consciousness. In an extrapolation of this position, Timothy Jacobs argues that the wraith's lexical control can be extended to incorporate the entire narrative. Jacobs suggests that the wraith is 'the text's mediator, the centering and orienting presence that organises the entire narrative structure,' and that its presence can implicitly be felt from the first page of the novel, with the pronouncement 'I am in here' attributable to the wraith's possession of the entire narrative (*Eschatological* 56–9). The wraith, Jacobs argues, is the master mediator:

> All is mediated, the polyphonic voices collated, by the wraith [...] the narrative is dialogic, yet also complexly monologic in the sense that the wraith assembles the many voices through his own voice. (75)[22]

Jacobs' suggestion that 'the wraith [...] serves as a transmission of the author's embedded consciousness' (62) positions Wallace in a simultaneous 'flickering' enactment and defiance of the 'dead' author; the wraith remains as a trace of authorial presence (Jacobs does not believe that the wraith literally *is* Wallace, thus disagreeing with LeClair's alignment). Whether or not one agrees that the wraith mediates the *entire* novel, Jacobs' conflation of the wraith's 'centering and orienting presence' with Wallace himself engenders an important question, one fundamental to Wallace's representation of possession: what exactly are the ramifications of this 'dialogic, yet also complexly monologic' model in terms of the novel itself? In interviews while writing and publicizing *Infinite Jest* Wallace oscillates between guardedly suggesting to McCaffery that 'fiction's duty [is not to] edify or teach' (26) and more prescriptively asserting that 'principles and values in this country [...] [seem] to me like something our generation *needs to feel*' (60, emphasis mine). Is there a risk that, through the ideological 'centering and orienting' of *Infinite Jest*, Wallace's 'possession' of the narrative comes at the cost of a 'plurality of consciousnesses not linked to a single ideological common denominator' (Bakhtin, *Problems* 17)? Jacobs recognizes the monologic ramifications of the 'centering and controlling' wraith, stating (in a comparison between the wraith and Eliot's Tiresias in 'The Waste Land') that 'to posit a governing consciousness risks the attenuation of the [work's] many individual voices' (Jacobs, *Eschatological* 99).

While it is difficult to reconcile these positions, I read the presence of the wraith in *Infinite Jest* and the attendant development of the companion ghost as representing a *moving towards* an engagement with dialogism in Wallace's work through awareness of his monologic tendency. LeClair argues that there is a direct correlation between the wraith's version of 'radical realism' and Wallace's own fiction (32–3), but the wraith's iteration of radical realism is *not* identical to Wallace's approach as it is framed within the narrative of *Jest* as the work of a failed artist. A more useful correlation between Wallace and the wraith's methodologies can be found in LeClair's later explanation that while 'Infinite Jest' (the film) is 'single-voiced', *Infinite Jest* the novel is 'multifarious and multivocal' (34): Boswell makes a similar suggestion (*Understanding* 170). This is a useful approach to thinking about how Wallace begins to address the 'single-voiced' monologic tendency in his own work. By embedding into his own novel the monologic work of a failed artist (an artist whose filmography bears some significant similarity to Wallace's own previous work), and framing that artist's gestures towards polyphony within a *dialogue* with a character (Gately) who chastises the artist for his self-centred approach (835), a monologic artistic tendency is critiqued within a dialogic framework. While this may not entirely rescue *Infinite Jest* from monologic tendencies, the objective of the episode is a movement towards its dissolution, a dramatization and transfer of monologic power that is *enacted* in the uneven possessor–possessee relationship between Gately and the wraith. This technique not only operates as a simultaneous dramatization and critique of monologism within a polyphonic framework, but also draws attention implicitly to the conflation between the wraith's power of possession and extradiegetic control of the narrative by an author figure.[23]

This approach is complemented by a change in the materiality of the companion ghost. The absent possessors of Wallace's earlier work have a fundamentally *hidden* quality, either through not being physically present or hiding figuratively behind the mask of irony. Conversely, the companion ghost is always in some sense *present*. This presence has a gradual adverse effect on the degree of possession afforded, before leading (in 'Octet' and 'Good Old Neon') to a more equilateral, co-creative relationship between speaker and listener. The wraith and Neal also have a 'quantum' quality that allows them to move almost imperceptibly between places and consciousnesses, an ability identified with polyphony by Bakhtin when he describes Dostoevsky's method in the following terms:

The fundamental category in Dostoevsky's mode of artistic visualising was [...] *coexistence* and *interaction*. He saw and conceived his world primarily in terms of space, not time [...] Dostoevsky strives to organize all available meaningful material [...] in one time-frame, in the form of a dramatic juxtaposition [...] he strives to perceive all existing contradictions as various stages of some unified development; in every manifestation of the present he strives to glimpse a trace of the past, a peak of the present-day, or a tendency of the future; and as a consequence, nothing for him is arranged along a single extensive plane. (Bakhtin, *Problems* 28, emphasis original)

If this passage recalls the wraith's ability to move at the speed of 'quanta', it is even more redolent of Neal's experiences of simultaneity of time and space after death.[24] While the wraith's mode of possession remains yoked to elements of monologism, the simultaneous availability of 'everyone's room' after death in 'Good Old Neon' dramatizes a systematic totality of empathy whereby possession no longer operates in a hierarchical manner, and the matter of 'telling' that so constricts Wallace's earlier protagonists has been dissolved. This dissolution of possession has also been informed in part through the aforementioned 'opening out' of control of the narrative to the reader in 'Octet'.

## The Revenant Author

McCaffery: Had you considered writing a more direct autobiographical novel? Why go to such lengths to hide yourself?
Wallace: Because that's how hidden I was then. (41)

These 'ghostly' approaches towards dialogism and metafiction lead inexorably to the question of Wallace's own authorial presence in his texts. As I have illustrated, Wallace's own nominal appearances in his fiction, like those absent possessors, are initially hidden before emerging, by gradations, in an apparition commensurate with the introduction of the companion ghost in the later work. I believe that this slow accretion of presence, rather than a simple brute reassertion of authorial control, operates in tandem with Wallace's approach to *apophrades* to create a contingent, *revenant* author figure, 'killed' by Barthes' essay, who has reasserted their presence on the basis of material contingency and through a process of dialogism. Wallace's revenant author accepts 'the birth of the reader', but refuses to submit to its own effacement, instead proposing an author–reader relationship that is explicitly dialogic.

Wallace's authorial presence in the diegetic world of his fiction materializes under more than one name (Dave, David Wallace) and none of these personae should, of course, be taken as exactly commensurate with the author himself (the name 'Foster' is itself an amendment to David Wallace, the name by which he went to friends and colleagues). Moreover, in the earlier fiction Wallace actually moves to disguise or efface some explicit authorial references. In the original draft of *Broom* Lenore was born in 1962, the same year as Wallace (Box 3.7), but in the published text the date is 1966. Bonnie Nadell later suggests moving the date of the action to 1986, to which Wallace replies that he 'needed an Olympic year', which doesn't explain how the novel ends up being set in 1990 ('Letter to Bonnie Nadell, Oct 31st 1985'). This refining out of explicitly biographical data from a novel that Wallace later described to McCaffery as 'a coded autobio' (41) is more dramatically enacted in a couple of changes made to the published version of 'Westward'. Firstly, the name of the abusive counterfeiter with whom 'Dave' shares a cell is not Mark, but Barth (Box 14.6). Secondly, the mysterious 'L——', for whose death Dave is convicted, is called Gale (Box 15.2), which is the name of an ex-girlfriend of Wallace's (Max 58). In a letter to Gerald Howard in April 1988 about the legal fallout caused by the use of real names in the manuscript of *Girl*, Wallace explains that 'the first draft's use of a real person's name is testimony to my stupidity in terms of balancing literary and real-world considerations [...] I need the circularity of "Westward"'s character contriving a fiction in which I as real person am character'. Later in the same letter, Wallace indicates that L 'stands for Lenore, if anything' ('Letter to Gerald Howard, April 25th 1988'). While Wallace is prepared here to use his real name for the first time, it still occurs within a complex amalgamation of registers. It does, however, represent a degree of progression from the coded and redacted biographical data from the drafts of *Broom*. Two Davids appear in the drafts of *Infinite Jest*, and both are subsequently erased. In the first iteration of the 'professional conversationalist' scene, which appears to date from 1986 and has the title 'What are you exactly – unadorned autobio – automabiography', Hal is called David. The scene is set in 1974 and 'David' is 13: Wallace would have been 12 (Box 15.6). In a subsequent draft the character later named as Marlon Bain is called David Foster Wallace (Box 16.5).

From *Broom* to *Infinite Jest*, this process of 'hide-and-seek' appears to bear out Wallace's response to McCaffery that 'I'm an exhibitionist who wants to hide, but is unsuccessful at hiding' (43). However, the encroachment of Wallace's presence in his own fiction is also concurrent with the transition of the absent possessor to the companion ghost, and their attendant associations with monologism and dialogism. The change in the mode of Wallace's presence in 'Octet' and 'Good Old Neon', a development from the earlier manifestations in *Broom*, *Girl* and *Infinite Jest*, mirrors the difference between the absent possessor's remote orchestration of narrative action (*Gramma* in Broom, the 'hidden' Wallace) and the companion ghost's presence in and sacrifice of control of the narrative to their dialogic partner (Gately, the reader in 'Octet'). While the presence of an author in a text might initially be taken as a *reinforcement* of monologism, reminding the reader of exactly who is controlling the narrative, Wallace's appearance in 'Good Old Neon' actually has the reverse effect, one comparable to Bakhtin's assertion that the dialogic author creates 'free people, capable of standing *alongside* their creator'. At the climax of 'Good Old Neon', where Neal's ghost reveals the dialogic simultaneity of 'this whole seemingly endless back-and-forth between us' with the actions of 'David Wallace', a repositioning of Wallace's implied presence from monologic remote orchestrator to dialogic companion has been strongly effected. 'David Wallace' has been separated out from both absent possessor and companion ghost to stand, in a literalizing of Bakhtin's formulation, 'alongside' his own characters in a moment of diegetic temporal simultaneity.

Bakhtin explains that a dialogic character's word does not 'serve as a mouthpiece for the author's voice […] it sounds, as it were, *alongside* the author's word and in a special way combines […] with it' (Bakhtin, *Problems* 7, emphasis mine). At the climax of 'Good Old Neon', Neal's voice does exactly this, simultaneously combining with Wallace's experience of reading about Neal's suicide and allowing 'David Wallace' himself the final word of the story. Like *Broom*, this final word is itself 'word', but rather than provide a fallacious ambiguity of 'openness', this final word affords the revenant author the recognition of the contingent survival of his own voice.

2

# Spatiality

## 'In the Middle of the Middle of Nowhere': Regionalism and Institutions

Within David Foster Wallace's large archive of notes is a notebook titled 'Midwesternisms' (Box 31.12). This book, which consists almost entirely of Midwestern colloquial phrases and appears to date from the composition period of *The Pale King*, operates as a kind of ethnographic source text of Midwestern language and was presumably intended to be consulted throughout that novel's composition. 'Midwesternisms', a portmanteau that combines region with a suffix commonly associated with academic practice, suggests a subsumption of the phraseology of the Midwest into the categorizing discourse of the academy. Accordingly, in Wallace's fiction the Midwest is rarely, if ever, afforded the chance to exist as an unmediated environment. In this chapter, I read Wallace's uneasy relationship with the Midwest as a deep ambivalence over his own sense of regional identity, framing this argument within a critical discourse based on what I term 'performative' regionalism and the cultural and literary oscillation between the Midwest and the East coast as centres of literary production. Subsequently, I read this mediation of region by institution as a facet of a broader spatial conflict between institutional and non-institutional areas that characterizes Wallace's writing ever more forcefully and abstractly.

This conflict is not identical with the mediation of voice analysed in Chapter 1 but is still thematically related to Wallace's concerns over the monologic and the dialogic: those concerns are also expressed *spatially*, as an encroaching disquietude over the institution's ability to possess the space outside of itself. At times, this possession is explicitly spatial, with the institution actually physically shaping the landscape itself. Elsewhere, the possession occurs at the level of cultural discourse, whereby the institution presumes to produce a simulacrum of the space outside that it then monologically appropriates into a version of itself. In Wallace's work, the Midwest is a key battleground for this system of spatial relations, but he does not ultimately limit his scope to this region.

## Gardens and Institutions

In American letters, the Midwest has long existed in a geographically dialogic relationship with the coastal and national centres of cultural production. Paul Giles argues that regional American literature of the nineteenth century 'tends not only to be saturated in locality but also to understand that locality as a guarantee of its own authenticity and its patriotic allegiance [...] the relationship between the local and the national becomes self-allegorizing' (*Global* 11). Tom Lutz, analysing the historical development of American regionalism, goes further and in doing so invokes the question of dialogism, arguing that '[r]egionalist literary texts represent both sides of the major cultural debates of their time [...] but not with the intention of resolving them. Instead of settling these debates, they opt for an oscillation between the sides, a kind of contrapuntal unresolved Bakhtinian symphony of cultural voices and positions' (28). However, this 'symphony' also carries with it the prospect of monologism, embodied in the accusation that the disproportionate cultural weighting of the East coast (which, then as now, houses the lion's share of the US publishing industry) effectively implements a particular form of easily digestible regional Midwestern stereotype which effaces the region's true qualities. Lutz glosses this as 'strip-mining [...] selling a mythic vision of rural and marginal cultures to jaded city folk interested in buying images of the quaint or degraded' (25). An early manifestation of this anxiety, which I use here for its striking concordance with an element of Wallace's late story 'The Suffering Channel', can be found in the Massachusetts poet William Cullen Bryant's 1832 poem 'The Prairies'. Bryant's characteristically Romantic poem fetishizes the Midwestern landscape in terms of both its Edenic beauty ('the Gardens of the Desert [...] fresh as the young earth, ere man had sinned' [1042]) and prospective diffusion via the arrival of the coastal visitor (Bryant himself visited the prairies during a trip from Boston). Bryant implicitly acknowledges that the act of viewing itself prefigures a physical incursion into the virgin territory, immediately thereafter marked by the entrance of 'my steed' (1043).[1] This incursion initiates a lengthy and highly ideologically inflected reverie on the history of the peoples of the prairies, which characterizes the 'red man' as the instigator of genocide against an earlier race, 'that long has passed away' and is now remembered only as the constructor of 'the mighty mounds/That overlook the rivers' (1043). The ascription of murderous qualities to the Native American tribes currently being eradicated by colonists provides, of course, a convenient naturalizing of the rise and fall of prairie civilizations. Finally, Bryant considers with disquiet 'that advancing multitude/Which soon shall fill these deserts' (1044). The poem ends on a note of ambiguity that derives its power from the implied synthesis of the narrative position of the coastal poet with those 'multitudes' who will efface the region's peculiar qualities (the mounds return in 'The Suffering Channel', discussed towards the end of this chapter).

Bryant's anxiety over the effacement of regional identity is itself a component of a broader cultural concern over what Leo Marx famously refers to as 'the machine in the garden': the American cultural conflict between 'an undefiled, green republic' and an 'urbanized landscape' (6). Marx describes an American pastoralism that sets 'a natural landscape, a terrain either unspoiled or, if cultivated, rural' against 'an "artificial" world, a world identified with "art"' (9).[2] I use Marx's quote here specifically for its collapsing together of art, the urbanized and the artificial. The threat to the pastoral landscape is not simply configured as urban-industrial: there is also implied danger in the very contrivance of art itself. While Marx's study refers particularly to works of nineteenth-century American Romanticism, of which Bryant's poem is clearly an example, the distinction between 'natural' and 'art' is also relevant to the locational and cultural disquiet described in Wallace's writing. In Wallace's earlier fiction in particular, this can manifest as an anxiety over the spatially inflected encroachment of culture described by Fredric Jameson in *Postmodernism*, whereby society undergoes 'a prodigious expansion of culture throughout the social realm, to the point at which everything in our social life [...] can be said to have become "cultural" in some original and yet untheorized sense [...] to the point where our now postmodern bodies are bereft of spatial coordinates and practically (let alone theoretically) incapable of distantiation' (48–9).³ However, in this chapter I want to move away somewhat from Wallace's relationship to postmodernism and towards consideration of a less discussed element of Wallace's spatial anxiety: the relationship between the idea of the region and institutional/extra-institutional space.

Wallace's fiction teems with descriptions of institutional spaces: retirement homes, universities, sports academies, halfway houses and tax examination centres. In an essay on *The Pale King*, Brian McHale remarks on Wallace's interest in the 'subuniverses' created by certain institutions. Drawing from Peter Berger and Thomas Luckmann's *The Social Construction of Reality*, a foundational text on institutionalization, McHale argues that Wallace has 'a long-term fascination with institutions as microcosms and world-building engines [...] their world-sustaining apparatus, and [...] their self-perception as scale models of the world at large' (204). It is McHale's description of the 'scale model' that particularly interests me here, as it circumscribes the institution spatially. Institutions in Wallace's fiction, I suggest, are primarily *spatial* entities that dictate the behaviour of those within them in strongly spatialized terms. In this sense, and building on McHale's analysis, I see accordance between institutions in Wallace's fiction and Berger and Luckmann's description of the perceived totality of institutional reification:

> The institutions, as historical and objective facticities, confront the individual as undeniable facts. The institutions are there, external to him, persistent in their reality, whether he likes it or not. He cannot wish them away. They resist his attempts to change or evade them. They have coercive power over him, both in themselves, by the sheer force of their facticity, and through the control mechanisms that are usually attached to the most important of them. The objective reality of institutions is not diminished if the individual does not understand their purpose or their mode of operation. He may experience large sectors of the social world as incomprehensible, perhaps oppressive in their opaqueness, but real none the less. Since institutions exist as external reality, the individual cannot

understand them by introspection. He must 'go out' and learn about them, just as he must to learn about nature. This remains true even though the social world, as a humanly produced reality, is potentially understandable in a way not possible in the case of the natural world. (78)

I believe that Wallace spatializes this process of institutional reification in his fiction: Berger and Luckmann's individual, confronted with an abstract set of institutional 'facts', becomes progressively concretized in Wallace's fiction into a character who is physically, as well as psychologically, constrained by a physical institutional environment. This spatial constraint is initially described in putatively dialogic relation to an area outside the institution: in the earlier fiction, this space is defined as strongly regional, and specifically Midwestern. Later, the space outside the institution becomes more abstracted and effaced, before Wallace stages a qualified return to the matter of region in his late fiction.

I would also suggest that Berger and Luckmann's uneasy invocation of a colloquy between the institutional and natural worlds is played out spatially in Wallace's fiction, which ironizes their suggestion that the individual must 'go out' to learn about the institution: institutions in Wallace's fiction progressively *impede* egress, becoming increasingly abstract and imprisoning spatial structures and, as I will argue in regard to Wallace's late fiction, actually begin to *efface* elements of the 'natural' world outside. Of course Wallace is himself, to quote a famous note from his drafts for *The Pale King*, a 'creature of the system' (*Pale* 546). Institutionally bound for much of his life in various universities where he alternately studied, wrote and taught, he writes about these problematic spaces from within: Wallace's work is both institutionally sceptical and *produced*. In this sense, Wallace's institutions can also bear traces of Erving Goffman's famous formulation of the 'total institution': 'a place of residence and work where a large number of like-situated individuals, cut off from the wider society for an appreciable period of time, together lead an enclosed, formally administered round of life' (Goffman 11).[4] While Goffman deals primarily with prisons and asylums, the model of the total institution is torqued in Wallace's fiction to incorporate sites of learning: the school or, more frequently, the university.

This vexed position generally manifests in the work as a sustained and complex dialogue between a site of cultural production or education and the world outside that site. In describing this new approach, I diverge somewhat from Paul Giles' spatial attribution of 'sentimental posthumanism' to Wallace's work. Giles argues that Wallace 'flattens out the old binary opposition between city and suburb, center and margin, replacing it with a new model of the digital network [...] a level playing field where the mass media operate in all zones simultaneously' (*Global* 163–4). This strikes me as partially applicable to Wallace's spatial approach to region in his fiction, particularly in the later work, but this 'levelling' position does not take full account of Wallace's deeply ambivalent relationship with institutional space and its disproportionate regional weighting. I believe that it is crucial to incorporate the spatial situation, increasingly present in Wallace's writing, whereby 'the barrier that total institutions place between the inmate and the wider world' (Goffman 24) progressively broadens to encompass the region itself, which then becomes monologically *produced* and *subsumed* or *dominated* by the institution. This cultural matrix is produced in part via the ambiguous matter of Wallace's own regional identity.

## Performative Midwesterners: Region, Mobility and Institutional Identity

In a perceptive essay about the use of geography and space in Wallace's fiction, Paul Quinn quotes an interview he conducted with Wallace's sister Amy, where she outlines the spatial dislocation that underpinned their regional identity while growing up in the Midwest:

> The kids who had been here for generations treated us as if we were East-Coasters, and then when David went off to the East-Coast and realized they treated him like a hayseed, he realized he was from a place no one else was. *Somewhere in the middle*, I think that was David's Midwest, *the neither here nor there*. (Quinn 95, emphasis original)

This is a useful point from which to begin to understand the complex question of Wallace's regional identity, because to locate Wallace specifically as a Midwestern author is to commit something of a category mistake. While it would be correct to observe, as Giles does, that Wallace has 'affiliations to a tradition of Midwestern realism' (*Global* 175), I would argue that it is most accurate to term Wallace a 'performative Midwesterner': he can stage, when expedient, a Midwestern persona. Despite his birthplace (Ithaca, New York) and later residence in Boston, Wallace never adopted what could be described as an East coast literary persona in his fiction or non-fiction, instead describing himself as a 'native' of the Midwest, even when reporting for an East coast publication such as *Harpers*, as in his essay about the Illinois state fair (*Supposedly* 84). However, when required Wallace can also abstract himself from this persona and towards a cooler, more observant register. This can be detected in a somewhat anthropological tendency towards the simultaneous valorization of certain stereotypical Midwestern qualities (community, sincerity, isolation, worship) and the denigration of others, with the most notorious example being the reference to the 'subphylum' of 'Kmart people' in his state fair essay (120). This unedifying description balances both the observing eye of an educated visitor ('facts are facts') and the authority of an insider ('I went to high school with Kmart people. I know them' [120–1]).[5]

A useful comparison might be made here with William Gass, a writer whose work Wallace admired enough to cite *Omensetter's Luck* as one of the five 'direly underappreciated U.S. novels' published since 1960 (*Flesh* 203). Gass, like Wallace, is frequently identified as a Midwestern writer both by the subject of his fiction and his personal location. However, the circumstances of both writers' relationship to the Midwest are different and connected to factors both regional and institutional. Gass was born in North Dakota and latterly raised in Ohio by a father who worked as a school clerk (Gass xix). Conversely, Wallace is an East coaster by birth, born to parents who relocated to the Midwest to advance his father's nascent academic career at the University of Urbana-Champaign (Max 1). While Wallace lived for a sustained period during childhood and adolescence in Illinois, his later life is marked by a similar institutional itinerancy (he lived, learned and taught for various periods in higher education institutions in Boston, Illinois, Arizona and latterly California). In accordance with Amy Wallace's reminiscence, perception of his regional identity changed dependent upon his location. It is striking to compare the characteristics ascribed to the geography of the Midwestern town in Gass' autobiographical introduction to *In the Heart of the Heart of the Country* with the counterpart descriptions in Wallace's writing. In the introduction to his collection, Gass characterizes his adolescent frustrations with his Midwestern upbringing via descriptions of the *small* and *enclosed*, while the less regionally anchored Wallace tends, in his state fair essay, towards an observation of Midwestern geography as terrifyingly, sublimely *disclosed*, in a description which notably ends with his movement away to Amherst College on the East coast, and is itself a reflection of his description of Illinois in 'Westward the Course of Empire Takes Its Way'. Tellingly, both of Wallace's descriptions here are framed from the perspective of East coasters, from without rather than within:

> Warren, Ohio – factory smoke, depression, household gloom, resentments, illness, ugliness, despair, etcetera, and *littleness, above all, smallness*, the encroachment of the lean and meagre. (Gass xix, emphasis original)
>
> To people from the Coasts, rural IL's topography's a nightmare [...] the land flat and dull and endless [...] For me, at least, it got creepy. By the time I left for college the area no longer seemed dull so much as empty, lonely. Middle-of-the-ocean lonely. (*Supposedly* 84)
>
> Central Illinois is [...] the most *dis*closed, open place you could ever fear to see. (*Girl* 242, emphasis original)

The divergence of these centrifugally inflected descriptions of the Midwest from the fundamentally centripetal spatiality of Gass' landscape, coupled with the rather abstracted, anthropological approach to Midwestern qualities in the examples above, serve to illustrate the fundamental observational *mobility* that is afforded to Wallace's unfettered regional identity. This mobility affords Wallace the opportunity to become, in his words, 'an enormous eyeball floating around something, reporting what it sees' (Interview, Charlie Rose). This choice of image is significant, as a floating, orbiting eyeball is not only disembodied but also necessarily regionally dislocated.[6]

Wallace's putative 'Midwestern' literary persona is also useful because of its stereotypical concordance with the valorization of 'single-entendre principles' (*Supposedly* 81) that explicitly inform his thesis from *Girl with*

*Curious Hair* onward. While there may be a temptation to ascribe a kind of essentialist 'Midwestern' quality to the work because of this concordance, I believe that it is problematic to read regional identity directly as precursor to literary manifesto in Wallace's writing precisely *because* of this performativity and mobility observable in his register. However, while this performative persona may give the lie to any inherent sense of regional 'rootedness' in the work, Wallace's mobility affords him the ability to observe how locations progressively interact with or subsume one another from a pan-regional perspective.

In Wallace's work (and, indeed, his life) regional mobility is often aligned with residency within educational institutions, and particularly with creative writing classes. Accordingly, Wallace can be seen to perform, with some ambivalence over coastal cultural authority, an exegesis of a contemporary literary development in the cultural dialectic between the region, the East coast and the educational institution, a dialectic most succinctly synopsized in the title of Chad Harbach's influential 2010 essay 'MFA vs. NYC'. Harbach outlines the situation of 'two literary fiction cultures' in the United States, 'one condensed in New York, the other spread across the diffuse network of provincial college towns that spans from Irvine to Austin to Ann Arbor to Tallahassee' (12). While much of Harbach's essay, as the title indicates, proceeds from an adversarial position, this 'diffuse network' does not ultimately calcify the ambiguous cultural relationship between the East coast and the 'province'. In fact, as Mark McGurl outlines in his celebrated study *The Program Era*, it has only intensified and problematized that 'oscillation' to which Tom Lutz refers. McGurl outlines how the historical development of the famous Iowa Writers' Workshop has incorporated both regional specificity and, latterly, international diffusion. The workshop initially emerged 'amidst a thriving, self-consciously Midwestern cultural scene' implicitly opposed to a 'dislocated mass culture and to a deracinated cosmopolitan high culture' (*Program* 148). However, it also appeared at 'a moment of crisis for regionalism, since the very sense of cultural difference from the national, New York-centered mainstream which had been its inspiration was here confronted with the possibility of its dissolution by expansion', providing an 'emblem of regionalism's increasingly outward orientation [...] with an eye to acquiring national prestige'. McGurl then traces the further expansion of Iowa's geographical remit and its attempt to position itself as 'a prestigious *international* centre for writers [...] a complex palimpsest of cultural geographies' (149–50, emphasis original). The regional creative writing programme is caught in a double bind, a victim of the success of its own geographical economy. It is faced with two options, both of which will efface its regional identity: to become enmeshed with the 'New York-centred mainstream' or to diffuse its Midwestern specificity within a broader framework of international writing.

Through his performative Midwestern persona and his residency within a series of educational institutions, Wallace is aligned with Harbach's historical model of the 'talented' and 'ambitious' novelists of the latter half of the twentieth century who 'carved out for themselves a cultural position that depended precisely on a combination of public and academic acclaim [...] writing with one eye on the academy and the other on New York': Nabokov, Gaddis, Bellow, Pynchon and DeLillo are cited alongside Wallace (24). Harbach is so confident in the alignment of Wallace's career with his model that he associates Wallace's death with 'the end of this quasi-popular tradition' (24). Like many of those writers described by Harbach as belonging to that category, Wallace is itinerant. However, he is also at least a generation younger than any other writer on Harbach's list, and while some taught at universities (Nabokov's tenure at Cornell being probably the most famous example) Wallace is the only writer who came through the creative writing programme as part of his literary apprenticeship. Therefore, Wallace's relation to what McGurl calls the 'shelter of institutions' ('Institution' 30) is both more developed and more ambivalent.

## Inside and Outside the Institution

Across Wallace's pre-*Pale King* fiction there is a progressive developing relationship between institutional and non-institutional spaces which can be described as alternately separatist, co-operative, symbiotic and cannibalistic. While the early fiction generally describes this relationship with recourse to some fairly well-worn paradigms of postmodern spatiality, the increasing focus in the later fiction of the cross-pollination of these spaces rehearses an ambivalent anxiety central to Wallace's fiction: the institutional site will come, both figuratively and literally, to dominate, subsume and exterminate the space outside of itself.[7] The manner in which this anxious dialectic is depicted in the fiction is fundamentally connected to that aforementioned quality of mobility ascribed to Wallace's register, as it is more often than not dramatized as a spatial question of *movement* and *constraint*, of the ability to move or not move freely within and between these spaces. To this end, Wallace also deploys in his fiction a series of small-scale frameworks of geometric and directional movement (these frameworks also closely associated with questions of entropy and solipsism, the focus of several earlier critics of Wallace).[8] These operate as a counterpoint to the broader macro-scale of cultural anxiety (an anxiety that mirrors that expressed over the monologic effacement of voice described in Chapter 1) over the traversing and subsumption of extra-institutional space by the institution that is not just total, as in Goffman's formulation, but *totalising*.

*The Broom of the System*, submitted by Wallace as one of two theses in Amherst College in 1984 (Max 41), was originally titled *Inside* and divided into two parts subtitled 'The Broom of the System' and 'Interactive Cable', both of which were accompanied on the original contents page by the graphic of an arrow pointing eastward (Box 3.4). While the two-part split remains in the published novel, this original title refers more explicitly to the prevailing spatial models that underpin the narrative: this *bildungsroman* is, after all, predicated upon the importance of escape from linguistic, systemic and institutional structures. While the novel's preoccupation with linguistic constraint and systems theory has been discussed extensively[9] less has been written about the importance of the spatial movement of characters within the institutional environments of the novel's futuristic iteration of Ohio (*Broom*, like *Infinite Jest*, depicts an era only a few years ahead of the novel's publication) and the form of those environments themselves. As befits a novel divided, and later described by Wallace to Larry McCaffery as influenced 'in terms of distinct problems and univocal solutions' (32), many of *Broom*'s trans-environmental motifs present as reasonably clean-cut. Perhaps the prevailing spatial image of *Broom* can be found within Dr Jay's lengthy digression on 'membrane-theory':

> The membrane must be a strong, clean membrane. The strong, clean membrane chooses what to suck inside itself and lets all the rest bounce dirtily off. Only the secure can truly pretend, Lenore. The secure have membranes like strong, clean ova. Like ovums. These membranes withstand the onslaught of the countless Other-set, ceaselessly battering. (330)

However, a closer look at the novel's two-part structure, and the environments within that structure, illustrate a rather more complex, if still formative, spatial model. The first half of the novel establishes a series of institutional environments that are generally 'monadic' (76). The novel's prologue, which takes place in Lenore's older sister's dorm room in Mount Holyoke College, distinguishes strongly between the interior and exterior of the building through an invasion of the dorm room by sexually threatening male students, among them Lenore's future partner Andrew Sealander Lang. Lenore's first substantial action in the novel is to physically escape from the room, negotiating 'a hall door, a stair door, a hall door, and a front door, all locked tight from the inside' in order to escape to the 'well-lit' street outside, where she experiences another microscopic breaking of a monadic barrier, 'a brief nosebleed' (21). The prologue dramatizes the novel in miniature: at the climax of *Broom* Lenore 'gets out, finally she does' (21) after negotiating five apparently 'tightly locked' monadic environments (her apartment, Shaker Heights nursing home, the Bombardini building, Dr Jay's office and her physical imprisonment by Rick Vigorous in the Great Ohio Desert [G.O.D.]) and escapes from the novel itself.

The constructed environments and institutions incepted in part one of *Broom* all dramatize physical and directional constraint in one way or another. East Corinth, the eastern suburb of Cleveland which incorporates Shaker Heights and Lenore's apartment and in which much of the novel's action takes place, is an invention of Wallace, but is roughly geographically contemporaneous with the real Corinth, Ohio, which is an unincorporated community and therefore not locally self-governed, thematically complementing Lenore's lack of autonomy.[10] Within East Corinth, Shaker Heights' nursing home is 'broken into ten sections [...] each roughly pentagonal in shape', these sections arranged in a circle, 'each accessible by two and only two others' with a pool in the centre made of 'concentric circles of colored water' under 'a translucent plastic roof' (37–8). This bizarre architectural description, almost as hard for the reader to picture as it is for the residents and visitors to negotiate, locks the inhabitants into a kind of artificially engineered centripetal orbit, within which Lenore's great-grandmother's room is kept sealed and artificially heated at 98.6 degrees (39).[11] Similarly, in her apartment Lenore possesses 'one of two square bedrooms' with an 'inoperative' fireplace (94). Lenore's place of work, the Bombardini building, is located outside of East Corinth, but is hemmed in by Lake Erie to the north and 'slowly eaten' by the shadow of the Erieview Tower (46) on a daily basis. Lenore's physical position in Dr Jay's office is similarly constrained, as her therapist controls and operates a mechanical chair on a track (61). Conversely, the placing of the most formatively traumatic event in the lives of Lenore's family (the violent and traumatic birth of Lenore's brother LaVache) at the beginning of the second half of the novel (262) figuratively permeates the monadic membrane of the two halves of the book by performing an analepsis that reaches back prior to the beginning of the narrative, also allowing the reader to reflect upon the diffusion of that previously unrevealed narrative across the body of the entire novel. In his personal copy of Tom LeClair's *In the Loop*, Wallace annotated a section about the two-part structure of DeLillo's *Ratner's Star* with the note 'pt I – discrete pt II – continuous' (120), and the structure for *Broom* does appear to cleave broadly to this form, with the individually separate and distinct units described in part one opening up into a continuum in part two that retroactively operates across the entire narrative.[12]

It is in part two of the novel that the action finally enters the G.O.D., a putatively natural environment which is in fact institutionally constructed. The G.O.D., a somewhat unsubtle dramatization of the Baudrillardian 'desert of the real' (Baudrillard 1), has been senselessly imposed by state government upon the site of Wayne National Forest, in a sequence which acts as an embryonic iteration of the more elaborate creation of the Great Concavity in *Infinite Jest* (*Jest* 400–5).[13] The postmodern spatial context of the G.O.D. is boosted by the fact that this event takes place on 21 June 1972, just a month before the destruction of the Pruitt-Igoe housing development in St Louis that Charles Jencks famously aligned with the inception of postmodern architecture. 1972 is also the year of publication of Don DeLillo's *End Zone*, a novel with a significant influence on Wallace's fiction, which takes place in an institution (Logos College) in the middle of the desert landscape of West Texas.[14] However, while DeLillo's protagonist Gary Harkness, who describes the location as 'the middle of the middle of nowhere' and redolent of 'the state of being separated from whatever is left of the center of one's own history' (29–30), nevertheless finds the desert a suitable space for reflection and meditation ('a lovely interlude' [29]), the G.O.D. is characterized as a fundamentally compromised location because of its institutional artificiality. Tellingly, when Lenore and Rick finally travel to the interior of the G.O.D. at the climax of *Broom* they participate in an immobilizing re-enactment of the climax of *another* novel, Frank Norris' *McTeague* (440), an ironic fulfilment of Governor Zusatz's promise that the G.O.D. will be a 'point of savage reference' (54).[15]

The G.O.D. lacks the sophistication of the institutional spaces in Wallace's later fiction, and this is reflected by its geographical distinction from the locations in which the rest of the novel's action takes place. The stratified topology of the G.O.D gestures towards the kind of complex spatial colloquies to be found in *Girl with Curious Hair* onward, but is nevertheless still a circumscribed space that must be physically entered. However, scattered around the narrative of *The Broom of the System* are a number of references to the convoluted geographical and cultural position of the Midwest that will soon develop into something more substantial and make evident that Wallace, writing a broadly Midwestern-set novel while in attendance at Amherst, an East coast college, is increasingly preoccupied with the cultural position of an area 'both in the middle and on the fringe [...] the physical heart, and the cultural extremity' (*Broom* 142). For example, Wallace has a secondary character, nursing home administrator Mr Bloemker, deliver a flatly undramatized speech on region and culture:

Midwesterners [...] stand in such an ambiguous geographical and cultural relation to certain and other less occluded parts of the country that the very objective events and states of affairs that are proper objects of a social awareness must pass in transit to the awareness of the residents here through the filters both of subjectively colored memory and geographical ambivalence. (369)

As clunky as this speech is, it looks forward to a more sustained, spatially complex engagement with the tension expressed between the immobility of Midwesterners (they 'stand') with the mobility of objective events (which 'pass in transit') that they experience, a geographical anxiety also implicitly expressed in the novel through the juxtaposition of the eastward-bound arrows that accompany the beginning of chapters and the subtle invocation of westward-bound egress that pepper the narrative: East Corinth juts 'precipitously westward' (45); the Frequent and Vigorous switchboard and offices are located on the 'western side' of the Bombardini building (47); two of Lenore's apartment windows face west (94). Lenore's definitive escape from her institutional structures at the climax of the novel suggests that the inside/outside binary which governs much of *Broom* extends to Wallace's concept of space: at this point, it is still possible to 'get outside'.

While *Broom* does not explore areas west of Cleveland, *Girl with Curious Hair* is much more directly focused on the Midwest as problematized cultural territory. The collection is framed by Midwestern vistas, with the opening story 'Little Expressionless Animals' beginning in 'a field, in the wind' under a 'cerebral' sky 'low and full of clouds' (3) and the closing novella 'Westward the Course of Empire Takes Its Way' immersed within the 'cartographic obelisk' of the Central Illinois countryside (299). The effect of this framing is to encase the collection, despite its diverse range of environmental locations, within a sense of Midwestern geography: all of the stories are figuratively bound by this horizon. Furthermore, the opening image of the 'cerebral' sky operates as a kind of overture to the collection, indicating a collapsing together of an image of the intellectual and geographical and the relative permeability of both qualities, a conflation echoed in a speech given by Lyndon Johnson in 'Lyndon' where the president announces to students of Amherst College that he 'hitchhiked fifty miles to get back into the classroom' from his manual job as a Highway worker (*Girl* 98).[16] Throughout *Girl with Curious Hair*, the classroom and the region permeate and inform one another, culminating in the subsumption and containment of the Illinois countryside in 'Westward' via the institutional environment of the creative writing workshop. This relationship is fallaciously dialogic: while it has the appearance of a cultural dialogue between regions, the Midwest ultimately becomes spatially circumscribed according to the rules of the institutional workshop.

While the university plays a notable role in the history of the Beadsmans in *Broom*,[17] it remains largely separated from region and does not occupy the dominant role that it assumes in *Girl*, where 'institutional thinking' subjectively transforms the Midwestern landscape into a systemized diagram, as when graduate student Bruce in 'Here and There', struggling to orientate himself emotionally, visualizes 'a unit of memories [...] laid out and systematised like a colored print on the gray, chewed-looking two-lane road ahead of me' (157). In a further development from *Broom*, where Rick's stories originate outside of a university setting, *Girl with Curious Hair* stages a process whereby the tropes of fiction writing are captured and held within the educational institutional spaces that subsequently begin to dominate the environments without. The prevailing focus on educational institutions is unsurprising, since most of the stories in the collection were produced and workshopped while Wallace was attending the MFA programme in the University of Arizona in the mid-1980s (Max 60). The release of the collection is also roughly contemporaneous with the essay 'Fictional Futures and the Conspicuously Young', in which Wallace describes a form of contemporary writing he terms 'Workshop Hermeticism [...] over which Writing-Program pre- and proscriptions loom with the enclosing force of horizons' (*Both* 40). Wallace's employment of an explicitly *spatial* metaphor for bad MFA fiction is a useful way of understanding the frameworks of geographical mobility and hybridity of institutional and regional space in *Girl with Curious Hair*. Of course, as Kasia Boddy has argued *Girl with Curious Hair* is itself an 'exemplary product' of the program era, though while the collection does indeed act as 'an interrogation of that era's modes and mores' (23), its emergence from *within* the MFA programme also establishes the book's own delimited horizons.[18]

This 'nesting' of the collection and its generative context locates the regional space that frames the opening and closing stories of *Girl with Curious Hair* within a claustrophobic formulation whereby it is continually reconstituted and remapped according to the ideology of the institution that has engendered its cultural and literary function. This containment and reconfiguration of Midwestern space is most obviously evident in 'Westward the Course of Empire Takes Its Way', where the sublimity of the Illinois cornfields fuses symbiotically and claustrophobically with the oppressive politics of the East Chesapeake Tradeschool Writing Program through the subjectivity of the story's principal narrator, who is most likely an unidentified member of the workshop. This spatial enclosure speaks to the anxieties expressed recursively across the collection over confinement: the televisual 'psychic split between surface and interior' (Boswell, *Understanding* 75) in 'Little Expressionless Animals'; the ever more occluded parking lots in 'Luckily the Account Representative Knew CPR'; the encroaching buzzards at the window in 'John Billy' (142); Bruce's climactic entrapment behind a stove in 'Here and There' (170). In addition to these dramatizations of claustrophobic situations, the collection is often spatially characterized by a preoccupation with 'englobement', a term I derive from John Ashbery's poem 'Self Portrait in a Convex Mirror', the third stanza of which Wallace quotes in 'Little Expressionless Animals' (*Girl* 42). Marshall Boswell has analysed the importance of the poem to the collection:

> The portrait [of Parmigianino] in the painting as well as in [Ashbery's] poem is 'life englobed' – that is, life transmitted into mediated territory – and although 'One would like to stick one's hand/Out of the globe, ... its dimension/What carries it, will not allow it.' The world within the text/poem looms out into the world but cannot break through [...] Like Wallace's story, then, Ashbery's poem both entertains the fantasy of escaping textuality, of breaking through, and rejects it simultaneously. (*Understanding* 74)

While Boswell's analysis here is phrased in response to Wallace's use of television in his fiction, and also speaks to the ongoing anxiety expressed in Wallace's debut over whether the self is 'nothing but a linguistic construct'

('Interview with Larry McCaffery' 41), I diverge somewhat here in my discussion of how 'englobement' operates in the collection to incorporate the idea of spatial containment and the 'englobing' of particular areas by institutional spaces. The motif of the globe, and particularly the *curve* implied by the shape of the globe, occupies a recurrent, vexed position throughout the collection. A sustained and ambivalent description can be found at the climax of 'Lyndon':

> Forget the curved circle, for whom distance means the sheer size of what it holds inside. Build a road. Make a line. Go as far west as the limit of the country lets you – Bodega Bay, not Whittier, California – and make a line; and let the wake of the line's movement be the distance between where it starts and what it sees; and keep making that line, west, farther and farther; and the earth's circle will clutch at that line [...] and the giant curve that informs straight lines will bring you around, in time, to the distant eastern point of the country behind you, that dim master bedroom on the dim far eastern shore of the Atlantic; and the circle you have made is quiet and huge, and everything the world holds is inside: the bedroom. (117)

This convoluted description, much closer in register to the lengthy reverie that closes 'Westward' than anything else in 'Lyndon', appears to describe the making of a straight line that eventually becomes a global circle, subject to the 'giant curve that informs straight lines'. The aim of this gesture initially appears inclusionary, framing the world of President Lyndon Johnson, which must necessarily be politically commensurate with the whole globe, the bedroom within which Lyndon, his assistant Dave Boyd and Boyd's lover Duverger converge, and the interior world of Boyd himself. However, while this englobing movement might appear to represent a unification of disparate physical and figurative areas, the story ends in possible betrayal, as Dave discovers that his lover has concealed a relationship to Johnson of which he was previously unaware, reducing Boyd to an 'alien presence' (118). The englobing movement in this uneasy climax also indirectly and ambivalently echoes the sentiments of the first pronouncement by Johnson to Boyd in his office, which uneasily amalgamate institutional inclusivity and possession: 'I own the fucking floor you stand on, boy' (77), which is itself an apparently misjudged attempt at expressing affection, according to Johnson's wife ('You contain one another. He says he owns the floor you stand on' [116]). The englobing image in 'Lyndon' indirectly indicates a centripetal global subjugation to US territory, which acts as precursor to Wallace's more effective employment of the motif at regional level in 'Westward'.[19] It is also surely no coincidence that global presidential power in 'Lyndon' is often framed in the context of speeches within educational institutions: Wallace's alma mater Amherst College (which has already featured in *Broom* [98]), Columbia University (103) and, tellingly, 'Chesapeake High School' (92), which is pointedly located in the same region as the writing workshop in 'Westward', by which story the institution has essentially *become* the world, figuratively englobing the wild Midwestern territory within which the graduate student protagonists travel.

The curve repeatedly directs movement in 'Westward', while making it unclear where exactly that movement is directed. In similar fashion to how the 'curving orifice of the exit ramp' prevents the titular account representative from contact with the outside world earlier in the collection (47), the curves of the road in 'Westward' effectively prevent the travelling party from seeing their destination. The level landscape, 'flat right to the earth's curve', also seems to engender a feeling of disorientation, perhaps even a kind of Burkean terror ('it's almost hard to even look' [244]), while the evocation of the place where 'everything curves. So everything's right in front of your nose' (352) suggests a region that is both vast and intensely claustrophobic.[20] If these references are largely implicit, then Dave's decision to stand firm 'against every curve's wave-like surge' and not to rat on his cellmate in the story's closing section (which is itself set within a prison) posits the curve as an overbearing force (369). The repeated references in 'Westward' to this imprisoning, englobing curve, and the subsumption of the Midwestern location to corporate infrastructure (in this case, the McDonald's corporation), have generally been critically taken to indicate a working to exhaustion of particular tropes of postmodern metafiction.[21] While this is an important critical reading, I want to suggest that the implicit subsumption of the Illinois landscape within the englobing motion of 'Westward' is also indexed to the problematic historical relationship between Midwestern literature and the creative writing workshop, and Wallace's own mobile and performative Midwestern identity. While a straight reading of 'Westward' in the context of Wallace's famous essay 'E Unibus Pluram' would appear to direct the blame squarely at the co-opting of ironic postmodern fiction by corporate advertising, it is equally important to consider the association between the MFA and the market described by Caren Irr in *Toward the Geopolitical Novel*: '[p]rogram fiction's interest in technical competence can endorse neoliberal market logic just as easily as liberal pluralism […] American universities consistently align middle-class professionalism with capitalist market pragmatism' (19).

Correspondingly, during his aforementioned discussion of the waning regional identity of the Iowa Writers' Workshop in *The Program Era*, Mark McGurl traces the further expansion of Iowa's geographical remit and its attempt to commercially position itself as an international centre for writers:

> It was a complex palimpsest of cultural geographies, none of them succeeding in fully cancelling out the others; the common polestar of this regionalist/nationalist/internationalist tangle was the pursuit of institutional and individual prestige. As [Iowa Writers' Workshop director Paul Engle] put it […] 'I have the warmest feelings about the Midwest and have written much about it, but the Workshop had to strive for excellence, not localism.' In other words, 'localism' was no longer the path to 'excellence' it had only recently seemed. (150)

This 'complex palimpsest' is at the heart of 'Westward'. Wallace, a putatively Midwestern but effectively trans-regional writer, identifies the Midwest via the perspectives of members of a writer's workshop as an area of both expansion and imprisonment. The composition of the story is also roughly contemporaneous with Wallace's transplantation from the Midwest setting of his upbringing and his debut novel, to his experience in the workshop at Arizona, and his subsequent dalliance with the East coast literary establishment ('Westward' was largely written at Yaddo, in New York [Max 89]). In a neat concordance, McGurl outlines how 'the mythical personae' of 'the Midwestern pioneer' that underlies this regionalism ('a traveller with his eye on the next horizon') also necessarily engenders its diffusion (151).²² This is perhaps the clearest illustration of why 'englobement' is an important leitmotif in *Girl with Curious Hair*: it dramatizes an institutionally directed 'curve' that is simultaneously constraining ('regional') and outwardly engaged ('global'), with the caveat that this very outward engagement necessitates the waning of one's own regional identity.²³,²⁴

The final image of 'Westward', of a wheel that 'has lost its ringing hub, has disclosed a radial's spokes' (373) seemingly presents a systematic challenge to the motif of englobement that has characterized *Girl*. The image is a recurrence of JD Steelritter's earlier rumination on whether Ambrose Gatz's apparently self-serving question 'For whom is the funhouse fun?' might actually conceal something 'true and sad and hubless' (242). The removal of the wheel's hub (I presume that Wallace refers to the *hubcap*, as the image does not make sense otherwise) and the disclosure of the radial spokes implicitly describes a form that is putatively encircled but that also diverges outward in multiple directions. The extension of radial spokes outward from a central hub incorporates the aforementioned motifs of expansion, but also suggests an outward motion that is associated, by its proximity to the end of the story, with an act of outwardly bound communication and dialogue (the final line of the story is 'You are loved' [373]). The image simultaneously recalls and challenges the earlier sealed, constrictive centripetal orbit of Shaker Heights in *Broom*, suggesting that the 'spin against the spin, inside' (373) might enable an unconstrained action to be produced centrifugally from *within* a constrained spatial model: the spokes are, of course, still encircled by the wheel itself. Moreover, the climatic disclosure of the circular centre in the image of the hubless wheel, and its implicit correspondence to the bullseye at which the young archer and writer Mark Nechtr aims, diffuses the directional tension implicit in the employment of the counter-directional arrows that accompany the chapter headings in *The Broom of the System*. The implication in 'Westward' is that the climactic arrow is fired *outward*, in a vector outwith the boundaries of the story and 'right in the heart' (294) of the reader, at whom the final declaration of love is aimed.

The climactic use of this complex spatial model formally dramatizes both the constraint afforded by the institution in 'Westward' and also the possibility of escape from within that institution: the climax of the story is, of course, framed as a piece of fiction from the creative writing workshop itself. However, unlike at the climax of *Broom* this escape is contingent upon the modes of production of the institution itself. This model will characterize much of Wallace's fiction to come, and in its abstraction will also signal a move away (for a time at least) from the earlier focus on regional environments and towards a more abstract concept of institutional and extra-institutional space.

## Retreating Inside: *Infinite Jest* and *Brief Interviews with Hideous Men*

*Infinite Jest* forgoes the Midwestern spaces of the earlier fiction and is located instead within a series of educational and rehabilitation institutions within and around the adjacent coastal cities of Boston and Cambridge and describes a trajectory of progressive institutionalization that continues throughout Wallace's following collection *Brief Interviews with Hideous Men*. There are fewer substantial representations of extra-institutional spaces in these texts, and when these areas do appear they tend to be fundamentally compromised, adulterated or hostile: the streets of Cambridge in *Infinite Jest*, for example, are plagued with murder, drug abuse and violent crime (*Jest* 128–35, 719–21) and the mountains against which Marathe and Steeply hold their dialogue are uninhabitable. Adam Kelly notes that 'the point made consistently throughout *Infinite Jest* is that the world outside institutions is inhospitable to the contemporary individual' (Kelly, 'Dialectic'), and indeed these two texts gesture, in their description of polluted territories and paralysing social interactions, towards a literal *toxification* of the world outside the institutional space. It is no coincidence that three of the brief interviews (#15, #36 and #59) in the latter collection take place in secure facilities, while interview #28 is heavily inflected with institutional language. When coupled with *Infinite Jest*'s prevailing focus upon infantilization, it is tempting to think of the institution in these texts as both fulfilling and accelerating the function of Gaston Bachelard's famous description of the house, with the ontological peril that might lie outside its walls: 'Without it, man would be a dispersed being [...] It is body and soul. It is the human being's first world. Before he is "cast into the world," [...] man is laid in the cradle of the house' (7). Correspondingly, in a development of the spatial formulation of 'Westward' these texts also stage heavily mediated description of extra-institutional spaces *from within* the institution. In the most sustained example, the cartographic reconfiguration in *Infinite Jest* of the United States, Canada and Mexico into O.N.A.N. and the accompanying designation and pollution of the Great Concavity is reported through the narrative of a film made and screened within Enfield Tennis Academy (380–407), a hybrid home, school and sports training camp that is situated atop a hill that has been denuded for the purposes of its construction.

*Infinite Jest* and *Brief Interviews* stage an acceleration of the spatial constraint afforded by institutions in Wallace's earlier fiction. Both texts perform a retreat into institutional spaces and an accretive reduction of mobility under the proviso that a select number of those institutions (the most obvious example being Alcoholics Anonymous in *Infinite Jest*) can figuratively and spatially reconfigure constraint as a kind of freedom. *Infinite Jest*, which in manuscript form was originally divided into two parts in a similar fashion to *The Broom of the System*,[25] partially achieves this through enacting a narrative structure identified as 'fractal' by Michael Silverblatt and clarified by Wallace as resembling a 'lopsided' triangular-shaped fractal called a Sierpinski Gasket (Interview, *Bookworm* 1996).[26] Abandoning a two-part structure, Wallace instead constructs a series of associative, recursive relationships between discrete parts of the novel to create a narrative structure that is characterized by 'connectedness' across its entire body. This structural method is illustrated by a marginal listing in a draft of the novel that describes a number of individual sequences ('main body of Lenz-dog and Gately fight, with worked-in inserts of dialogues, Mario and Madame, Gately & Joelle on UHID, Orin & Slansker, Slansker CV') which are followed by the note 'This needs to be broken up' (Box 16.6).[27]

The constraint associated with the englobing motif in *Girl* is reconfigured by Wallace within *Infinite Jest* into a 'redemptive' circular image which is itself a development of the radial hubless wheel model described at the climax of 'Westward': a circular motif that at first suggests imprisonment before allowing the possibility of escape.[28] However, the pathological 'cycles' of behaviour that characterize a number of failed rehabilitations in *Infinite*

*Jest* are initially aligned with the physically constraining circularity of some of the institutions in the novel. For example, Ennet House Drug and Alcohol Recovery House is the 'sixth of seven exterior Units on the grounds of an Enfield Marine Public Health Hospital complex that [...] resembles seven moons orbiting a dead planet' (193). Enfield Tennis Academy, location of the increasingly dysfunctional Incandenza family and a series of nested institutions (school, sports academy and family home), is characterized by its four 'inward-facing' buildings (*Jest* 983n3) and convoluted series of interconnecting subterranean tunnels, within which matriarch Avril Incandenza prefers to travel. In an extraordinary sequence partially cut from the published text and roughly narratively contemporaneous with the description of Ennet House's 'orbit', Orin Incandenza dreams that he is 'dangling upside down with his mother's permeated face strapped around his own face, eyeball to eyeball, in a decaying orbit around the planet earth' (Box 16.3).[29]

This constraint performs a kind of calcification of the body, one that recalls a hyperbolic acceleration of the subjugation of the individual to the 'facticity' of the institution as described by Berger and Luckmann: the patterning of the movement of the body, and sometimes even the physical corpus itself, into an institutional 'shape'. As Heather Houser has argued, drawing attention to the mapping of physical organs on to architecture in the novel, 'social norms, values and symbols sediment in built spaces and are taken up by the bodies that move through them' (129).[30] Correspondingly, *Infinite Jest*'s institutionally corrupted wilderness, the Great Concavity, operates in a degraded form of the englobement afforded to the Midwestern landscape in 'Westward', with the 'total, menacingly fertile' corn crop of that story (*Girl* 275) entropically transfigured via the process of annular fusion into a perpetual *cycle* that alternates between 'overgrown to wasteland to overgrown several times a month' (*Jest* 573). Despite originating from a governmental policy predicated upon a monadic sense of separate clean and toxic spaces, the Concavity does not behave in the same manner as the G.O.D., which in a reflection of *Broom*'s prevailing focus on monadism retains a sealed border. The Concavity, conversely, *encroaches* upon the areas around it: 'displacing waste means displacing people' (Houser 125). The encroachment of the exponentially toxic region accordingly necessitates a retreat back indoors, inside the institutions within which the characters of *Infinite Jest* retreat into themselves.

Such cyclical constraint therefore acts in opposition to the breakthrough promised by the centrifugal 'spin against the spin' at the end of 'Westward'. However, the overcoming of pathological behaviour in *Infinite Jest* is ultimately posited as being generated from *within* the constrictive spatial institutional model itself. This process is a development of what is hinted at by the radial wheel model in 'Westward': the solution to institutional constraint can only be found by retreating further into institutional behaviour. The most obvious example is the 'traditional huge circle' (*Jest* 503) employed during AA meetings, during which the 'vicious cycle' can be reappropriated into an act of sharing and communion. Don Gately, stoically battling against his substance addiction, is the novel's exemplar of how submission to institutionally directed regulations, themselves apparently constrictive and arbitrary, will ultimately lead to freedom:

> [Gately] hits the knees in the A.M. and asks for Help and then hits the knees again at bedtime and says Thank You, whether he believes he's talking to Anything/-body or not, and he somehow gets through the day clean. This, after ten months of ear-smoking concentration and reflection, is still all he feels like he 'understands' about the 'God angle'. (443)

Gately's ritualized behaviour is echoed in the sports pedagogy of Enfield Tennis Academy's Gerhard Schtitt, aggressively headhunted by James Incandenza 'as a kind of antidote to reductionist sporting strategies' (Burn, 'Machine' 42). Schtitt has formulated a psycho-geometric spatial theory of tennis as a system of self-transcendence, whereby

> Real tennis was really about not the blend of statistical order and expansive potential that the game's technicians revered, but in fact the opposite – *not*-order, *limit*, the places where things broke down, fragmented into beauty. That real tennis was no more reducible to delimited factors or probability curves than chess or boxing [...] a matter not of reduction at all, but – perversely – of expansion, the aleatory flutter of uncontrolled, metastatic growth – each well-shot ball admitting of n possible responses,

> 2n possible responses to those responses, and on to what Incandenza would articulate [...] as a Cantorian continuum of infinities of possible move and response. (81–2, emphasis original)[31]

However, Schtitt's assertion that through this formula the player can 'transcend the limited self whose limits make the game possible in the first place' (84) is grounded within some decidedly suspect political ideology and iconography. Schtitt, a septuagenarian Austrian, is presented as a caricature of fascist disciplinarianism. News of his dismissal from another academy as a result of 'a really unfortunate incident involving a riding crop', as well as references to his 'shiny black boots' and 'old F.R.G.-era BMW cycle' (*Jest* 79) further embellishes the image of fascistic severity. It is perhaps unfair to suggest, as Mark McGurl does, that 'neither Wallace nor Wallace's novel has any serious problem' ('Institution' 40) with Schtitt's implied fascism: Schtitt's lopsided dialogue with Mario Incandenza, bathetically complemented by Schtitt's subsequent revelation that he once fell in love with a tree (83), indicates that Schtitt himself is not himself playing an even game.[32] However, McGurl's suggestion that 'it is only in submission to the human institutional order that individuals have a chance to survive and thrive' ('Institution' 40) and Kelly's argument that 'true freedom [...] is now to be found in recognizing limits and submitting oneself to boundaries' (Kelly, 'Dialectic') undoubtedly speak to the spatial formulation of *Infinite Jest* which problematizes extra-institutional space in the narrative.

However, while Mary Holland's related criticism that when the 'limitations from which the characters suffer and through which they are defined equally shape and bind the world and structure of the novel, no room for critique remains' (*Succeeding* 84) is based within an astute reading of the novel's approach to narcissism, this approach discounts the importance of the aforementioned 'fractal' structure to an outwardly directed reader comprehension of the novel's discrete component parts.[33] As the reader performs a linear rearrangement of the novel's disparate spatial and temporal elements, they create a hermeneutic space which mirrors the 'huge circle' of communication. It is this reader-directed framework that ultimately characterizes the major territorial shift within *Infinite Jest*. As spatial restriction becomes more exponential, egress can be found in the erection of a communication loop between narrative and reader whereby the reader reconstructs the narrative. However, this approach does *not* stage a recovery of the non-institutional space lost in the narrative of *Infinite Jest*, with the final ordinal reference to a mysterious 'continental emergency' (934) suggesting that the shoring up of the redemptive power of the institution may have come at the cost of the space outside itself.[34]

Accordingly, the vast majority of *Brief Interviews with Hideous Men* takes place indoors or in artificially constructed natural surroundings. Wallace was blustery about the content of the collection in interviews ('there isn't really an agenda with this book' ['Interview with Patrick Arden' 95]) but a letter to Michael Pietsch reveals that the internal structure of the book was considered at length ('I feel pretty good about both the mss's constituents and their order as they stand. I like the way they play off one another and the way certain leitmotifs weave through them' ['Letter to Michael Pietsch, August 17th 1998']).[35] While Boswell calls the collection a 'recapitulation' that does 'not significantly advance its author's art' (*Understanding* 181), I believe that the retreat into institutional space enacted in *Brief Interviews*, and the associated eclipse of the area outside, does represent a demonstrable development of Wallace's spatial preoccupation. It is not insignificant that the collection begins with a history of post-industrial life that is 'Radically Condensed', and this condensation of space continues throughout the collection, from the aforementioned institutionalized hideous men to the toilet attendant's residence in 'the vortex' in interview #42 (73). However, perhaps the most revealing spatial juxtaposition occurs between 'Death is not the End' and 'Forever Overhead', the first two full-length stories in the collection.

'Forever Overhead' was, by Wallace's admission, a story that had never found a suitable home. He admits to Larry McCaffery in 1993 that 'I did the first draft of that story in college and it's been through about twenty drafts over the course of about eight years' (42), and D.T. Max accordingly places the composition at Arizona (Max 55), but I would suggest that the earliest iteration of the story can actually be found in Rick's memory of Vance's childhood in *Broom*, which is remarkably similar in both narrative register and subject matter ('the pool gives birth to clean new red-eyed children [...] the red sun lowers to melt into the blue bath of clean chlorine' [299]). Considering how problematic Wallace clearly found 'Forever Overhead', even going so far as to tell Larry McCaffery it was a 'failed' story (42), it is significant that he chooses to incorporate it adjacent to 'Death is not the End', which is also a story about a male character and a pool. While the protagonist of 'Death is not the End' is 56, the boy in 'Forever Overhead' is only 13, and the placement of the stories and similarity of subject matter positions 'Forever Overhead' as an implicit analepsis that pivots around the function of the pool and associated environment. The young boy on the diving board is on the verge of entering a pool that is referred to variously as 'public' (5), a 'system of movement' (7) and, on three occasions, as a 'machine' (7, 10). The implication of the story's fairly unsubtle central metaphor is that an entry into the pool is an immersion in the public, adult world ('the board will nod and you will go' suggests the inevitability of the event [13]) but it is also significant that the moments before the immersion in the pool afford the boy a view of a layered vista beyond the pool area:

> Beyond this a hot black parking lot full of white lines and glittering cars. A dull field full of dry grass and hard weeds, old dandelions' downy heads [...] And past all this, reddened by a round slow September sun, are mountains, jagged, their tops' sharp angles darkening into definition against a deep red tired light. (5)

Conversely, the poolside environment in 'Death is not the End' within which the middle-aged poet lounges horizontally is described as an 'enclosed tableau', a hermetically sealed environment surrounded by 'enclosing fauna' (3). This static scene, 'wholly still and composed and enclosed' (3) reconfigures the natural vista of 'Forever Overhead' into a womb-like constructed border, which prevents the intrusion of any other outside element, including sound. The juxtaposition of these stories at the beginning of the collection stages an overture to the trapped, constrained characters the reader is about to experience, from the interviewees to the infamous 'Depressed Person', whose exponential paratextual thought process threatens to spatially eclipse her principal narrative.[36] Moreover, the shift in natural environment between the two poolside stories effectively dramatizes the steady effacement of extra-institutional space that has occurred throughout the preceding fiction, through the employment of natural flora and fauna to create an artificial hermetic border within which the older and thoroughly institutionalized individual resides: the story lists the poet's many institutionally awarded prizes in the same detached register that describes his physical form.[37]

From this perspective, perhaps the most strongly institutionally inflected brief interview in the collection is interview #59, in which a male character in 'Harold R and Phyllis N. Engleman Institute for Continuing Care' recounts a sexual fantasy about stopping time (181). The interviewee's fantasy is specifically drawn from the 'State Exercise Facilities' where his military father was posted (182) and is based around the thoroughly institutionalized 'young women of the military or civilian atomic engineering services' (183). The interviewee explains how his fantasy, which has increasingly little to do with the actual act of sex itself and more with situational control, became progressively more difficult to sustain due specifically to the lack of hermeticism afforded to the facility. The interviewee requires the kind of institutional 'barrier' described by Goffman for psychological stability:

> [The facility] is in truth public, open to all those of the post's personnel with proper documentation desiring to exercise; therefore, some person at any time could with ease stride into the facility in the midst of the hand's seduction [...] To me this was not acceptable. (186)

The increasingly ridiculous mental gymnastics required to sustain the fantasy lead to the interviewee's proposal that his imagined freezing of time must extend beyond 'one bleak Siberian defense outpost' to incorporate 'the freezing of the entire state' (187) before realizing that 'the state itself existed in close ideological and defensive alliance with many neighbouring satellite states, and, of course, also was in communication and trade with countless other of the world's nations' (188). The interviewee finally suffers a breakdown at the point at which he tries to make the fantasy incorporate the orbit of planets within the solar system (190–1). Once again, the orbiting motif is associated with a loss of autonomy. At the point of interview, the speaker is, of course, captive in another much more secure institution. The reference to a Siberian landscape, which indirectly echoes the frozen 'tableau' of 'Death is not the End', is one of a small number of references made in the collection to the world outside the institution, the interviewee's inability to square his fantasy with a non-institutional public space causing a breakdown that necessitates enclosure within an even more spatially constricted area.

Despite this accretive process of institutional constraint there is, perhaps, an implicit counterforce contained within both 'Death is not the End' and interview #59, one that incorporates a recognition of a world outside the protective sealed space. The final, gnomic footnoted pronouncement in 'Death is not the End', that the description of the 'enclosing flora's motionless green' as 'vivid and inescapable' is 'not wholly true' (3), seems to defy the hermetically sealed space of the story both by its contrarianism and physical placement outside the body of the main narrative. Similarly, the entry of an interviewer into the secure institution that houses interviewee #59 and brings his story into the environment outside suggests that through a repositioning of the account as a kind of case study, that diagnosis can lead to cure. Despite this possibility, the sense of institutional encroachment and the toxic nature of the outside world permeates the narratives of *Brief Interviews* and has progressed exponentially by the publication of *Oblivion*.

## 'That Carved Out Square of Something Green': *Oblivion*

The progressive effacement of non-institutional space in Wallace's fiction is effectively illustrated by the manner in which the enclosure of the stories in *Girl* with two Midwestern vistas is mirrored by the two skyscrapers that bracket *Oblivion*, a collection within which the retreat into the institution has been fully performed.[38] The stories in *Oblivion*, some of which were composed at the same time as *The Pale King*, have a stronger ambivalence about institutional structures than that text, tending towards a description of offices and classrooms in terms of their ability to inspire horror and disorientation. Marshall Boswell accurately describes the spatial model in *Oblivion* as the opening up of 'an outer layer of interiority into which the story's principal layer has been nesting all along' ('Constant' 152), a process strikingly illustrated when the narrator of 'The Soul is not a Smithy' describes how his Civics class had 'built papier mache models of the branches of government' (68), thus constructing a physical model of an institution inside a class based around the function of government which is being taught within another institution, a school classroom. In an important shift, while the receding space outside the institution in the earlier fiction is at least representative of a tactile, corporeal environment, in *Oblivion* the perceived exterior becomes just another institutional stratum. With 'Mister Squishy' and 'The Suffering Channel', *Oblivion* also performs an exploration of the toxic spatiality of corporate institutions which seek, through market strategy, to mould the world outside themselves into their own image, thus representing a development of that 'totalising' effect afforded to the educational institution in the earlier fiction. Much of the disorientation felt by the characters within the disorientatingly stratified institutions of *Oblivion* can be aligned with an iteration of Kevin Lynch's warning about the risks pertaining to the visual incomprehensibility of the urban environment, where 'if there is little relation between levels' there is an 'extra burden of organisation on the observer' (Lynch 86). It is precisely a misunderstanding about literal and figurative 'levels', extended within *Oblivion* to incorporate the physical corporate hierarchy implied by the floors of skyscrapers and office buildings, which traps the characters ever more in their delimited interior worlds. Furthermore, the climactic novella 'The Suffering Channel' also marks a pointed return to the Midwestern territories of Wallace's earlier fiction, but the Midwest appears here in a strikingly mediated form, a simulacrum engendered by a combination of regional mobility and performativity and the cultural power of the coastal publishing institution.

The accretive process of institutional constraint is strongly illustrated in 'Mr Squishy' and 'The Soul is not a Smithy', the two stories that open the collection. Both make indirect geographical reference to the urban environments of *Broom*, with 'Mr Squishy' taking place in a large tower adjacent to a great lake and 'The Soul is not a Smithy' located in the same state, Ohio. The return to the Midwest in the latter story is striking for its difference from the environments last seen in 'Westward', with the view from the narrator's classroom window (which are tellingly located in the east side of the room, rather than the west [*Oblivion* 70]) presenting only 'grey skies and bare trees' chassis' (71). Like the tinted windows in 'Mr Squishy' that the downtrodden product tester Terry Schmidt prefers, having 'stopped looking at the sky' or 'opening the lightproof curtains' (33), the window in 'Soul' is not looked *through* to the environment outside, but instead looked *at*, with the narrator creating a fantasy narrative in the wire mesh embedded in the glass. The response to the world outside the institutional window in these two stories is characterized implicitly by a fear of contamination and, indirectly, downward social mobility: Schtitt fears for his job in the broader global hierarchy of the Reesemeyer Shannon Belt corporation, while the narrator of 'Soul' imagines a series of increasingly horrific events taking place within a 'shabby neighbourhood' (79). Neither protagonist realizes that they are so implicated within the institution itself that the world that presents itself outside of the window is simply a reflection of the environment taking place inside. The product testers of 'Mister Squishy' occupy a vantage point similar to the protagonist of 'Forever Overhead', but are so 'implicated' (25) within the corporation that the view has become immaterial. Schmidt, who views the confections made by his employer 'with the expression of an urchin at a toystore's window' (14) is about to be confronted through the window of the conference room with a giant corporate emblem, unveiled by a clambering Mr Squishy employee who may also be operating as a tester to prove the ineffectiveness of the very class of facilitators to which Schmidt belongs (62).[39] Similarly, the increasingly violent and sordid narrative that appears within the mesh window in 'The Soul is not a Smithy' is a subconscious reflection of the physical threat posed by the narrator's substitute teacher, Mr Johnson, who is having a psychotic breakdown in the classroom. The culmination of the story's window motif occurs with the narrator's nightmare vision of 'a number of men at desks in rows in a large, brightly lit room', where 'if there were windows, I do not remember noticing them' (103). The nightmare is poignantly juxtaposed with the narrator's mental image of his father 'looking at that carved out square of something green', the circumscribed grassy area adjacent to his office where he spent his lunch break 'year after year' (106).[40,41]

The narrator's nightmare climaxes when 'I look up and into the lens of the dream's perspective and stare back at myself, but without any sign of recognition on my face' (110). This horrific moment of involution illustrates the degree of recursivity that has been obtained in the bleak institutional environments of *Oblivion*, where the possibility that a constraining institutional structure can be reconfigured into a communicative space has been obliterated by the sheer spatial 'facticity' of the institution itself. Perhaps the most acute example occurs in the climactic conversation in 'Mr Squishy' between Scott Laleman and Alan Britton of Reesemeyer Shannon Belt on the future of Team Δy, the market research firm of which Terry Schmidt is a member. It is revealed that 'in Belt and Britton's forward-looking vision, the market becomes its own test. Terrain = Map. Everything encoded [...] Team Δy would become 100% tech driven, abstract, its own Captured Shop' (64). This strategy, with the latter term (which appears to be Wallace's own neologism) neatly incorporating the language of both physical enclosure and corporate capital, performs a comprehensive cartographical eliding of any environment outside the institutional space.[42] In this way, Wallace dramatizes the metastatic spread of the totalising institutional environment and its reconfiguration and appropriation of the world outside of itself to its own image and design.

In the collection's concluding novella, 'The Suffering Channel', Wallace returns to the Midwest for the longest sustained period since 'Westward'. It is a qualified homecoming: in 'The Suffering Channel' the Midwest, in a calcification of the 'englobed' environment from 'Westward', has become a different kind of 'captured shop', a simulacra of all the cultural tropes of the 'Midwest' generated within the American coastal media. Skip Atwater, a native Midwesterner employed at *Style* magazine in New York City, knows 'the shape of the terrain that *Style*'s WHAT IN THE WORLD feature covered' (*Oblivion* 240), pursuing 'the triumph of creative achievement in even the unlikeliest places' (245), the latter sentence pointedly conflating Brint Moltke's colon (which produces exquisitely rendered faecal sculptures) with the Indiana locale in which he resides. Lee Konstantinou proffers an acute model of the coastal-Midwestern relationship in 'The Suffering Channel':

> The closed loop of the US media system is [...] geographically bifurcated. At the core of the system, we have those coastal Americans, the highly professional, extremely thin interns at Style [...] who produce US culture. At the system's periphery, midwestern Americans [...] do little more than consume the nobrow culture [their] counterparts in New York produce [...]

> Skip Atwater, born in the Midwest but now working for the East Coast culture industry, serves as a bridge figure, shuttling between these social zones. ('World' 74)

Konstantinou's reference to the 'closed loop' (which could also adequately describe the annular processes of the Great Concavity or the hermetically sealed environments of Brief Interview #59 and 'Death is not the End') establishes a spatial model of the constricted Midwestern environment in 'The Suffering Channel'. His argument that the 'world' implied by this frivolous human-interest column 'refers to anything but the world' (77) is also important, as it unites the motif of the 'englobed' Midwest of 'Westward' with the heavily circumscribed Midwest-as-perceived-through-East-coast-institution described here. In both cases, the Midwest is spatially enclosed and defined by the constricting curve of a putative 'world' which is in fact only the generated ideology of an institution *that perceives itself to be the world* (the writing workshop, the East coast media). This model is accentuated by the heavily policed length of Atwater's WHAT IN THE WORLD column, which is restricted to 'one 400 word piece every three weeks' (243), a limit implicitly and ironically contrasted with the amount of energy Atwater expends in getting the story, and indeed the length of 'The Suffering Channel' itself.

Those Midwestern 'mounds' described by Bryant in 'The Prairies' reappear in 'The Suffering Channel' in a conversation between Atwater and Brint Moltke's wife Amber, 'less a person than a vista, a quarter ton of sheer Midwest pulchritude' (*Oblivion* 250). Amber remarks on how Atwater has partially effaced his regional accent, noting that 'sometimes I can hear it and then other times you sound more... all business' (277). Atwater explains that he is originally from Anderson, Indiana, to which Amber responds 'Up by Muncie you mean. Where all the big mounds are', remarking that 'they still say they don't know who made all those mounds. They just know they're old' (278). Despite its brevity, there is a striking concordance between the ideological function of Bryant's reference to the mounds and their indirect appearance in the story. The invocation of the mounds in Atwater and Moltke's conversation is, I would argue, indirectly evocative of the imposition of one physical and ideological landscape over another, a mediation that recalls the stratification of the respective civilizations that have colonized the land in Bryant's poem (Atwater's work is produced from within a new kind of 'mound', a skyscraper). This evocation is significant because the cultural moment within which 'The Suffering Channel' takes place represents, as seen through the eyes of the returning Atwater, a contemporary institutional reconfiguration; that of the ideology of the East coast publishing industry upon the geography of the Midwest. The close proximity of Atwater and Moltke's discussion of the mounds to Amber's remark on the effacement of Atwater's accent brings into alignment the reporter's inability to truly return to the Midwest of his birth, seeing instead only the cultural simulacra of the Midwest (obesity, corn, vast space, sincerity) mapped on to the region by his journalistic training at *Style* magazine. Moreover, the asinine and mercenary ideology of *Style* is itself depicted as having colonized the mindset of those who live in the Midwest, with Amber, who aggressively pursues the enshrinement of her husband's 'talent' to the detriment of his mental health, deferential to Atwater because 'he lived and worked in New York City, the cultural heart of the nation' (*Oblivion* 276).

The loss of the authentic, non-mediated Midwest in 'The Suffering Channel' and its replacement with a culturally encoded 'Midwest' is accompanied by an alternating irrational repulsion and attraction to the simulated differences of Midwestern people and places. This is explicitly dramatized when Skip's intern, Laurel Manderley, suffers a nightmare during which her imagined representation of the Moltke's duplex initially gives the impression of 'something generic or vague or tentative, like an abstract or outline' before that sensation is replaced by an 'overwhelming sense of dread [...] a creeping, ambient evil' (301).[43] This nightmare combines the fear of downward social mobility accorded to the low-income neighbourhoods by the narrator of 'The Soul is not a Smithy' with a particular spatial sense of the generic informed by Manderley's ignorance of anything other than the simulated model of the Midwest produced 'in-house' by *Style*. That this nightmare is experienced by a character who was voted 'Most Rational' in high school (244) demonstrates how thoroughly inculcated the employees of *Style* have become in the production of regional simulacra perpetuated by their industry. The obverse of this sensation is the sexual attraction Atwater feels to Amber Moltke, whose 'Anne Rice paperback' (251) neatly encapsulates the motifs of regional snobbery and vampirism that underpin their relationship. The consummation of their sexual attraction involves Atwater effectively being consumed by Amber's 'vista' (250), a less than subtle dramatization of Atwater's fear of returning home and being absorbed by the amalgamated model of the Midwest that he has generated during his absence on the East coast.

It is not difficult to perceive a correlation between Atwater and the performative Midwestern persona practised by Wallace in his non-fiction. Christoph Ribbat sees Atwater himself as a 'cartoonish stand-in for Wallace' (96) with Quinn describing his pieces as 'extreme parodies of Wallace's own assignments as Midwestern village-explainer' (98). Indeed, Skip's real name, Virgil, only emphasizes his role as guide to a disturbing topographic space, descending into the Midwest and parsing accounts of grotesquery for the delectation of others, in an account that carries unmistakeable and unsettling echoes of Wallace's own accounts of 'Kmart people', who 'tend to be overweight' and 'aspire to own mobile homes' in his state fair essay (*Supposedly* 120–1).[44] Accordingly, there are two separate references made to Atwater's experience with Midwestern county fairs, in one of which he 'assumed that all county fairs were roughly similar' (274). In the final substantial piece of fiction published during Wallace's lifetime, an implicitly Wallacian figure is positioned within this ruined, simulated, culturally constrictive middle space, unable to return home to the denuded terrain of his birth but equally alienated from an East coast institution which will never fully culturally absorb him.

It is this lack of shelter that Mark McGurl argues acts as the provocation in Wallace's fiction for retreat and reabsorption into the body of the institution. Positioning the institution as 'the safe space in between exteriority and interiority' ('Institution' 37) McGurl correctly describes Wallace as 'deeply embedded in the culture of the school' (32) and as a figure of the '*normalization* of the emergent conditions of institutionalization' indicated by the program era (31, emphasis original). McGurl's provocative and persuasive essay, which aligns Wallace's institutionalism with a form of social and political conservatism, illustrates the comfort that the institution provides in some of Wallace's fiction, positing the aforementioned 'bound infinity' of Schtitt's tennis philosophy in *Infinite Jest* (and thus, the novel's fractal form) as a maximalist version of Hemingway's 'clean, well lighted place'. I have argued that I do not believe that the binary relationship characterized by the 'predatory nothingness of the great outdoors' cited by McGurl (37) as the motivation for a retreat back 'indoors, under the shelter of institutions' (30) necessarily speaks to the relative porousness of the institutional and non-institutional spaces across the body of Wallace's fiction. While a significant element of McGurl's criticism here is aimed at the institutional model in *The Pale King* (and I will return to the essay in Chapter 4) I have suggested here that the steady process of elision of that very 'outdoors' across Wallace's fiction presents a more complex and problematic image of the institution itself.

While I concur with McGurl's description of the institution in *Infinite Jest* as 'a communal antidote to atomism, a laboriously iterated wall against the nihilism attendant to solitude' (38), the institution also performs an *accretive* process of constriction as Wallace's fiction develops. The institutions depicted in *Brief Interviews* and particularly *Oblivion* have a relationship with the space outside themselves that is fundamentally antipathetic, but crucially, also parasitic. In *Oblivion*, the institutionalization of space that has steadily accreted throughout Wallace's fiction operates in tandem with an ideological toxification of wild space *by the institution itself*. The predatory quality referred to by McGurl might be evident to those trapped, institutionalized characters in *Oblivion*, but it is a quality that is generated from *within* that very space in which they shelter and which claims to offer comfort and security. The topography of the Midwest in 'The Suffering Channel' is still, literally, as 'real' as it ever was, but has become institutionally inflected, effectively enclosing both Midwesterners and East coasters within a cultural simulacrum. In *Oblivion*, in a development of the nascent and simultaneously vast and claustrophobic englobing 'curve' in 'Westward', the view on to the 'predatory nothingness' outside is characterized not by the Burkean sublimity of vast disclosed areas, but by the institutional window that reflects your own image back at you.[45] The institution is indeed the only viable space in *Oblivion*, but it is not a shelter. It is a trap, a 'captured shop'. Atwater's fate is to be stuck between the englobed cultural space of the Midwest and the East coast institution that *produces* this simulacrum, never fully absorbed into either. This is reflected within Atwater's own awareness of his spatial constriction. He knows 'in his heart' that he is 'polished but about two inches deep' (270) and, climactically, considers himself 'just a bodyshaped area of space itself, impenetrable but empty, with a certain vacuous roaring sensation we tend to associate with empty space' (313). The reference to vacuity implies, of course, the banality of his journalism but also the disturbingly airless image of the fundamental loss of physical space occupied by Atwater.

Accordingly, Bryant's ambivalent premonition in 'The Prairies' of an 'advancing multitude' on the body of the Midwest is fulfilled in Wallace's fiction, but not through the material occupancy of space implied by the poem. Instead, it is the institutionalization of space in Wallace's fiction that is pervasively concomitant with a figurative loss of territory. The institution, a highly ambiguous space in Wallace's fiction, does indeed offer the 'shelter' that McGurl outlines. However, as the progressive material and cultural elision of extra-institutional space in Wallace's later fiction demonstrates, the rapacious nature of the institution leads not only to a figurative and cultural geographical colonizing, but also a generation of the area outside itself as toxic and predatory. To paraphrase Thomas Wolfe, himself an early proponent of the program era that Wallace occupies, even the performative Midwesterner, blessed with geographical mobility, can't go home again.

3

# Visuality

## 'Seeing by Mirror-Light': Wallace on Reflection

In December 1988, Wallace sent a letter to Bonnie Nadell with which he enclosed a very short story titled 'Las Meninas'. He described the piece, which would later appear in *Infinite Jest* as Clenette's monologue (37–8), as 'a 2-page story that has been distilled to its fictional essence', adding that 'I like it rather a lot' ('Letter to Bonnie Nadell, Dec 31st 1988'). *Las Meninas* is, of course, also the name of Velazquez's 1656 painting of the court of King Philip IV of Spain (Figure 3.1). While the relationship between title and content in Wallace's story might at first seem arbitrary (notwithstanding a loose connection between Clenette's low-paid cleaning job and the English translation of the painting's title, *The Maids of Honour*) I believe that Wallace's invocation of *Las Meninas* at this juncture in his career is a matter of some serious significance. The objects central to Velazquez's painting – the appearance of the artist himself, and the mirror within which the subjects of the artwork are themselves reflected – are an interwoven leitmotif throughout Wallace's fiction, and an awareness of its function in Velazquez can aid an understanding of the complex and often deeply ambivalent relationship Wallace had with the concept of visual reflection and 'modes of seeing' in his work. As indicated in the examples from *Oblivion* in the previous chapter, mirrors and reflections abound in Wallace's fiction, but their representational function changes periodically, from a dramatization of the worst excesses of narcissism or entrapment within the narrative to the possibility of dialogic communication with the reader outside the text. Mirrors are also used by Wallace as a fundamental referent for the image of the cinema or TV screen. The screen is, of course, a motif of immense significance in Wallace's fiction.

**Figure 3.1** Diego Velázquez, *Las Meninas* 1656.

To relay the crucial importance of the mirror in Wallace's fiction, I want to outline how this formal model of 'reflection' operates and changes, with Velazquez's painting as a useful starting point. First, I want to contextualize the multivalent functions of Wallace's model of reflection in relation to certain critical frameworks accorded to *Las Meninas*, and modes of representation in visual art, by Clement Greenberg, Michel Foucault and Lucien Dällenbach. These three critics advance certain models of interpretation – 'flatness', 'reciprocity' and '*mise-en-abyme*', respectively – that can be helpfully used towards a theorizing of the function of the mirror and reflection in Wallace's writing. This is not to downplay the importance of other critics – Jacques Lacan, Roland Barthes, Christian Metz and Fredric Jameson – to whose models of flatness and reflection Wallace is indebted, and their work will remain important to my analysis. However, to constructing a theoretical framework I want to turn first to Greenberg, Foucault and Dällenbach.

In 'Modernist Painting' Greenberg makes a distinction between the medium specificity of the work of the 'Old Masters' and that of Modernist painters:

> The Old Masters had sensed that it was necessary to preserve what is called the integrity of the picture plane: that is, to signify the enduring presence of flatness underneath and above the most vivid illusion of three-dimensional space [...] The Modernists have neither avoided nor resolved this contradiction; rather they have reversed its terms. One is made aware of the flatness of their pictures before, instead of after, being made aware of what the flatness contains. Whereas one tends to see what is in an Old Master before one sees the picture itself, one sees a Modernist picture as a picture first. (87)

While not explicitly about *Las Meninas*, this distinction helps us to better understand the multivalent visual strategies within that painting and Wallace's use of its title. In accordance with the strategy attributed to the Old Masters, Velazquez's painting immediately foregrounds the scene itself (the royal court) rather than 'the flatness' of its medium. However, *Las Meninas* also exhibits strong self-reflexivity via the appearance of Velazquez himself and his canvas within the picture. 'Flatness' is particularly pertinent here because Velazquez makes use of two planar surfaces – the blank reverse of his canvas and the mirror at the back wall of the scene within which the royal couple, the apparent subject of the painting, are reflected – to indicate the painting's metatextual dimension. Moreover, when upon sustained contemplation the viewer begins to query their own position in relation to the painting – surely it should be *their* reflection in the mirror, as they are physically positioned where the king and queen stand, outside the painting looking in – and consider the centrality of the artist himself to an image of which he is not the purported subject, the picture reveals a complex system of what Foucault and Dällenbach term 'reciprocity'.

Foucault's essay on *Las Meninas* in *The Order of Things* foregrounds the problematic relationship between artist and viewer, querying the extent to which the viewer is participant or acknowledged presence. Foucault begins by outlining this contradictory dialogue, making reference to Velazquez's own appearance in the painting:

> The painter is turning his eyes towards us only in so far as we happen to occupy the same position as his subject. We, the spectators, are an additional factor. Though greeted by that gaze, we are also dismissed by it [...] But, inversely, the painter's gaze, addressed to the void confronting him outside the picture, accepts as many models as there are spectators. (4)

Foucault subsequently suggests that the viewer, while ostensibly invited into the picture, is ultimately shut out, lost:

> We are observing ourselves being observed by the painter, and made visible to his eyes by the same light that enables us to see him. And just as we are about to apprehend ourselves, transcribed by his hand as though in a mirror, we find that we can in fact apprehend nothing of that mirror but its lustreless back. (6)

However, the viewer's recognition of the mirror at the back of the painting 'offers us at last that enchantment of the double that until now has been denied us' (7) and ultimately provides 'an oscillation between the interior and the exterior' (11). Foucault concludes with some tentative optimism about the communicative function of this oscillation:

> The entire picture is looking out at a scene for which it is itself a scene. A condition of pure reciprocity manifested by the observing and observed mirror [...] That space where the king and his wife hold sway belongs equally well to the artist and to the spectator: in the depths of the mirror there could also appear [...] the anonymous face of the passer-by and that of Velazquez. For the function of that reflection is to draw into the interior of the picture what is intimately foreign to it: the gaze which has organized it and the gaze for which it is displayed. (14–15)

Foucault's metatextual model of *Las Meninas* presents the painting as a possibly dialogic space that permanently hovers on the cusp of monologism. It is perhaps unsurprising, given the attention afforded to depth and depthlessness, dialogism and monologism in Velazquez's painting, that *Las Meninas* preoccupied Wallace to the extent that he used the title for his own work. It is also unsurprising that Wallace's use of the title should emerge at a time when he was fundamentally recalibrating several of his earlier ideas about authorial effacement and communication with the reader: the appearance of 'Las Meninas' in 1988 falls between the completion of *Girl with Curious Hair* and the composition proper of *Infinite Jest*. Those properties of *Las Meninas* outlined above, particularly its simultaneous depth and depthlessness, are also relevant to some of the critical and theoretical models that influence Wallace's writing in this period, as his fiction becomes more specifically occupied with the viewing of screens and planar surfaces. I will return to the theoretical problem of 'flatness' in detail later in this chapter, but I want now to address the question of *Las Meninas*' 'reciprocal' qualities in order to explore the third model of interpretation, Lucien Dällenbach's use of *mise-en-abyme*, that will ultimately assist the construction of a workable theory of the mirror and reflection in Wallace's fiction.

Dällenbach's brief analysis of *Las Meninas* in *The Mirror in the Text* is also preoccupied with reciprocity. Dällenbach reiterates Foucault's sentence about oscillation verbatim, suggesting that this process makes 'the image "come out of the frame," while inviting the visitors to enter the picture' (11). However, this mode of reciprocation is based within a different theoretical model: *mise-en-abyme*. The term, coined according to Dällenbach by Andre Gide, has no literal English translation but can most commonly be understood as the replication of an image or narrative within itself. The terminology comes from heraldry, where it involves 'putting a second representation of the original shield "en abyme" within it' (Gide, quoted in Dällenbach 7). Gide's theoretical model of *mise-en-abyme* is somewhat delimited (e.g. he rejects the example of the play within *Hamlet* as it is not an *exact* replica of the narrative around it), and Dällenbach's study is aimed towards the establishment of a more stable and inclusive terminology. It is this slightly 'looser' approach that proves useful towards constructing a theory of reflection in Wallace's fiction. Dällenbach outlines his three-part structure of *mise-en-abyme* as follows:

(a) Simple Duplication: a sequence which is connected by *similarity* to the work that encloses it (e.g. the play in *Hamlet*)
(b) Infinite Duplication: a sequence which is connected by similarity to the work that encloses it and which *itself* includes a sequence that itself includes a sequence etc. (e.g. an image on a book cover of someone holding that same book cover, and so on to infinity)
(c) Aporetic Duplication: a sequence that is supposed to enclose the work that encloses it. This is the most difficult model to extrapolate. It is perhaps most clearly illustrated by the reference made in Borges' 'The Garden of Forking Paths' to the night in *The 1001 Nights* where Scheherazade starts to tell the story of the 1001 nights again from the beginning (Borges 51).[1]

Of this three-part model, the most relevant to a discussion of reflection in Wallace's fiction are (a) and (b). While 'Infinite Duplication' immediately calls to mind the title of Wallace's most famous work, and 'Simple Duplication' recalls that same novel's kinship with Gide's *The Counterfeiters* (which, like *Infinite Jest*, features in its plot a work with the same title as the novel itself), these initial similarities only constitute the tip of Wallace's use of *mise-en-abyme*. To return to *Las Meninas*, Wallace's use of such nested, 'reflective' narratives also comes to foreground that double bind which Foucault observes in Velazquez's painting: the oscillating, ambiguous image of the painter's gaze, which is a by-product of the artist's appearance in their own work.

It is not difficult to see why such enquiries preoccupied Wallace. Much of his writing was generated within academic environments at a time when literary study was undergoing a theoretical scrutiny that constituted a vexed cultural development of some of the same problematic narrative qualities suggested by Velazquez's painting. For example, Fredric Jameson's landmark 1991 study *Postmodernism, or the Cultural Logic of Late Capitalism* (which emerged first in article form in 1984, when Wallace was at Amherst) foregrounded the question of 'depthlessness, which finds its prolongation both in contemporary "theory" and in a whole new culture of the simulacrum' (*Postmodernism* 6) with a specific attribution of the term to the visual plane of painting and visual art (9). Lacanian psychoanalytic theory, with its focus upon the importance of the reflection as a constitutive component of the Imaginary and Symbolic order, began its major transition to the English-speaking academy between 1982 and 1987, when 'important explications of Lacan were published in English [and] key essays by Lacan began to appear in anthologies of theory for use in English-speaking classrooms' (Ryan 80).

There was also a compositional and theoretical tension between the metafictionally inflected literature that preoccupied and strongly influenced Wallace in this period (Barth's *Lost in the Funhouse*, Barthelme's 'The Balloon' from *Unspeakable Practices, Unnatural Acts*) and, as explicated in Chapter 1, the problematic post-Barthesian ontology of the author's position in the work. This tension informs a great deal of Wallace's fiction from the period of *Girl with Curious Hair* onward, the writing often fluctuating between what Linda Hutcheon refers to as 'overt' and 'covert' narcissism, moving from the overt revelation of textual self-awareness to the internalization of the same process, where 'such a text is self-reflective but not necessary self-conscious' (*Narcissistic Narrative* 7). Hutcheon's model is useful to a discussion of Wallace's fiction because it takes a less pejorative position on the term 'narcissism', which she glosses as 'process made visible' (6) rather than always directly conflating it with involution or solipsism. Indeed, Hutcheon's suggestion that the use of *mise-en-abyme* in metafiction as a replacement for the more traditional mimetic mirror helps to '[make] the mirror productive' (42) will prove helpful when considering Wallace's model of reflection in his later fiction. The late 1980s was also the period in which the focus of Wallace's writing turned strongly towards the social problems engendered by another planar image: the screen, and its concomitant association with narcissism and solipsism. A number of novels name-checked by Wallace around the late 1980s and early 1990s, including Pynchon's *Vineland*, DeLillo's *Americana*, *White Noise* and *Running Dog* and McElroy's *Lookout Cartridge*, make explicit use of television or cinema not only as a plot component, but as a motif of mystery, chaos and social breakdown.

Wallace's writing also responds, often explicitly, to certain other pre-existing philosophical and literary-critical models of reflection, their structural function in artistic composition and relatedly, the shifting position of the artist within the work. The reference to the 'Stendhalian mirror that reflects the blue sky and mudpuddle' in 'E Unibus Pluram' (*Supposedly* 22) indicates Wallace's familiarity with Stendhal's famous model of the novel in the epigraph to chapter 13 of *The Red and the Black* as a mirror carried along a roadway, a model glossed by Morris Dickstein as the representation of 'constantly shifting images, each fleetingly accurate yet framed into meaning by choice, happenstance and sequence' (Dickstein xiv). Relatedly, Wallace's familiarity with Goethe's *The Sorrows of Young Werther* (he occasionally referred to himself as 'sorrowful Werther' [Max 147] and uses the apparent neologism 'Werther's Axiom' in brief interview #20 [*Brief* 268]) indicates his conversancy with the model of the page as mirror of the soul expounded by the eponymous protagonist ('Oh couldst thou only express, couldst thou breathe forth upon this paper, all that lives so full and warm in thyself, that it might becomes the mirror of thy soul' [quoted in Abrams 44]).[2] Wallace's later attribution of the title of Richard Rorty's neopragmatic 1979 work *Philosophy and the Mirror of Nature* to one of the stories in *Oblivion* is a reminder of Wallace's continuing dialogue with the work of, and philosophical responses to, Wittgenstein and the problems of regarding language as a 'mirror' of reality.[3] It is also important to remember that Wallace's description of television as a 'mirror' in 'E Unibus Pluram' (*Supposedly* 22) locates the motif of reflection in direct conjunction to contemporary televisual and advertising culture, a culture with which Wallace was particularly preoccupied around the time of the composition of 'Las Meninas' and which saturates the narrative of the novel, *Infinite Jest*, of which that short story eventually becomes a part.

Having outlined the contexts of the mirror motif in Wallace's writing, I want to address how Wallace posits a sustained and progressive response to these problems – depthlessness, authorial ontology, metatextuality, mimesis, narcissism, monologism and dialogism – by constructing a formal model of 'reflection' that develops across his fiction. This model follows an imbricated, interwoven four-part structure that is connected to the contexts and narrative modes described above. Firstly, Wallace employs *the reflection of the text within the text* (*mise-en-abyme*). Secondly, he displays *the reflection of the author within the text* (authorial presence). Thirdly, he describes *the absorption of the character in the text within the reflective image, be it a mirror or screen* (narcissism). Finally, Wallace develops a fourth trope, a motif of *refraction* that is often in deliberate conflict with the preceding three: a specifically communicative gesture between character and character, text and reader or authorial presence and reader. If the previous three motifs reflect the text, author and character, the fourth attempts to refractively pass through the 'reflective' surface and dialogically communicate with whoever is through or outside that surface. If, as outlined in Chapter 1, speaking is eventually framed within Wallace's work as a possible gesture towards communication, then watching or looking is generally presented as uncommunicative, solipsistic and narcissistic. I want to suggest that via this four-part model of reflection, Wallace displays a desire to reframe looking and watching as a communicative, dialogic gesture.

However, this communicative model is not unproblematic. In concluding this chapter, I explore the move towards what might be described as an 'ethics of watching' in Wallace's fiction, an approach characterized by a collapsing of boundaries between the fiction and the non-fiction and a focus upon extremes of visual content (pornography, snuff) that results in an amalgamation of authorial personae that predicates some of the compositional problems that ultimately attended the construction of *The Pale King*.

## 'Second Order' Stories: Early Reflections

In Wallace's earliest published work of fiction, the 1984 story 'The Planet Trillaphon as It Stands in Relation to the Bad Thing', a narrator who suffers from the depressive delusion that he has 'a really huge and deep wound' on his face describes how his belief in the existence of this wound is confirmed by the fact that 'whenever I'd look in the mirror, there it would be' (6). In a prototypical version of a characteristic Wallace double bind, the protagonist ultimately mutilates his own face in an attempt to stitch the wound, resulting in the appearance of a real wound in the same location. The mirror reifies the protagonist's delusion by appearing to reflect the existence of his wound in the real world, while in fact it merely acts as a reflection of his own self-consciousness. It is possible here to see an embryonic version of the function of the mirror in *The Broom of the System*, which makes extensive recourse to motifs of reflection (the climax of that novel also mirrors the ending of 'The Planet Trillaphon…' in its withholding of the final word of its final sentence). While mirrors are often used in *Broom* as a way of dramatizing narcissism, Wallace also begins to develop the more complex, multivalent narrative model of reflection outlined above. An early version of this model is advanced through four elements within the narrative of *Broom*: Rick Vigorous' pseudonymous stories, Rick's estranged son Vance, Lenore's cockatiel Vlad the Impaler, and the bizarre, contrived 'family theater' performed by the family of Lenore's sister Clarice.

Rick's telling of stories to Lenore, a recurrent event throughout the narrative of *Broom*, begins in Chapter 2 of the novel when he describes a tale about a man who suffers from 'second order-vanity […] Vain about his appearance, obsessed with his body, but also obsessed with the desire that no one know of his obsession' (22–3) who ultimately alienates his partner. This doubled self-consciousness, an early example of what will become a mainstay of Wallace's fiction, is particularly important because it occurs within a nested narrative that we later discover has been written by Rick himself and pseudonymously disguised from Lenore. It takes little effort to understand that Rick's stories are thinly dramatized iterations of episodes of his own life, with later stories fictionalizing his obsession with his young neighbour Mindy Metalman (the story 'Love' [321]) and his belief that Lenore is being controlled by others (the tree-toad story discussed in chapter 1 [191]), but the sustained focus upon 'second-order' in Rick's early story is useful in drawing our attention to Wallace's convergence of the motifs of *mise-en-abyme*, authorial presence and narcissism. This story stages a version of Dällenbach's 'Simple Duplication' by dramatizing the events of the novel in miniature inside a nested narrative (similar, though not identical, to the function of the play in *Hamlet*). This iteration of *mise-en-abyme* is explicitly linked to a dramatization of authorial presence (the reader knows that Rick wrote the story) and poisonous narcissism (Rick's self-obsession with the dramatization of his own life will ultimately claim his relationship with Lenore). All of these elements are united by the image of the mirror in Rick's story, which explicitly reflects the face of the narcissistic protagonist while implicitly reflecting Rick's authorial presence and narcissism to the reader. The totality of these elements also covertly indicates Wallace's own interest in metafiction and self-referring narratives.[4]

This conflation of reflection and narcissism is explicated further in the chapter where Rick describes his problematic relationship with his estranged son Vance, whom he adored as a child. For Rick, the infant Vance was a boy 'whom from the age of independent decision and movement reflected the world in his own, special, wobbled mirror. Vance for me was a reflection' (75). However, his interest in Vance begins to wane when the child starts to imitate, in bizarre fashion, the events in Vietnam unfolding on the family TV. 'I miss my son', says Rick, 'Which is not to say that I miss an eighteen-year old […] I miss my *son*. My child […] a special and hilarious infant' (75). Rick initially adores Vance because he is a 'reflection', a mirror of his father, but when Vance advances to another 'mirror', television, Rick starts to lose interest and misses only his 'infant'.[5] In this episode it is also possible to see Wallace's response to another 'reflective' theoretical framework: the 'mirror stage' of Lacanian psychoanalysis. Marshall Boswell offers a sustained analysis of Wallace's response to Lacan in *Infinite Jest* (*Understanding* 128–32, 151–6, 159–60) but I want to suggest here that Wallace's engagement with Lacan can be traced back to this episode of *Broom*, and that Rick's obsession with the reflection of his son develops the association between the mirror and narcissism in Wallace's 'reflective' model. Vance's recognition of himself in the secondary mirror of the television, itself a perversion of the point at which the infant recognizes itself as an object in the Symbolic order ('the time at which the specular I turns into the social I' [Lacan 79]), seems to inversely and retroactively position *Rick* in the infantile Imaginary order: he remains fixated on infancy, while his own infant has moved on into the social world.[6] Crucially, while this episode clarifies Rick's narcissistic and infantile position on reflection and initiates Wallace's dialogue with Lacan, it also proposes that television acts as a kind of secondary mirror. This suggestion is advanced further in two more episodes in *Broom* which prepare the ground for Wallace's more sustained conflation of the mirror and the screen in his later fiction.

A subplot of *Broom* involves Lenore's cockatiel Vlad the Impaler, who has become hyper-talkative after ingesting a supplement that stimulates the pineal gland, repeating whatever is spoken in his presence. Vlad's repetitive phrases attract the attention of TV evangelist Reverend Sykes, and in the novel's climax the bird, renamed 'Ugolino the Significant', co-presents Sykes' show 'The Partners with God Club', repeating Sykes' phrases in a grotesque parody of evangelical call-and-response. When Vlad's cage is first described, it contains 'a mirror so dull and cloudy with [...] bird-spit that [Vlad] could not possibly have seen anything more than a vague yellowish blob behind a pan of pure mist'. Nevertheless, the bird continually returns 'to dance in front of its own shapeless reflection, straining and contorting always for a better view of itself' (96), with a 'patch of chewed wall' behind the cage where Vlad 'had gnawed on the wall in the dark when the mirror-show had closed' (96–7). When Vlad becomes a television celebrity, the cloudy mirror is removed (274), Lenore speculating that 'Vlad's probably got a cage entirely lined with full-length mirrors now [...] in a state of constant bird-orgasm' (293). The comedy of this subplot sometimes overshadows its significance to Wallace's fiction: for the first time, Wallace combines the motifs of the cage and the mirror, suggesting a concordance between the narcissism of the bird and its imprisonment. When the 'mirror-show' ends, Vlad becomes aware of his cage and makes a vain attempt to escape by gnawing through the wall, only to become entranced once more when the mirror-show begins anew the following day. Finally, his narcissistic desires granted beyond his imagination, Vlad is presumed to be in a state of constant ecstasy in his mirrored cage at the same time as he appears on television. Here Wallace initiates a deft conflation of several motifs (the cage, the mirror, television, the ecstasy of narcissistic fulfilment) that will characterize his fiction for the rest of his career. Through the image of a mirror-lined cage, Wallace combines the recursive *mise-en-abyme* motif of 'Infinite Duplication' (reflections of reflections of reflections *ad infinitum*) and thematically ties it to both narcissism and physical constraint. By placing the bird 'behind' the television screen in the climactic pages of the novel, Wallace proposes a further level of mediation, locating Vlad behind the secondary mirror that has so entranced Vance Vigorous, in a state of infinitely recursive entrapment disguised as narcissistic fulfilment.

This process is compounded in the bizarre episode that depicts Lenore's sister Clarice and her family participating in 'family theater', during which they wear masks of their faces while facing a video recording of an audience and cardboard cut-outs of themselves positioned next to the television (166). This process, a parody of family therapy, involves Clarice, her husband and her children physically performing figurative oscillations between the family group and individual freedom. Clarice's husband recites by rote how over-association with the family unit 'made the people in the family not as much people anymore' (167) before attempting to rectify this by 'attaching themselves to things in the world, extrafamilial objects and pursuits' (169) before concluding that 'what they needed to get their feelings of being themselves from was *themselves*' (172, emphasis original). At the end of this grotesquely comic spectacle, the pre-recorded audience on the TV pointedly rise 'as one' (173). By having the family act out this ritual of their lives within a discrete narrative episode, Wallace performs a form of 'Simple Duplication' that reveals 'family theater' to be an enclosed, constraining process. The family repeat, time and again, a pre-recorded dramatization of their lives, their faces obscured with masks, invisible to one another: the process has an implicit kinship with Rick's narcissistic masked presence in his own fiction. A self-conscious spectacle, the family's response to a pre-recorded image of an audience on television, gives only the illusion of dialogic communication and distorts the message at the end of the ritual (that one can only find true validation from within the self) into a kind of narcissistic performance, which is only amplified by the fact that the family are performing this ritual to images of themselves.

## The Mirrored Cage

Wallace's preoccupation with the relationship between television and the 'mirrored cage' of narcissism develops substantially in the period after the completion of *Broom*. This phase, between 1986 and 1993, incorporates the composition of several major pieces of writing, including the stories that comprise *Girl with Curious Hair*, the initial drafts of sections of

*Infinite Jest* (including 'Las Meninas'), the essays 'Fictional Futures and the Conspicuously Young' and 'E Unibus Pluram: Television and U.S. Fiction' and the lengthy interview with Larry McCaffrey for *Review of Contemporary Fiction*.[7] As this exceptionally rich period of Wallace's writing is often characterized by the simultaneous composition of pieces (the stories from *Girl* overlap with 'Fictional Futures', and the pieces of *Infinite Jest* overlap with both the stories from *Girl* and the composition of 'E Unibus Pluram', which began life as a commission for *Harpers* in 1990 [Max 148]), it is a fair assessment to suggest that they enjoy a thematically symbiotic relationship. For example, the material on television in the first part of 'E Unibus Pluram' is reflected in the televisual focus of certain plot elements of the stories 'Little Expressionless Animals', 'My Appearance' and 'Westward the Course of Empire Takes Its Way'. Both essay and stories mark an advancement of the model of reflection established by Wallace in *Broom*, connecting it much more explicitly to television while retaining and developing the narrative motifs of *mise-en-abyme*, authorial presence and narcissism.

This advancement involves the explicit unification of the television screen with the earlier reflective surfaces of *Broom*. While the juxtaposition of Vlad's mirrored cage and his appearance on television and the rituals of 'family theater' point towards a connection between narcissism and the screen, 'E Unibus Pluram' concretizes and theorizes this correspondence in detail. Wallace, who begins the essay by describing fiction writers as 'born watchers' (21), spatially aligns television with embedded frames of glass: 'the screen's glass' perceived by the viewer and the 'second layer of glass [...] the lenses and monitors via which technicians [...] hurl the visible images at us [...] that terrible blank round glass stare' (24–5). While Wallace refers to the viewer as being 'outside the glass', he concedes that 'television, even the mundane little business of its production, has become my – our – own interior' (32). This refusal to accord a stable space to the viewer, who is located both inside and outside that simultaneously deep and depthless glass screen, is compounded by Wallace's description of television as 'reflecting what people want to see. It's a mirror' (22). While this problematic depth model recalls the ambiguous monologic/dialogic status afforded to reciprocity in Foucault's analysis of *Las Meninas*, Wallace suggests that in the case of television this ambiguous spatial position is potentially harmful because of the ultimate *lack* of reciprocity engendered in the audience by contemporary televisual entertainment. Simply put, the mirror presented by television presents 'what we as Audience want to see ourselves as', making it 'not the Stendhalian mirror that reflects the blue sky and mudpuddle' but 'the overlit bathroom mirror before which the teenager monitors his biceps and determines his better profile' (*Supposedly* 22). Crucially, this vexed spatial description of the televisual mirror in 'E Unibus Pluram' informs the reflective model that Wallace uses in *Girl with Curious Hair*: the stories that most profitably illustrate this interconnection are 'Little Expressionless Animals' and 'Westward the Course of Empire Takes Its Way'.

The conversation held by lovers Julie and Faye via a make-up mirror 'bordered by bulbs' (*Girl* 41) in 'Little Expressionless Animals' might be a more engaged dialogue than the pensive back-and-forth in the barroom mirror between Rick and Lang in *Broom* (223), but Wallace nevertheless couches the scene in ambiguity. If Faye's initial declaration of 'I love you' (*Girl* 40) appears heartfelt, its status is necessarily compromised by being spoken into a mirror, and Julie's response, which is made directly to Faye's face, is more qualified ('That's when I love you, if I love you' [41]). The environments of the story are characterized by glass, notably Faye's glass-walled apartment (4), the aforementioned make-up mirror and the television studio where Julie appears on *Jeopardy*. Marshall Boswell describes *Girl* as a book that, in dramatizing the lives of characters within television and the media

> holds a mirror up to our mirror, and in so doing seeks a [...] way out that allows us to recognise the omnipresence of mediated reality while at the same time pointing *away* from the mediated reality and toward some undepicted, yet still vital, reality – the reality *surrounding* those two mutually reflective mirrors. (*Understanding* 69, emphasis original)

I concur with Boswell that Wallace's strategy becomes increasingly about recognizing the limitations of the mirror, but I would make the distinction that in Wallace's reflective model during and after *Girl* this 'vital reality', which is increasingly configured as a communication with the reader outside the text, does not *surround* the mirrors but must ultimately be refractively perceived *through* the mirror. This can be understood as the difference between 'looking at' (as one does to a mirror) and 'looking into' (as one does to another's eyes), a distinction of some importance for Wallace's reflective model during and after this period. For example, Julie 'cannot stand animals, because animals' faces have no expression' and believes that men's faces 'move through different configurations of blankness' (41). Her frustrated desire for communication, and her fear of the blank stare that looks *at* rather than *into*, recalls Wallace's description of 'that terrible blank round glass stare' of the television camera (25). The terminology of the final line of the story ('Julie and the audience look *at* each other' [42, emphasis mine]), with its escalation of the audience/performer dynamic from 'family theater' and its implied lack of communication and deliberate eliding of whether 'audience' refers to the studio audience or the audience at home, indicates the kind of entrapment imposed upon those behind the 'second layer of glass', unable to look *into* or *through* that glass but only *at* it. The veiled quotation in this story from Ashbery's 'Self Portrait in a Convex Mirror' is here contextualized in terms of the mirror's unbreakability: the inability to reach through the glass to the other side.

This problem is addressed differently in 'Westward...' when the failed 'diplopic ad actor' Tom Sternberg (*Girl* 235), a man with one eye 'completely turned around in his head' (250), studies his face in a men's room mirror. Sternberg, who is 'maybe about the most claustrophobic individual in the history of his generation' (277) and whose failed acting career is connected to his optical disability, has a vexed relationship with the qualities ascribed to actors by Wallace in 'E Unibus Pluram':

> The man who can stand the megagaze is a walking imago, a certain type of transcendent semihuman who, in Emerson's phrase, 'carries the holiday in his eye.' The Emersonian holiday that television actors' eyes carry is the promise of a vacation from human self-consciousness. Not worrying about how you come across. A total unallergy to gazes [...] It is also, of course, an act, for you have to be just abnormally self-conscious and self-controlled to appear unwatched before cameras and lenses. (28)

Sternberg's inverted eye cannot undergo a vacation from self-consciousness: it is literally *looking at his brain*. Moreover, the presence of a purple cyst on his forehead leads Sternberg to compulsively check his appearance in the mirror. A paragraph deleted from the published story by Wallace illuminates and draws together some of the motifs of self-consciousness in 'Little Expressionless Animals' and 'Westward …' and is worth quoting at length:

> But you need to be able to see yourself, if you're going to be an actor. Hence the idea of mirrors. Sternberg, idea man, has evolved a bunch of ideas about looking at himself. For instance that he definitely prefers mirrors to photographs, in terms of having to look at himself. They're inverse ideas, the two. A photo gives you no time to see yourself or arrange yourself before it's shot, you're photo'd, shot by a good shot, and then you get a forever to look at the unfailingly ghastly result of an unarranged, shot you […] And but mirrors are the inverse: you can take as much self-seen time as you need to prepare and arrange what you decide is really you. You can make your face how you want it. Within limits, of course; would that a mirror could will away a cyst. But you can still <u>compose your expression of self</u>. For you alone. A perfect moment. You're rapt. Then look away and it's gone, ridden away, a knight on a nighttime plane, pricking: gone but not forgotten. He likes it. Mirrors are polite. They respect the careful privacy the times call for. (Box 15.2, underlining original)

Like Rick Vigorous, Sternberg needs a mirror. Unlike Rick, he doesn't need another individual to act as a mirror image of himself but desires an actual mirror to 'compose' himself. However, in another cut passage, Sternberg reveals his fear of being seen while doing so:

> If somebody right there in there with you <u>sees</u> you composing, if somebody is clued in that it's this conscious act of arrangement, because <u>he's doing it too</u>, then the whole transformation, is it still that? Are you still transformed as you wish? (Box 15.2, underlining original)

This passage performs an involuted development of the mirror conversations between Rick and Lang and Julie and Faye: the appearance of another in Sternberg's mirror engenders a retreat into intense self-conscious enquiry. It is no wonder, then, that he suffers under the delusion that 'a body is a prison and not a shelter' (305) and fears most 'whatever he's inside' (337). In his personal copy of Christopher Lasch's *The Culture of Narcissism*, Wallace underlined the following passage: 'the narcissist depends on others to validate his self-esteem. He cannot live without an admiring audience [...] for the narcissist, the world is a mirror' (Lasch 10). Television actor Sternberg's narcissism, which follows this model to the letter, is dramatized through this process of looking *at*, in a similar manner to Julie's entrapment behind the make-up mirror and the 'glass stare' of the camera in 'Little Expressionless Animals'. In a similar torquing of the Lacanian model as in *Broom* (whereby Rick replaces Vance in the infantile position), the appearance of another in the mirror, represented by the infant's association with the mother in Lacan's mirror stage, invites not social communication but *involution*: a regressive move into infantile solipsism.

How then does Wallace propose that the blank reflective eye of television can be penetrated, looked *through*? Wallace notes in 'E Unibus Pluram' that, when watching television, we are seeing 'analog waves and ion streams and rear-screen chemical reactions' (*Supposedly* 24) rather than real people. This stages a modification of Greenberg's assertion that viewing modernist art involves resisting the desire to see the illusory depth of the image and instead being aware of its materiality. Wallace suggests that by seeing the technological materiality of the medium, we become more aware of its artificial, mimetic qualities and might avoid the delusion of imagining the screen as mirror or as reality. However, this is surely only a partial solution, as it actually involves collapsing *any* possibility of depth into surface: another version of looking *at* rather than *through*.

A more coherent proposal is advanced in the interstitial sequences in 'Westward...' which address, via 'a really blatant and intrusive interruption' (264) both the story's metafictional framework and Mark Nechtr's desire to progress beyond and through metafiction to communicate with the reader outside the story, despite the framework of metafiction apparently posing the greatest threat to communication. In this story metafiction, via a thinly dramatized and grotesquely commercialized reification of John Barth's funhouses, represents a communicative form of literature that has become fundamentally compromised. Wallace draws our attention to this by sketching a franchise of Barthian funhouses that are mirrored on the inside ('mirrored discotheque franchises' [240]; a 'crowded, mirrored place' [280]). This elision of metafiction in 'Westward' with an internally mirrored structure not only recalls the narcissistic ecstasy of Vlad the Impaler in his mirrored cage in *Broom*,[8] but also draws a distinction between the reflection of the mirror and the possible refraction offered by the motif of a window:

> [...] metafiction [...] a required postmodern convention aimed at drawing the poor old reader's emotional attention to the fact that the narrative bought and paid for and now under time-consuming scrutiny is not in fact a barely-there window onto a different and truly diverting world, but rather in fact an 'artifact,' an object [...] and is thus in a 'deep' sense just an opaque forgery of a transfiguring window, not a real window, a gag, and thus in a deep (but intentional, now) sense artificial [...] this self-conscious explicitness and deconstructed disclosure supposedly making said metafiction 'realer' than a piece of pre-postmodern 'Realism' that depends on certain antiquated techniques to create an 'illusion' of a windowed access to a 'reality' isomorphic with ours. (265)

Conversely, in Mark Nechtr's subsequent fantasy of his new form of metafiction, the importance of 'egress' is paramount:

> [...] the Exit would never be out of sight. It'd be brightly, lewdly lit [...] clearly marked, and straight ahead, and not even all that far. It would be the stuff the place is made of that would make it Fun. The whole enterprise a frictionless plane. Cool, smooth, never grasping, well lubed, flatly without purchase, burnished to a mirrored gloss. The lover tries to traverse: there is the motion of travel, except no travel. More, the reflective surfaces in all directions would reflect each static forward step, interpret it as a backward step [...] The Exit and Egress and End in full view the whole time. (331–2)

The 'mirrored gloss' here is not congruent with the internal mirroring of the commercially co-opted funhouse. It resembles instead an amendment of Wallace's earlier suggestion about focusing on the materiality of the medium of television: the always-visible exit will allow the inhabitant of Mark's funhouse/fiction to recontextualize the materiality of the mirrored surfaces.

One will simultaneously be able to look *at* (the mirrors) and look *through* (the exit, which resembles the window that was previously 'illusory').

This process recalls Hutcheon's reading of metafiction as 'making the mirror productive' (42). However, Wallace's idea of mirror productivity differs from Hutcheon, who implicitly praises Barth's methodology in *Lost in the Funhouse* for '[preventing] the reader's identification with any character and [forcing] a new, more active, thinking relationship upon him [...] the reader can share, with the author, the pleasure of its imaginative creation' (49). Mark Nechtr's new funhouse, a development of Barth's model, is based less around sharing than the author being 'one cold son of a bitch [...] who could hate enough to feel enough to love enough to perpetrate the kind of special cruelty only real lovers can inflict'. In fact, 'the story would barely even be able to be voluntary, as fiction' because 'metafiction is untrue, as a lover, it cannot betray, it can only reveal. Itself is its only object' (332). Wallace suggests that by combining the motifs of mirror *and* exit, Mark constructs a recalibrated form of the 'the transfiguring window' mentioned above that allows reciprocal communication between reader and author.

Hutcheon's idea of mirror productivity is also connected to the mode of *mise-en-abyme* (Hutcheon 42), and indeed 'Westward' makes accompanying use of *mise-en-abyme* as a complementary, but implicit, exit strategy. It is surely no coincidence that Wallace displays a preoccupation in 'E Unibus Pluram' with the famous 'most photographed barn in America' scene from DeLillo's *White Noise*, and its focus on the infinite regress and 'metastasis of watching' as diagnosed by the 'would-be transcender of spectation' Murray (*Supposedly* 48–9).[9] In his analysis of this Infinite Duplication, Wallace aligns DeLillo with the narrator Jack Gladney, who 'eloquently diagnoses the very disease from which he, Murray, barn watchers and readers all suffer' (49). Katherine Fitzpatrick reads this scene differently, critiquing Wallace for granting DeLillo himself a form of immunity to the whole metastatic watching process (121–2). However, while Wallace might be guilty of according an artificially transcendent position to DeLillo, he thoroughly implicates himself in the duplicated and nested narratives of 'Westward', where his employment of *mise-en-abyme* progresses from Simple Duplication (the climactic embedding of Mark's story, which is clearly a dramatization of the events of the earlier narrative) to Aporetic Duplication (the ultimate collapse and folding inward of the finale of 'Westward', where Mark's story begins to enclose the work that encloses it). This final moment of Aporetic Duplication provides a metatextual version of the egress promised by Mark's funhouse: rather than repetitive or infinite embedding, Mark's story breaks the frame of 'Westward's' narrative and provides a visible exit. This 'exit' is the final line of the story, which is enunciated simultaneously by Mark, the narrator of 'Westward' and, implicitly, Wallace himself. The line, 'You are loved' (373), is a pointed divergence from the mirror-bound 'I love you' uttered by Faye to Julie in 'Little Expressionless Animals' at the beginning of the collection. It is enacted *through* the embedded layers of metafiction and *mise-en-abyme* to the reader: its aim is not narcissistic (looking *at*) but communicative (looking *through*), recalling that sustained 'oscillation between the interior and the exterior' in Foucault's reading of *Las Meninas* and freeing the reader from the 'mirror maze of the story' (Hutcheon 57).

## Breaking the Mirror

Throughout the period in which he published 'Westward' and 'E Unibus Pluram', Wallace was working on discrete portions of what would become *Infinite Jest*, most of which was composed in a sustained burst of creativity between 1993 and 1995. During the process of writing his second novel, Wallace's fixation with the 'mirrored cage' and the association between television, narcissism and reflection expanded to incorporate another medium: film. The reflective model in *Infinite Jest*, which is predicated on a blurring of the distinction between cinematic and televisual modes, comingles the motif of the flat, planar mirror and the cinema screen.

The encyclopaedic narrative of *Infinite Jest* teems with examples of both reflection and refraction. Mirrors abound, usually in the context of a moment of supreme narcissism or solipsism: the 'mirrored series' of Hal Incandenza's fingers just before his breakdown in the Year of Glad (3); the mirror tellingly placed above the anxiety-paralysed Ken Erdedy's Teleputer (22); the drugged narcissistic girl dancing 'in the full-length mirror' at Molly Notkin's party;

the 'dirty lit mirror' that displays Joelle Van Dyne's face before her suicide attempt (238); the use of a mirror during sex by the narcissistic Orin Incandenza (566).[10] The most sustained single episode involving reflection and narcissism is the digression on the socio-economic failure of videophony (144–51), wherein the rapidly proliferating self-consciousness engendered by the appearance of users faces in video calls stages a hyper-acceleration of the paralysing regressive problems of 'arrangement' experienced by Tom Sternberg in the mirror in 'Westward', leading ultimately to the production of masks of 'form-fitting polybutylene-resin' (148) whereby consumers can hide their true faces from one another in an echo of the masking process in *Broom*'s 'family theater'. However, among these reflective episodes are motifs of *refractive* communication. Towards the midpoint of the novel, ETA student Trevor Axford repeats 'a mnemonic limerick about Brewster's Angle for the Leith-taught Quadrivial colloquium "Reflections on Refraction."': Brewster's Angle is an angle of incidence that allows light to be transmitted directly *through* a transparent surface without reflection (*Jest* 511). When the narrative refers to addicts who have failed in the recovery process by trying to 'avoid the mirror AA hauls out in front of them', it implies that some of the successful recovering addicts in the novel have learned to treat a potentially reflective surface as a refractive one, conversely seeing in their reflection their appearance in the world as object.

However, the centrality of film to the narrative of *Infinite Jest* offers a substantial new direction for Wallace's reflective model. Initially, one would assume that the kind of passive entertainment that certain types of cinema provide might act as an amplification of the problems of narcissistic or solipsistic entrapment that characterize responses to television in *Girl*. In an analysis that aligns the motifs of cinema with the depth of the picture frame, Stanley Cavell, with whom Wallace was familiar, writes in *The World Viewed* that

> The world of a painting is not continuous with the world of its frame; at its frame, a world finds its limits. We might say: A painting *is* a world; a photograph is *of* the world. What happens in a photograph is that *it* comes to an end [...] The world of a moving picture is screened [...] It holds a

projection, as light as light. A screen is a barrier. What does the silver screen screen? It screens me from the world it holds – that is, it makes me invisible. (24)[11]

In defining this 'screening' Cavell stages that same moment of dismissal afforded to the viewer in Foucault's reading of Velazquez. However, the possibility of that fully reciprocal relationship between viewer and artist ultimately suggested by Foucault is denied by Cavell, who pointedly characterizes the viewer at the film screening as 'present not at something happening' (26). Wallace's personal library contains a heavily marked-up copy of Walker Percy's novel *The Moviegoer*, in which he has underlined the section where Percy's protagonist Binx Bolling, bound within a reverie whereby his cinemagoing reflects his detachment from the world outside him, says 'The movies are on the search [for a true understanding of oneself], but they screw it up. The search always ends in despair' (Percy 13).[12]

The 'screening' of the moviegoer from both the artist and the world outside themselves in Cavell and Percy is in some respects indebted to Horkheimer and Adorno's famous warning in 'The Culture Industry' about the individual who 'perceives the street outside as a continuation of the film he has just left', with cinematic entertainment creating 'the illusion that the world outside is a seamless extension of the one which has been revealed in the cinema […] the simple reproduction of mind does not lead on to the expansion of mind' (99–100). Andrew Sayers, in an essay on entertainment in *Infinite Jest*, suggests a different model: the idea of the cinema screen as gigantic narcissistic mirror. For Sayers, the genuflection of the spectator to the screen presented by Roland Barthes in 'Upon Leaving the Movie Theater' connects this moment of identification with infantilism in Lacan:

> For Barthes, drawing on Lacan, childhood is characterised not only by rapt spectation but also by narcissistic (mis)identification […] Barthes draws an analogy between the relationship of the spectator to the image onscreen and the relationship of the infant to his reflection in the mirror. (Sayers 109)

Sayers subsequently aligns this position with that of Metz, who pronounces in *The Imaginary Signifier* that 'film is like the mirror' (Metz 45). However, Metz's position on the film-as-narcissistic-mirror is not necessarily as straightforward as Sayers' citation indicates. In a departure from Lacan, Metz suggests that film differs from 'the primordial mirror' in that while 'everything may come to be projected, there is one thing and one thing only that is never reflected in it: the spectator's own body'. Metz argues that 'In a certain emplacement, the mirror suddenly becomes clear glass' (45). The screen is not like a mirror in the sense that 'the perceived […] is entirely on the side of the object […] it is always the other who is on the screen; as for me, I am there to look at him'. Subsequently, 'this perceived-imaginary material is deposited in me as if on a second screen'. This results, in Metz's formulation, in the spectator identifying with himself, but fallaciously: 'this mirror returns us everything but ourselves, because we are wholly outside it, whereas the child [in the Lacanian model] is both in it and in front of it' (48).

This is a complex process, but I believe that Wallace's reflective model in *Infinite Jest* pivots on the precise pre-narcissistic moment when the mirror of the cinema screen 'becomes pure glass'. This, of course, is a moment of refraction, a *looking-through*, occurring just before the viewer processes the perceived-imaginary material and erroneously identifies it with himself, transfiguring the screen into a reflecting surface. This moment, during which the cinema screen, like the amended funhouse in 'Westward', becomes a window rather than a mirror, affords the possibility of a communicative process between viewer and either the artist or the world outside the viewer, a process that can transcend the 'screening' and self-identifying problems of the cinema screen evidenced in Cavell, Percy, Barthes and Metz. The possibility of this communicative moment in *Infinite Jest* rests on a distinction that Wallace made between art and entertainment, which Wallace perceived as operating on a 'continuum' (Lipsky, *Although* 80). At the entertainment end of this continuum are works that simply want to give the viewer 'a certain kind of pleasure that I would argue is fairly *passive*' (80, emphasis original), a position that can be aligned with Metz's reflective moment of self-identification. At the other end lies art: this is identified with the kind of 'special cruelty only true lovers can inflict' that is exhibited by Mark in 'Westward'. This cruelty is glossed by Larry McCaffery (in a definition accepted by Wallace) as performed by writers who 'care enough about their audience […] a process that's going to strengthen [the audience] in the end' (24). In this model, art is a *refractive*, not reflective process. It proceeds not from a narcissistic position on behalf of the writer but from an urge to communicate dialogically with the reader, a process that must involve the reader '[putting] in her share of the linguistic work' (34). The alignment of 'work' and 'cruelty' with art in Wallace's thesis suggests a continuation of the focus on materiality of form pursued in 'Westward': art foregrounds *awareness*, rather than oblivion. The art-entertainment continuum exists in its most developed form yet in *Infinite Jest* because Wallace bases the novel around film to which, unlike television, he ascribes the possibility of *both* qualities. Television, in Wallace's fiction and criticism, is 'the epitome of Low Art in its desire to appeal to and enjoy the attention of unprecedented numbers of people [...] It's all about syncretic diversity: neither medium nor Audience is faultable for quality' (*Supposedly* 37).[13] Film, with a spectrum that ranges from avant-garde to Hollywood blockbuster, can encompasses a broader, less capitalistically inflected range of possibilities, essentially *embodying* the art-entertainment continuum itself.

Accordingly, the most sustained and directed meditation on reflection and refraction in *Infinite Jest* directly addresses film itself, via the work of cinematic auteur James O. Incandenza. I believe that Incandenza's cinematic career, which is substantially and satirically catalogued in a lengthy filmography in the endnotes of *Infinite Jest*, is absolutely fundamental to an understanding of how Wallace enacts the difference between art and entertainment in the novel and, connectedly, to the formal development of the modes of *mise-en-abyme*, authorial presence and narcissism in his reflective model. This development of the model can be detected in the degree of alignment between Wallace's own methodology and James Incandenza's filmography, and the positioning of their work on the art/entertainment continuum. Sayers, observing 'the double bind in which [Wallace] finds himself, stuck between a rock (entertainment, "commercialism") and a hard place (art, demanding too much of the reader without sufficient reward)' (110), partially quotes the response by Wallace to Lipsky about relative degrees of exposure to art and entertainment: 'I mean art requires you to work. And we're not equipped to work all the time. And there's times when, for instance for me, commercial fiction or television is perfectly appropriate' (Lipsky, *Although* 174).[14] The often disastrous oscillations between art and entertainment in James Incandenza's filmography, which end with the misjudged creation of the most dangerously entertaining film ever made, act as an illustration of this quandary and an interrogation of Wallace's own methodology. To this end, the filmography is also the most concentrated model yet of the reflective tropes of narcissism, *mise-en-abyme* and authorial presence in Wallace's fiction. Therefore, when Boswell suggests that Incandenza's filmography 'reads like an extended parody of the postmodern canon' (*Understanding* 162), that 'Incandenza's intentions are sound; it's his methods that are the problem' (160), but that ultimately 'he remains hidden behind its mirrors and reflecting surfaces' (164) he suggests a model of Incandenza's work with which I only partly concur. While the filmography undoubtedly satirizes elements of both avant-garde fiction and filmmaking, Incandenza's methodology is more malleable than Boswell suggests, and a close reading of the filmography suggests that the director, and indeed Wallace, displays his authorial presence more nakedly than might at first be apparent.[15]

Many of the works in the filmography are parodies of real art films, and these parodies often indirectly indicate accelerated processes of narcissism. For example, *Every Inch of Disney Leith* (*Jest* 989) implicitly parodies Willard Maas' short film *Geography of the Body*, but while both films consist of macroscopic photography of body parts (a literal representation of 'navel-gazing') Incandenza's film is nearly four and a half hours longer than Maas'. Takahiko Iimura, mentioned twice in the filmography and the dedicatee of Incandenza's *Dark Logics*, directed the films *Self-Introduction* and *TV Confrontation* which show, respectively, the filmmaker interviewing himself and two television sets facing and reflecting one another: the generational inheritance of this narcissism is indicated by Orin Incandenza's enjoyment of watching films of himself playing sport (298).[16] Moreover, Incandenza's mirror-related films 'The Medusa vs. the Odalisque' and 'The Joke' indicate, like the mirrored franchised funhouses of 'Westward', the problems that attend a superannuated version of self-reflexivity which does not care for its audience. These films involve, respectively, the murder and ridicule of viewers. The literal transformation of the screen into a mirror in 'The Joke' (a film that works at the expense of a real-world, rather than diegetic, audience) suggests the worst excesses of the kind of narcissistic cinematic self-identification theorized by Barthes and Metz, and a kind of self-indulgent directorial sadism unlike the 'special cruelty' perpetrated by Mark Nechtr in his communicative story at the end of 'Westward'.

The slow convergence between 'Cage' and 'Infinite Jest', two ongoing series of films in Incandenza's filmography, involves a dramatization of many of the motifs of narcissism used thus far by Wallace in his fiction. 'Cage' is a 'parody of a broadcast-television advertisement for shampoo, utilizing four convex mirrors, two planar mirrors, and one actress' (986), 'Cage II' involves two men, one blind and one deaf mute, trying to 'devise ways of communicating' (987), while 'Cage III', about two audiences undergoing 'unspeakable degradations' and mutations at a carnival sideshow, cleaves closely to the model of audience cruelty in 'The Medusa vs. the Odalisque' and 'The Joke'.[17] While 'Cage IV' and 'Cage V' are both listed as unfinished, the latter has the subtitle 'Infinite Jim', which connects it to the simultaneous series of 'Infinite Jest' films, of which 'Infinite Jest (VI)' is the lethal entertainment that drives the novel's plot. While all the iterations of 'Infinite Jest' remain 'unseen', the nominal convergence between 'Cage' and 'Infinite Jest', and the catastrophic effects of 'Infinite Jest (VI)', unite the problematic motifs of narcissism and lack of audience communication dramatized in much of Wallace's earlier fiction (the cage motif first appearing, of course, in *Broom*). Furthermore, the filmography is *itself* a mediated reproduction, an article from the *ONANite Film and Cartridge Studies Annual* (985), compiled by a collective of unreliable critics who are narcissistically interpreting Incandenza's work through a critical methodology informed by parody and pastiche. For example, the entry for the film 'Wave Bye-Bye to the Bureaucrat' suggests that the film is a 'possible parody/homage to B.S. public-service-announcement' (*Jest* 990) without taking into account that Incandenza could be attempting to make a sincere statement about communication, a possibility given credence by the fact that it is Mario's favourite of his father's films precisely for its 'unhip earnestness' and that the outwardly unaffected Hal 'secretly likes it' (689). The most substantial clue to the unreliability of the critics is the attribution of quotes from those who have seen 'Infinite Jest (VI)', despite the addictive nature of the film rendering people critically and physically inarticulate. The fact that one of the reviews is anonymous (993) does not help their case.

Initially, the function of *mise-en-abyme* in the filmography appears to only amplify the narcissistic motifs of reflection therein. In a process of Simple (and potentially Infinite *and* Aporetic) Duplication, each successive version of 'Infinite Jest' is itself a remake of all the prior versions, these versions enclosed, of course, by a process of Simple Duplication within the novel *Infinite Jest*. While the subject matter of the 'Infinite Jest' films may not exactly match the content of the novel, Wallace's use of *mise-en-abyme* suggests a concentric, embedded sequence of narcissistic reflections. However, like the 'egress' promised by Mark's funhouse in 'Westward', Wallace embeds into this apparently centripetal model of internal reflection the possibility of an exit, of a refractive process whereby the screen becomes, as in Metz's formulation, 'pure glass'. This is achieved via engagement with the cinematic theory of 'auteurship', which is aligned with the modes of authorial presence previously employed in 'Westward', and involves Wallace offering a critique of his own methodology as a palimpsest narrative.

James Incandenza has a combative relationship with film theorist Andre Bazin, founder of *Cahiers Du Cinema*: he is observed on one occasion 'making a tormented face' at the mere mention of Bazin's name (745). The dislike goes back to Incandenza's childhood, as he recalls 'reading something dull by Bazin' as a boy (491). The most likely explanation for Incandenza's dislike of Bazin lies in the latter's theorization of cinema as 'objectivity in time' (Bazin 14) and his opinions on the automatic process of photography, whereby 'an image of the world is formed automatically, without the creative intervention of a man' (13). The kind of self-conscious auteurship with which Incandenza begins his career in cinema stands in stark opposition to Bazin's position; Incandenza's films operate as a *reinforcement* of authorial presence, rather than as an effacement of it, and his appearance in several of his own films supports this position. Furthermore, the foregrounded materiality of Incandenza's cinema acts against Bazin's suggestion that 'a [picture] frame is centripetal, the screen centrifugal' (166) in much the same manner that Greenberg ascribes to modernist painting; Incandenza is not interested in cinema as a window to the world, but as a reflection of the auteur: a monologic art.

However, as the filmography progresses, fault-lines begin to appear in this position. Joelle Van Dyne, initially classifying Incandenza's work as 'oddly hollow, empty' and with 'no emotional movement towards an audience [...] like a very smart person conversing with himself', goes on to recognize that 'there had been flashes of something else [...] when he dropped the technical fireworks and tried to make characters move [...] and willingly took the risk of appearing amateurish' (740–1). Indeed, Incandenza's career is littered with films that occupy a strange liminal space between reflection and refraction: films that are *implicitly*, not overtly, about the auteur and that seem to constitute a cry for help. Some of these films are direct dramatizations of episodes from Incandenza's life that also appear elsewhere in the narrative of *Infinite Jest*. 'As of Yore', in which 'a middle-aged tennis instructor, preparing to instruct his son in tennis [...] subjects his son to a rambling monologue while the son weeps and perspires' (991) and 'Valuable Coupon Has Been Removed' are filmed versions of the events from Incandenza's childhood on pages 157–69 and 491–503, while 'It Was a Great Marvel that He Was in the Father Without Knowing Him' refers to Incandenza's relationship with his own son Hal on pages 27–31.[18,19] These films, which are dramatized so that only those familiar with Incandenza's life (which pointedly does *not* include the critics who compiled the filmography) can detect the traces of real-life events and traumas, concern a desire for intergenerational communication. This desire becomes more desperate as Incandenza's career progresses. While recalling another of his father's films, 'Good-Looking Men in Small Clever Rooms That Utilize Every Centimeter of Available Space with Mind-Boggling Efficiency', Hal's narration offers a direct rebuff to critical consensus on Incandenza's relationship with his audience:

> The art-cartridge critics and scholars who point to the frequent presence of audiences inside Himself's films, and argue that the fact that the audiences are always either dumb and unappreciative or the victims of some grisly entertainment-mishap betrays more than a little hostility on the part of an auteur pegged as technically gifted but narratively dull and plotless and static and not entertaining enough – these academics' arguments seem

> sound as far as they go, but they do not explain the incredible pathos of Paul Anthony Heaven reading his lecture to a crowd of dead-eyed kids [...] all the time weeping. (*Jest* 911)

The weeping appears to derive not from a lack of desire for communication but from sadness at the lack of communication itself. It is this desperation that leads, via a dreadful miscalculation, to the creation of 'Infinite Jest (VI)'.

If we consider Incandenza's hide-and-seek authorial presence in the context of Wallace's admission that *The Broom of the System* is 'a *coded autobio* that's also a funny little post-structural gag' ('Interview with Larry McCaffery' 41, emphasis mine) the distinction between Incandenza and Wallace partially collapses. Rather than a patriarch for his patricide, Wallace positions Incandenza's work as a partial reflection of his own presence in his fiction in a differently directed example of the materializing authorial presence I describe in Chapter 1. While references in the filmography occasionally revisit nominal elements of Wallace's earlier novels ('Death in Scarsdale' shares a location with *Broom*; the 'convex mirrors' of 'Cage' recall the invocation of Ashbery in 'Little Expressionless Animals'), the development from self-reflexivity to a desire for communication in Incandenza's work also evokes comments made by Wallace about his dissatisfaction with his earlier writing. *Broom* is a 'self-obsessed little bildungsroman', while in 'Westward' 'I got trapped one time just trying to expose the illusions of metafiction the same way metafiction had tried to expose the illusions of the pseudo-unmediated realist fiction that came before it [...] it came out just as what it was: crude and naive and pretentious' ('Interview with Larry McCaffery' 40–1). At the time of the novel's publication in 1996, both Incandenza and Wallace's most recent works are titled 'Infinite Jest'. *Infinite Jest* the novel acts in a similar manner to 'Infinite Jest (VI)' the film: an endpoint of experimentation with previous narrative forms and an attempt to communicate more directly with an audience, but by placing the rapacious 'Infinite Jest (VI)', in a *mise-en-abyme* gesture of Simple Duplication, inside his own novel, Wallace encloses the lethally entertaining film within his own, more deliberately communicative, narrative. While Boswell and LeClair have made similar points about this asynthesis between 'Infinite Jest' and *Infinite*

*Jest* (*Understanding* 164; 'Prodigious' 34), I do not believe that the novel is simply the corrective element and final stage of this process: it is not the kind of 'univocal' solution that Wallace disparages. Rather, the breakthrough in communication is made possible through an ongoing triangulated process: an internally reflective dialogue between Incandenza, the implied presence of Wallace himself and the reader outside of the novel, putting in the 'linguistic work' to piece the fractured narrative together. Like Mark Nechtr's funhouse, this complex series of reflections points to the exit, allowing 'egress'.

Correspondingly, on one particular occasion Wallace employs a more aggressive alternative strategy to refraction in *Infinite Jest*, one that involves actually 'breaking through' reflective surfaces and foregrounds the importance of the reader in the process of constructing the narrative of *Infinite Jest*. Quebecois separatists drag 'huge standing mirrors across US Interstate 87' where 'naively empiricist north-bound U.S. motorists [...] would see impending headlights and believe some like suicidal idiot or Canadian had transversed the median and was coming right for them' (311). While 'empiricist' drivers swerve to their deaths at the last minute, a valium addict 'saw the sudden impending headlights in her northbound lane as Grace' (312) and drives straight ahead, shattering the mirror and surviving, and saving the lives of others by alerting them to the plot. This episode suggests, as elsewhere in Wallace's work, that identification with the object in the mirror, a process that leads here to fatal attempts at self-preservation, is potentially lethal. Seeing through the mirror (the valium addict interprets the mirror as communication with 'Grace') leads to salvation. Stendhal, whose 'mirror in the roadway' is explicitly invoked by this sequence, proclaims in *The Red and the Black* that 'the man who carries the mirror on his back will be accused by you of immorality! His mirror shows you the mire, and you blame the mirror! Blame, rather, the road in which the puddle lies' (80). The 'man who carries the mirror' here is a hybrid of terrorist and implied author, who by placing the mirror in the roadway performs the act of 'special cruelty' that illustrates the danger of narcissism and the possibility of a literal and figurative breakthrough. I read the process of internal reflection produced by the implied presence of the author in *Infinite Jest* as offering an implicit dialectical and co-constructive framework *both inside and outside* the bound world and structure of the novel, one which can address the problems of narcissism in terms of 'looking through' and, latterly, 'breaking through'.[20]

## After the Breakthrough

Wallace continues to explore the motif of narcissistic self-identification with the screen immediately after *Infinite Jest*. In May 1997, he typed an early outline for a long work titled *Sir John Feelgood or, The Genesis of a Great Lover*. Certain elements of this project, such as the character name Drinion and the use of the IRS as a location, are an early manifestation of the colossal, protean project that would eventually be called *The Pale King*, which would inform almost all the fiction Wallace wrote until the end of his life. However, the principle plot notes for *Sir John Feelgood*, which are not present in *The Pale King*, revolve around technological advances in video pornography:

> IRS Special Agent becomes actor in his own digitized porn movies [...] 'Virtual reality goggles', but instead of piping a VR scene into your eyes they pump a view of you – the goggles wearer – from outside, from the camera's eye view. So what you see is not what you're 'looking at' but rather you looking at it [...] This exteriorized perception of self can cause disorientation, like trying to cut your hair in a mirror or move a mouse on a computer screen. (Box 37.4)[21]

Drinion eventually becomes an actor in these films because 'for some reason he's unusually easy to erase from [the] shot', being 'unnaturally pale'. Finally, 'Drinion/"Sir John Feelgood" becomes the void the viewer is projected onto' (Box 37.4). The reciprocity of the relationship between the viewer and onscreen pornography, a natural extension of the preoccupation with reflection, has a long history in Wallace's writing. In a letter to Bonnie Nadell in 1989, Wallace broaches the idea of writing 'a long piece of fiction that has something to do with the adult film industry', displaying a particular interest in why 'many of the movies have a kind of shadowy, dramatically superfluous character who seems to stand for the man watching film [...] and whose final access to female lead(s) effects film's closure' ('Letter to Bonnie Nadell,

May 11th 1989'). He begins to dramatize this reciprocal motif in his outline for *Sir John Feelgood*.[22] Wallace began to research the novel in early July 1989, visiting pornographic film sets in Los Angeles (Max 125). Despite this evidence, nothing substantial came of the research and none of the relevant notebooks or materials are present in Wallace's archive.[23] However, Wallace is still considering the question of self-identification with pornography during his 1996 interview with David Lipsky, in an exchange that clearly indicates that he was not only thinking about the genesis of *Sir John Feelgood*, but reading pornography in terms of the lethal effect of 'Infinite Jest (VI)':

> [...] in ten or fifteen years, we're gonna have virtual reality pornography. Now, if I don't develop some machinery for being able to turn off pure unalloyed pleasure, and allow myself to go out and, you know, grocery shop and pay the rent? I don't know about you, but I'm gonna have to leave the planet. Virtual. Reality. Pornography. [...] The technology's gonna get better and better at doing what it does. (Lipsky, *Although* 83)

In 1998 Wallace published 'Big Red Son', a long form non-fiction piece on the adult film industry, but the question of self-insertion into pornography explored in *Sir John Feelgood* remains unanswered in his fiction. However, even in this early outline it is clear that *Sir John Feelgood* was to accelerate some of the motifs of reflection, narcissism and *mise-en-abyme* that had preoccupied Wallace in *Infinite Jest*. For example, another plot note on the novel describes a scene combining narcissism and characteristic Simple Duplication: '[Drinion] and one IRS female are on couch watching video of him having sex w/ another IRS female – this so turns on the agent on couch that she and SJF have sex while watching SJF have sex w/ other agent on video' (Box 40.5). This constitutes both amplification and *reification* of the model of narcissistic self-identification with the screen proposed by Metz and Barthes: the onanistic viewer gains pleasure not only from watching the screen, but from watching *themselves* on the screen. In the outlined scene above, the screen mirrors the action in a grotesque, pornographic advancement of Incandenza's 'The Joke'. It is also a perversion of Foucault's suggestion that the viewer's recognition of the mirror at the back of the *Las Meninas* 'offers us at last that enchantment of the double that until now has been denied us', creating 'an oscillation between the interior and the exterior' (11). In *Sir John Feelgood*, this is less a dialogic oscillation than a narcissistic feedback loop.

Accordingly, both *Brief Interviews with Hideous Men* and *Oblivion* are informed by a mixture of narcissistic self-identification, 'mirroring' behaviour and sexual dysfunction, all traces of the unresolved *Sir John Feelgood*. By the nature of their piecemeal form, these collections also draw a stronger distinction between characters trapped within pathological, narcissistic behaviour and those who are afforded escape. While *Infinite Jest* weaves the lives of these characters together within a unified polyphonic narrative framework, the moments of dialogic communication in *Brief Interviews* are notable for their stark contrast with other standalone stories of extreme solipsism or narcissism-induced paralysis. However, as Mary Holland has suggested, the structure of the stories in the collection asserts 'a kind of integrity by implying echoes and connections among themselves and a logic to their placements in the collection [...] withholding overarching closure and coherence by comprising pieces and series of pieces that signify gaps, incompletion, and disorder as much as meaningful presence' ('Mediated' 109). I agree with this formulation to an extent, but I would argue that in 'Octet' the collection does have a specific 'heart', a central reflective and refractive surface that governs and mediates the collection around it.

I have described the dialogic alignment of reader responsibility and authorial presence in 'Octet' in Chapter 1, but the story also acts as a concentration of the reflective preoccupations of the rest of the collection, using *mise-en-abyme* and authorial presence to overcome narcissism by way of example. The stories surrounding 'Octet' contain multiple iterations of problematic reflection. 'Suicide as a Sort of Present' and 'On His Deathbed...' dramatize a kind of arresting of the Lacanian mirror stage, whereby the damaged child is unable to free themselves from identification with the image of the narcissistic parent and identify themselves as a discrete object in the Symbolic order. In doing so, these stories revisit the pervasive 'child-as-mirror-of-parent' theme that has recurred in Wallace's fiction since *Broom*.[24] Both stories involve the child performing a self-destructive narcissistic act that is implicitly aimed at the parent (respectively, suicide and the humiliation of the father through the staged dramatization of his dying moments by his 'reflectionless' son

[*Brief* 225]). In 'The Depressed Person' and the brief interviews themselves, a self-absorbed individual feigns refractive communication only as a way to burnish their own reflections. These individuals gesture towards dialogue but as evidenced by, respectively, the un-mourned death of the therapist and effacement of the interviewer's words, they actually perform a self-serving monologue, one which only consolidates isolation.[25] Elsewhere, 'Tris-Stan: I Sold Sissee Nar to Ecko', the most overt discussion of narcissism in the collection, updates the story of Narcissus and Echo to broadcast television and accordingly associates Sissee Nar's paralytic obsession with her own image: she is 'literally frozen [...] utterly static & passive & affectless' (214) before her impending destruction, 'ventilated [...] liberally' by the gun-toting Ecko (214).

Wallace was preoccupied with the placement of 'Octet'. In August 1998, in a letter to Michael Pietsch, he suggested that it was a 'strong piece', but 'I'm unsure if it's correctly placed [...] for a couple months I had placed it much nearer the end of the collection' ('Letter to Michael Pietsch, August 17th 1998'). On publication of *Brief Interviews*, it appears in the exact centre of the collection.[26] 'Octet' implements the refractive model developed within 'Westward' and *Infinite Jest*, marrying Mark Nechtr's metafictional funhouse model to a miniaturized version of the triangulated character-author-reader narrative structure from *Infinite Jest*. Its placement in the centre of the collection allows it to reflectively radiate upon the adjoining and surrounding stories, invoking both the internally mirrored structures of Wallace's earlier fiction and the refractive methodology developed later: the rest of the collection can be refractively viewed 'through' it.[27] It is the most intricate configuration of the reflective model advanced by Wallace throughout his fiction, and in retrospect perhaps the most complete dramatization of the interplay of reflection and refraction in Wallace's writing. The most substantial clue to the governing position of 'Octet' comes when the 'fiction writer' outlines his problem with the coherence of the 'Pop Quizzes' that make up the story:

> You are attempting a cycle of very short belletristic pieces [...] How exactly the cycle's short pieces are supposed to work is hard to describe. Maybe say they're supposed to compose a certain sort of '*interrogation*' of the

> person reading them, somehow – i.e. palpations, feelers into the interstices of her sense of something, etc… though what that 'something' is remains maddeningly hard to pin down, even just for yourself as you're working on the pieces […] You know for sure, though, that the narrative pieces really are just 'pieces' and nothing more, i.e. that it is the way they fit together into the larger cycle that comprises them that is crucial to whatever 'something' you want to 'interrogate' a human 'sense of,' and so on. (123)

The 'cycle' can refer simultaneously to the pop quizzes in 'Octet' and, in a gesture of Simple Duplication, the entire collection. In his disruptive placement of an apparently diffident authorial presence in the centre of the collection, Wallace accords judgement to the reader over not only the cohesion of 'Octet', but the whole of *Brief Interviews with Hideous Men*. This simultaneous use of *mise-en-abyme* (the collection in miniature embedded within itself) and self-effacing authorial presence reflects and frames the other stories in the collection, with their paralysed protagonists, as part of an overarching undertaking in defiance of narcissism.[28] Therefore, any narcissistic despair is ameliorated by its placement within a refractive system, which involves seeing the individual components of the collection not as discrete, monadic units but as an interdependent chain that can be looked *through*: an example, to cite the title used three times by Wallace in the collection, of 'the porousness of certain borders'.

## 'I Don't Want to Be *Seen* That Way'

The reflective model changes dramatically in *Oblivion*, where there appears little possibility of those modes of refractive communication that have developed in Wallace's fiction since 'Westward'. When Boswell describes the stories in the collection as, *contra* 'Westward', offering 'no way out', citing Corey Messler's blurb for the novel as resembling 'Russian dolls within Russian dolls' ('Constant' 162), he identifies the intensification of isolation in the collection with an explicit reference to a torquing of the process of *mise-en-abyme*. Rather than narratives nested within narratives, *Oblivion* describes selves trapped within layers of paralysing self-consciousness. Accordingly, the collection is full of claustrophobic arrangements of reflective surfaces, and the 'mirrored cage' motif returns with a vengeance: Neal's advertising agency in 'Good Old Neon' is described as 'one big ballet of fraudulence [...] a virtual hall of mirrors' (162); the sleep chamber in 'Oblivion' has mirrored walls (222); the gym in the World Trade Centre in 'The Suffering Channel' is 'lined with mirrored plate' (315); Skip Atwater enjoys 'periods of self-exhortation' in front of mirrors in the same story (241) accompanied by onanistic fist-pumping gestures.

However these mirrored environments, which are all explicitly connected to places of work, represent something of a change of focus for Wallace's model of reflection, one that increasingly revolves around the centralization of the figure identified in 'E Unibus Pluram' as 'Joe Briefcase', 'the average U.S. lonely person' (*Supposedly* 23). Joe Briefcase, with his everyman/worker drone nomenclature, is rather condescendingly presented in 'E Unibus Pluram' as something of an unenlightened test subject, drawn in contrast to the 'scholars and critics who write about U.S. popular culture' (27), with whom Wallace implicitly aligns himself. However, of the stories in *Oblivion*, 'Mister Squishy', 'The Soul is not a Smithy', 'Good Old Neon' and 'The Suffering Channel' centralize the world of white-collar office work and workers. With the availability of Wallace's archive, it is now understood that *Oblivion* developed in tandem with elements of *The Pale King*, and certain stories in the collection can be explicitly connected to parts of the evolving manuscript for that novel, which is based largely around workspace environments. This change of subject matter, and its ramifications for the reflective and refractive model developed by Wallace in his fiction, can be most succinctly analysed by considering the connection between narcissism and the title of the collection. Marshal McLuhan, in describing the effects of increased media saturation on the individual, glosses the word 'Narcissus' as deriving 'from the Greek word *narcosis*, or numbness' (McLuhan 41) and explaining that

> [...] such amplification is bearable by the nervous system only through numbness or blocking of perception. This is the sense of the Narcissus myth. The young man's image is a self-amputation or extension induced by irritating pressures. As a counter-irritant, the image produces a generalized numbness or shock that declines recognition. (42–3)

If the drug-fuelled descriptions of narcissism in *Infinite Jest* are often characterized with recourse to the 'narcotic' root of the word, the reactions to the 'irritating pressures' of the work environment in *Oblivion* might be understood as an amended version of McLuhan's model: the characters in *Oblivion* are not drug or alcohol addicts (they are, pretty much to a person, deathly sober), but they erect the same oblivious 'numbness or blocking of perception', an amputation of the world outside which, of course, leads to a sense of compounded isolation.[29] As described in Chapter 2, this sometimes manifests itself as the reverse of the process at the end of 'Westward' through the transfiguration of a window into a mirror, as in 'Mister Squishy' and 'The Soul is not a Smithy'. However, in the most severe cases, such as that of Terry Schmidt in 'Mister Squishy', the process of looking in the mirror itself 'declines recognition' and the vacuum is filled by the iconography of the corporation that employs him:

> [Schmidt] would call himself, directly to his mirrored face, *Mister Squishy*, the name would come unbidden into his mind [...] when he thought of himself now it was as something he called *Mister Squishy*, and his own face and the plump and wholly innocuous icon's face tended to bleed in his mind into one face. (33–4, emphasis original)

This is arguably neither reflection nor refraction. It is a total effacement of personality by the work environment, and a dramatized reversal of the Lacanian mirror stage. Schmidt's reflection moves from Symbolic to Imaginary, from a position of recognizability as an object in the world to the infant-like, 'squishy' face of his corporation. When Wallace explains that his childhood understanding of the adult world of work was characterized by the feeling that 'something terrible was coming' ('Interview with Steve Paulson' 129), the erasure of Schmidt's reflection seems to realize the criteria of that nameless fear. Accordingly, *Oblivion* lacks a 'refractive' story like 'Octet' to recontextualize the reflective isolation of the stories that surround it. The refractive breakthrough in the narrative of 'Octet' is certainly a prerequisite to the structure of 'Good Old Neon' with (as I have argued in Chapter 1) the latter performing a hitherto undramatized dialogic relationship between author, character and reader. However, 'Good Old Neon' does this in a position of isolation from the rest of the collection, as it does not perform the same *mise-en-abyme* function of Simple Duplication; it does not position itself as a miniaturization of the rest of the collection.[30] The other stories in *Oblivion* remain isolated, alone.

I want to suggest that this apparent arrest or reversal of the refractive model occurs as a result of a fundamental transition in the quality of authorial presence in Wallace's work in this period. *Oblivion* has a problematic standing in relation to *The Pale King*: archival evidence suggests that some of the stories in the collection are components of that larger work that have been hived off and polished into stand-alone pieces. While I will comment on that process in more detail in the next chapter, I want to establish here how Wallace's authorial presence undergoes a fundamental shift in *Oblivion*, a transition that is connected inextricably to his own developing public persona and his attempts to create a new, amended model of refraction, an amendment that is only partially successful. The best way to understand this transition is to look at the depiction of 'reporting' in 'The Suffering Channel' and an unfinished story from the same period, 'Wickedness'.

In an interview with Steve Paulson in 2004, the year of *Oblivion*'s publication, Wallace argues that '[The life of a writer is] also probably the life of [...] office workers, who we think of as having very boring, dry jobs. Probably all jobs are the same and they're filled with horrible boredom and despair' (129). The comparison is a little disingenuous: as a tenured academic and successful writer, Wallace is not beholden to the same environmental market forces as those workers depicted in 'Mister Squishy'. Nevertheless, this is important to an understanding of how Wallace was beginning to align his *public* persona with the subjects of his fiction. In the figure of Midwestern journalist Skip Atwater in 'The Suffering Channel' (whose correspondence with Wallace I have already outlined in some detail) Wallace implicitly dramatizes, for the first time, an iteration of his non-fiction reporting persona, a persona much more strongly conflated, however inaccurately, with a public idea of the 'real' David Foster Wallace (while *Infinite Jest*'s Steeply is a reporter, s/he is not an evident stand-in for Wallace in the same way as Atwater). It was inevitable in the work of a writer so obsessed with ideas of self-presentation that Wallace's public persona would at some point manifest itself in his fiction. Mike Miley, quoting Wallace's essay on Dostoevsky, unpacks how Wallace's concerns over the increasing emergence of his public persona are based explicitly around fears over inability to communicate:

> Wallace feared having that iconic status conferred upon himself would negatively affect his fiction because, as he claims in 'Joseph Frank's Dostoevsky', 'to make someone an icon is to make him an abstraction, and abstractions are incapable of vital communication with living people [...] once artists appear in the public eye, the public loses any ability to distinguish what is performance from what is genuine. As a result, everything, both sincere and not, becomes absorbed by the public persona'. ('And Starring' 192)

Wallace also displays nervousness about the function of his non-fiction persona when he distances himself from Hunter S. Thompson, who he criticizes for being 'far more interested in developing himself as a charismatic persona [...] than he is in writing *honest* or powerful nonfiction [...] most of his work bores me; it seems naive and *narcissistic*' ('Interview with Didier Jacob' 155, emphasis mine). In 'The Suffering Channel', Wallace attempts to forestall any potential lack of communication by actively dramatizing the conflation of his public and private personae in Skip Atwater. As Boswell has indicated, this conflation can also be extended to Brint Moltke, who embodies 'the conflict between [...] extreme personal shyness and need for privacy on one hand versus his involuntary need to express what lay inside him through some type of personal expression or art' ('Constant' 159). However, this modification of Wallace's authorial presence *itself* carries the risk of narcissism, of becoming a series of reflections of the artist on their own public persona: a public 'working out' of a personal problem. I believe that Wallace tries to sidestep the narcissistic possibilities of this formulation, and retain the refractive relationship with the reader, by couching this metapresence within a series of enquiries about the ethics of seeing and reporting. This amended model is also explored in 'Wickedness', an unfinished short story written by Wallace circa 2000 which, with its reporter protagonist and plot focused on tabloid sensationalism, likely constitutes an early version of 'The Suffering Channel'.

'Wickedness' can be found among Wallace's materials for *The Pale King*, though it is clearly not part of that novel. It concerns an undercover reporter, Chet Skyles, who is charged by his employer, the tabloid magazine *Wicked*, with entering the exclusive 'San Placido Institute' and secretly taking photographs of the Alzheimer's-stricken Ronald Reagan. Skyles is suffering from terminal oral cancer and is motivated by the prospect of a large payout on delivery of the photographs. The story appears to be related by an anonymous third-person narrator and published by an editor after Skyles' death. In a sustained passage, which I will quote at length due to the story's unavailability and its importance to the development of the refractive model, the narrator outlines *Wicked*'s strategy for publishing the pictures:

> Suppose a tabloid broke [a story about the secret son of a Hollywood actor who was institutionalised]. This would cross the line. The story would be riveting, of course, but it would also be bad business. The tabloids, just like the mainstream press, knew that a story was like a prism or jewel, with at least three reflecting surfaces. In tabloid editorial language this was called the three-in-one – every story is about (a) the subject, (b) the organ that runs it, (c) the person that buys it. [It would] reflect terribly on the tabloid that ran it [...] Nobody knew who or what owned filth.com [later called 'Latrine.com']. More important, people could pay their $1.25 and download it in private (a huge part of the third 'mirror' of people's sense of shame is public. It is well known that people will say, watch and do things in private that they would never even think of doing in public. For a long time, bathroom walls were the only venue of 'public privacy' – you could write all kinds of filth, depressing communiqués to people who'd read it but not even know you wrote it). (Box 39.5)[31]

This extract is important to Wallace's evolving models of reflection and refraction and to an understanding of his implied presence in 'The Suffering Channel'. The focus on extreme forms of pornography in *Sir John Feelgood* and 'Big Red Son' acts as an early indicator of an intensified preoccupation with the viewing of transgressive and damaging content which will reach its apex in 'The Suffering Channel' and 'Wickedness'. 'The Suffering Channel', which broadcasts images of extreme human suffering (*Oblivion* 291–2), and filth.com, which surpasses even the Suffering Channel's transgressive images by anonymously making the most intensely private moments of celebrities public (it partially enacts R Vaughn Corliss' fantasies of a medium 'devoted wholly to images of celebrities shitting' [*Oblivion* 295]), combine and advance one of the central motifs of *Infinite Jest*: the desire to view an image of something potentially damaging. However, in 'Wickedness' Wallace places this desire in the context of the 'three reflecting surfaces' of the 'prism or jewel' of the story. These three surfaces correspond to the subject, the medium and the viewer, and contained within the medium is the mediator themselves, the Atwater or Skyles who is charged with capturing the image.

The principal difference between 'Infinite Jest (VI)' and the model advanced by the Suffering Channel and filth.com is that the latter have a suffering 'subject' as well as a viewer. By explicitly connecting subject, medium/reporter and viewer in a 'reflective' chain Wallace erects, in an advancement of the triangulated character-author-reader dialogue from *Infinite Jest*, an ethically inflected model of refraction which dismantles the privacy of the viewer, requiring them to *look through* the 'prism' of mediation to the means by which the mediator retrieves the images of the suffering subject. By naming his reporters (in an implied gesture of authorial presence), giving them private lives and making them suffer, the process is also explicitly deanonymized. The anonymity that is enacted by filth.com's website works in both directions, separating viewer and subject and affording the viewer a desire to see that is based not in empathy but prurience and voyeurism. Once the reporter's role is explicitly detailed, the process of anonymity begins to be dismantled and the relationship between subject and viewer is made public. To partially amend Foucault's formula, 'in the depths of the mirror' there appears both the anonymous face of the viewer and the implied presence of Wallace himself. Ultimately, then, the authorial presence of Wallace in his reporter characters constitutes an attempt to dramatize his own public and private personae in the service of an 'oscillation between interior and exterior'.

The overlap of subject matter between 'Wickedness' and 'The Suffering Channel' acts as a reminder that after *Infinite Jest*, Wallace's fiction enters a phase of substantial cross-pollination and compositional complexity.

At the heart of this phase is Wallace's attempt to create a structure for his third novel, which will eventually become known as *The Pale King*. As I will explain in the final chapter of this book, this process presents Wallace with an unprecedented challenge, one that both unites and problematizes the formal approaches to vocality, spatiality and visuality that have characterized his fiction.

# 4

# Finality

## 'Not Even Close to Complete': The Many Forms of *The Pale King*

In the margin of a two-page document, titled 'Tornado of Characters', that attempts to make sense of the spiralling multitude of protagonists in the drafts of *The Pale King*, there is a note: '31 May 2005. Soon ten years after' (Box 39.1). At this time, Wallace had been attempting to seriously construct a third novel for eight years. This novel, which had already gone through several substantial plot changes and at least two working titles, was still failing to cohere, with Wallace describing the 'tornadic' nature of the process to Michael Pietsch as 'like wrestling sheets of balsa wood in a high wind' (*Pale* v). The reference in the note to the ten-year anniversary of the publication of *Infinite Jest*, the novel that cemented his status as a writer of fiction, hauntingly illustrates both Wallace's anxiety over surpassing that novel and his ongoing concern about the failure of coherence of the work in process.

A week later, on 7 June, Wallace writes a lengthy note to self in which he lays out his concerns about the compositional problems of the novel. This note betrays a deep anxiety over the amount of material that the third novel has generated and the attendant problems engendered by the retention of older drafts and material:

> The danger of re-reading all this old material is that it makes me think it all has to be preserved and used. As if the book were a puzzle and all these pieces had to fit into it. This is not so. The truth is that the book must be written – started afresh, and <u>continued</u> with. There are promising nuggets in this old stuff […] but none of them can just be re-used per se […] so much

time and work has apparently gone into these nuggets, and so many of them just stop [...] I so want it done, so want a key or clue in these old documents to how the book is to be done. I fear I have too much stuff, and too little [...] I do not have to write a book that is as good, or as well-received, as IJ. (Box 39.1, emphasis original)

This note clearly represents a crisis point in the life of *The Pale King*, one most likely exacerbated by the fact that a number of sections earmarked for the novel had been published in *Oblivion* the previous year, leaving Wallace with less workable material from which to draw.[1] In the period immediately following, Wallace devised a new narrative strategy that he clearly hoped would bring the disparate drafts together: he wrote himself into the novel. I will address the full formal ramifications of the appearance of 'David Wallace' in *The Pale King*, and its relevancy to Wallace's prior engagements with authorial presence, later in this chapter. Firstly, however, I must address the matter of coherency and the several different forms that Wallace's third novel took in its troubled and unfinished period of composition. Central to this enquiry is the question of what exactly *The Pale King* is, and how it evolved between 1997 and 2007, when Wallace withdrew from writing the manuscript while struggling with the onset of depression that would ultimately lead to his death the following year.

When Toon Staes and Luc Herman ask 'Can *The Pale King* Please Be a Novel?' they speak to a general desire, both readerly and scholarly, to be able to perceive the text as a coherent system.[2] They also speak, indirectly, to Wallace's own anxiety over the assembly of notes, drafts and chapters that comprise the fundamental materials of the novel. When approaching this unfinished text, the reader and scholar would be wise to recall Frank Kermode's assertion in *The Sense of an Ending* that

> No novel can avoid being in some sense what Aristotle calls 'a completed action.' This being so, all novels imitate a world of potentiality [...] They have a fixation on the eidetic imagery of beginning, middle, and end, potency and cause. (138)

In the unusual case of *The Pale King*, we have a literalizing of Kermode's formula: a text that exists as both a 'completed action' (an assembly of some of the drafts by Michael Pietsch into a novel-like format for publication) and 'a world of potentiality' (the public availability of the sprawling collection of compositional materials held in Wallace's archive). Accordingly, scholars have attempted to identify different ways of staging a reading of *The Pale King*'s form. Conley Wouters has speculated, on failing to find a central structural document within the archive, that if completed the novel might have taken the form of 'an almanac, or a narrative compendium' (185), while Simon De Bourcier suggests that 'Wallace knew what he wanted to say in this book, and largely said it' (369). I would argue that Wallace's 2005 note to self casts doubt upon the latter position, but there remains the question of how, if at all, the form of Wallace's third novel can be systematized.

Having examined all extant archive-based documentation and draft material pertaining to Wallace's fiction in the period 1997–2007, I will now outline a detailed genetic history of the novel's composition, which will comprise the first part of this chapter. Such an analysis allows us to formally systematize *The Pale King* project based upon the broadest spread of empirical evidence and will, I hope, help to advance a critical understanding of the nuances of Wallace's composition in this period by creating a map of his late fiction. In this respect I accord with Saverio Tomaiulo, who suggests that 'the lesson unfinished novels may teach those readers and critics interested in finished novels is to approach texts not as fixed entities but as "processual" events' (14). I believe that the form of *The Pale King* should be analysed 'processually' in order to ascertain how, if at all, the novel might have cohered. Once this processual analysis is complete, I will return to the questions of form and structure outlined in the previous chapters of this book to consider how the most coherent sections of *The Pale King* – most particularly those sections written after the novel's crisis point in 2005 – speak to the evolving questions of vocality, spatiality and visuality I have analysed in previous chapters. During this analysis I will return to the compositional materials when they suggest a matter of interest or problem pertinent to these formal modes. Of course, the lengthy and convoluted history of the novel, not to mention the sprawling and messy nature of the relevant archive material, presents a number of compositional aporias when addressing matters of teleological *development*, but I do believe that a coherent history of the novel's form, and its relationship to the formal preoccupations of the earlier fiction, can be established through this process.

## *The Pale King*: A History

In 'A Paradigm for the Life of Consciousness', Stephen Burn takes issue with D.T. Max's assertion that Wallace's creative history post-1996 can be framed as a struggle to surpass the reputation of *Infinite Jest*, arguing that Max 'mistakenly ascribe[s] a linear sequence of discrete projects, rather than emphasising a series of parallel compositions enlivened by creative cross-fertilization' (166 n4). I would argue that, on the basis of the archival evidence, the truth is somewhere between these two positions. There can be absolutely no doubt that as Burn suggests, the fiction post-1996 comprises a set of coexisting and co-evolving literary projects. However, I would also argue that the struggle to surpass *Infinite Jest* is absolutely central to the composition of *The Pale King* in that a significant number of the post-1996 fictions, most notably the stories in *Oblivion*, come into existence *because* Wallace is trying to write his third novel. Archivally, if one considers the 'shape' of Wallace's composition before *Infinite Jest*, he tends to write stories and novels discretely (an exception is 'Las Meninas', which ends up, rather awkwardly, in *Infinite Jest*). Even during the main period of composition of *Infinite Jest* between 1993 and 1995, this process is remarkably cohesive considering the size and sprawl of the undertaking, and unlike the period after publication in 1996, no other substantial fiction emerges out of the period of that novel's composition.

Essentially, then, the fiction after *Infinite Jest* could arguably be described as one huge linear 'discrete project' that shed or engendered other projects during its process. Of course, within this project there is just the kind of 'creative cross-fertilization' referred to by Burn which results in the creation of other fiction, but this tends to come about as the result of creative frustration or incompatibility with the macro project. I would therefore partially concur with Burn's suggestion elsewhere in the same essay that *The Pale King* project represents a 'summative work' (160), but I would incorporate an additional term: paralytic. Wallace's formal preoccupations advance and accrete in the most coherent sections of *The Pale King*, but the novel's composition is also marked by a juxtaposition and partial incompatibility of prevailing narrative voice and persona, an incompatibility which I read as partially connected to Wallace's increased visibility and public persona after 1996. *The Pale King* is, then, a narrative within which all of Wallace's prior formal concerns accumulate but are also in conflict.

Between 1997 and 2007, Wallace was continually working on his third novel. During this period, the novel progresses in three distinct but imbricated compositional stages, which I will now discuss in turn.

## 1. 1997–1999: *Sir John Feelgood* and *Brief Interviews with Hideous Men*

In the previous chapter I discussed some of Wallace's ideas from 1997 for *Sir John Feelgood*, a narrative based around an IRS agent named Drinion who becomes an actor in virtual reality pornography, and the connections therein to the modes of visuality explored in *Infinite Jest*.[3] However, despite these intriguing plot developments, *Sir John Feelgood* is not a stable project, existing only as an eight-page synopsis with a number of attendant, semi-related documents. What *is* clear is that the connection to the IRS is already firmly embedded within these early drafts. In *Sir John Feelgood*, Drinion is an 'IRS special agent' who 'first sees himself from outside in a special video made during a videotaped sting operation of a tax scam' where 'Drinion plays some sort of sham role as interested taxpayer' but becomes 'enraptured' with his image on video.[4] Through fraud enforcement, Drinion gets to know a pornographer named Steve Fast, who ultimately hires him as an actor.[5] The final part of the synopsis places the reader in more familiar territory: a short paragraph addresses the problem of 'desk names' in the IRS (this subsequently re-emerges in section 18 of *The Pale King*) and also provides an early reference to the 'incredible powers' possessed by IRS agents. However, these powers are not yet supernatural and instead refer to abuse of bureaucratic power by some agents (Drinion included) who become 'like mad royalty' (Box 37.4). The synopsis ends with the proposed opening paragraph of the novel:

> The sky lightened and the horizon greened. I sat in a tan Service vehicle on the Western edge of an immense system of cornfields, masturbating. It is curious that I jerked off hardly at all during adolescence but now as an adult have logged literally hundreds of hours masturbating, often on solo surveillance or alone at night in the district office. (Box 37.4)

This paragraph bears traces of what will become the first and third sections of *The Pale King* through its focus on the Midwestern landscape, IRS surveillance and masturbation. However, the *Sir John Feelgood* project is not only a template for *The Pale King*: it contains various motifs and thematic preoccupations that will form the bases of significant elements of *Brief Interviews with Hideous Men* and *Oblivion*. Indeed, in 1997 Wallace composes a network of semi-related stories and synopses that would underpin his future collections as well as his third novel.

This relational network is best illustrated via four pieces written by Wallace in 1997. The first, listed as 'BI#79', is a proto-'brief interview' featuring a blind date between an unnamed woman and a man named as 'Nugent/Keck', names that will later be given to IRS agents in *The Pale King* (Box 26.13). Subsequently Keck resurfaces in a second short piece, earmarked for *Sir John Feelgood*, as the narrator of a story about his own inability to pay attention as a child in a Peoria school in 1965. This piece is clearly the basis for 'The Soul is not a Smithy', a story that was slated for *The Pale King* before being included in *Oblivion*, but another iteration of the story from the same year also includes Drinion as a fellow pupil (Box 37.4; Box 39.3). Wallace writes a third piece in this period set in the late 1940s and titled, alternatively, 'What is Peoria for', 'Metamora' and 'Electric Girl'. This story, about a rural girl who suffers at the hands of her mentally ill family, is the basis of Toni Ware's story in section 8 of *The Pale King*. Written initially as part of *Sir John Feelgood*, it chimes thematically with the actions of hideous men in Wallace's 1999 collection before being subsequently listed for inclusion in *Oblivion* and then substantially rewritten in 2007 for *The Pale King* (Box 36.5). Finally, in some further notes for *Sir John*

*Feelgood* Wallace writes a short piece suggesting that the reason for Drinion's suitability for pornography might be that 'Drinion's penis is huge because after he got burned by hot water spilling into his diaper the doctors had to inject him with steroids, and this caused hypertrophy of the dick' (Box 37.4). This is, of course, a partial description of the synopsis of 'Incarnations of Burned Children' from *Oblivion*.

As well as these four pieces, which go some way to illustrating the complex processual counterpoint at the heart of the *Sir John Feelgood* project, Wallace wrote another short narrative that would eventually be included in Pietsch's assembly of *The Pale King*, a story with a compositional history that spans the full decade-long process. Usually titled 'Cede', it was first drafted in August 1997 before being revised in 2001 and again circa 2006–2007. It appears in *The Pale King* as section 36 and concerns a young boy who attempts to kiss every part of his body. 'Cede' is significant because Wallace comes to regard it as essential to locking together several disparate sections of his third novel, but can never make the story cohere fully with the rest of the narrative or connect an adult character to the boy. In this sense it stands as perhaps the most characteristic piece of writing in the whole process of writing the third novel. Wallace wrote to Bonnie Nadell in August 1998 suggesting that 'Cede' might be placed in *Brief Interviews with Hideous Men*, but that it was 'not even close to complete' ('Letter to Bonnie Nadell, Aug 29th 1998'). In its 1997 iteration the full title of the story is 'Americanid Rex: Adventures in Achievement: Dog, Creatus, Achiever: Cede' and the story of the self-kissing boy is intercut with two strange sections set in ancient Rome that deal respectively with the phenomenon of 'Pontic flights' (during which exceptionally thin people were carried into the air by the wind and mistaken for angels) and the use of Molossian hounds by Emperor Nero. Wallace ultimately abandoned the story for inclusion in *Brief Interviews with Hideous Men* and continued to revise throughout his composition process. I will return to it periodically.

Wallace's publication of *Brief Interviews with Hideous Men* in 1999 marks the end of the first stage of composition of the third novel, as much of *Sir John Feelgood*'s focus on sex, relationships and visual perception is sloughed off into that collection via stories such as 'Adult World' parts 1 and 2, 'Datum

Centurio' (which was written simultaneously with *Sir John Feelgood* and may well have been intended as part of it) and, of course, the interviews themselves. Wallace does not refer to the project as *Sir John Feelgood* after 1999, which suggests that the pornography element has been refined out of the project altogether. Instead, the peripheral focus on tax and the IRS assumes the main body of the narrative.

## 2. 1999–2005: *Glitterer/The Pale King* and *Oblivion*

The second period of composition can broadly be taken to begin around the publication of *Brief Interviews with Hideous Men* in 1999 and end in 2005, a year after the publication of *Oblivion*, with Wallace's note to self that opens this chapter. The compositional crisis that characterizes the end of this six-year span is in many respects characteristic of the problems of coherence that mark this stage of the novel's genesis. However, while the period 2005–2007 saw Wallace rework his novel with renewed energy and focus, several key elements of *The Pale King* were developed within this preceding interval.

An 'embryonic outline' for the novel from November 1999 sees the first appearance of 'two broad arcs' that are supposed to underpin *The Pale King*:

1. Paying attention, boredom, ADD. Machines vs people at performing mindless jobs.
2. Being individual vs being part of larger thing – paying taxes, being 'lone gun' in IRS vs team player (Box 38.8).[6]

This is substantially different from anything that appears in the notes for *Sir John Feelgood*. This document also sees the first appearance of Sylvanshine, 'Shane' Drinion, Glendenning, Lehrl, Bondurant and Stecyk as well as one Ellen Bactrian, who will later appear in 'The Suffering Channel'. In this outline Ellen Bactrian, described as 'assistant director for documents', is also 'Dave W's boss'. Indeed, this list of characters includes a certain 'David Wallace', who has 'trouble paying attention, sitting still, can't work' and 'disappears 100pp in' (Box 38.8). This is the first time 'David Wallace' appears in proximity to the third novel, but his presence does not become in any way substantial until after the crisis of 2005, and there is no reference at this stage to the appearance of the author persona that eventually narrates the 'Author Here' chapters. Notably, a two-line plot point on the same document refers to 'discovery of crude virtual-reality porn being developed at Fornir' and how 'Drinion being photographed has huge effect on him'. The relegation of the central narrative of *Sir John Feelgood* to a subplot suggests the sidelining of Wallace's interest in this idea.

Between 1999 and 2001, before settling on *The Pale King*, Wallace refers to the novel as *Glitterer*. It is not clear to what this title refers, though the use of the expression 'great glittering God' in 'The Suffering Channel' (293) might point towards a religious motivation. A document titled '*Glitterer* Pt 1 – Plot' partially refocuses the story on a character called Hurd who moves to Peoria from Rome NY to pass the CPA exam and 'after a life of selfish drifting wants to become a quiet hero' before losing his ID and facing humiliation at not being able to take the exam (Box 40.5). Hurd's story will eventually develop into both Sylvanshine's flight into Peoria in section 2 of *The Pale King* and the identification drama within which David Wallace finds himself in section 24. Wallace wrote the opening section of *Glitterer* in October 1999, and incorporated Hurd's flight as the second section, in much the way that Pietsch places Sylvanshine's flight in his 2011 assembly. The opening section of *Glitterer* employs an odd rhetorical register to describe the IRS agents coming to work:

> Look at the Internal Revenue Service agents coming to work at the Peoria/Lake James IL post at 116A-E Reed Road in 1989's first quarter.
> Look at them curve around from three directions and enter the parking lot and park their cars and exit their vehicles […] What color is the lot? How well ploughed? What is its capacity? Who designed it, and who hired that person? […] One imagines years of months of weeks of days seated under room-length fluorescent rods examining other Americans' tax returns […] Remaining for 7.25 hours daily sensitive to pattern and discrepancy and the nuance of attested fact […] Who are these men. (Box 40.3)[7]

This section is followed by a short devotional testimony that resembles an early version of Chris Fogle's epiphany:

> I'd always from early on as a child I think somehow imagined Revenue men as like those certain kinds of other institutional heroes, bureaucratic,

small-h heroes […] I don't mean the kind of heroes that 'put their lives on the line.' I suppose what I'm saying is that there are other kinds. I wanted to be one. The kind that seemed even more heroic because nobody applauded or even thought about them, or if they did it was usually as some enemy. (Box 40.3)

As evidenced in these extracts, *Glitterer* begins to work the more religious and heroic elements found in *The Pale King* into its narrative. Simultaneously with this opening, Wallace is writing a story titled '12 Hungry Men' which will eventually evolve into 'Mister Squishy' (Box 36.3), which itself occurs in the same world as *The Pale King* (*Pale* 47). Wallace said in 2004 that 'Mister Squishy' was 'part of a cycle, and the rest of the cycle kind of died' ('Interview with Michael Goldfarb' 138), but it is hard to ascertain from the available materials exactly what might have constituted this cycle. In any event, I find it hard to agree with Max's assertion that the composition of *Oblivion* was a 'smoother process' (276), as the collection does not come together organically as much as adumbrate the problems Wallace was having with his third novel. Notably, Wallace responded sharply to Mark Costello's suggestion that *Oblivion* could be 'the road map for *The Pale King*', responding 'You don't understand how tough the problem actually is' (Max 322 n8).

The 'problem' would appear to be that much of *Oblivion* essentially was *The Pale King*. At least three stories ('Mister Squishy', 'The Soul is not a Smithy' and 'Incarnations of Burned Children') were at one point part of the third novel. In October 2001, Wallace describes the stories in *Oblivion* as 'the best of the stuff I've been doing while playing hooky from a certain Larger Thing', but a cursory look at the evolution of some of those stories suggests that Wallace may not have been wholly honest here ('Letter to Michael Pietsch, Oct 13th 2001'). In the most glaring example, section 23 of *The Pale King* is clearly a partial draft of 'The Soul is not a Smithy'. When Wallace redrafts 'Cede' during this period, he attempts unsuccessfully to combine it not only with an early version of the Chris Fogle monologue (Box 38.6), but with 'Mister Squishy' ('juxtapose w/boy touching his own body?' [Box 24.5]) and 'Good Old Neon' (a note on the handwritten manuscript from 2001 suggests that Neal 'rescues kid in "Cede"' [Box 24.2]).[8] Another note to self suggests incorporating 'Cede' into one of the Stecyk sections and with 'Incarnations of Burned Children' (Box 40.2). Wallace evidently wanted the project to cohere, but the eventual publication of *Oblivion* suggests that he was having significant trouble corralling the narrative.

Around the turn of the millennium, Wallace engages a separate narrative strand in the *Glitterer* project based around journalism and non-fiction. This represents the first sustained attempt to address the question of the novel's narrating voice after the collapse of *Sir John Feelgood* and points towards the 'Author Here' sections that narrate *The Pale King*.⁹ In 1997, Wallace's notes suggest that *Sir John Feelgood* might take the form of a first-person memoir written by Drinion, while elsewhere he wrote that the novel could be narrated by a ghost. I will return to this in detail in the second part of this chapter when I refer back to questions of monologism (Box 41.1; Box 37.4). *Glitterer* does away with any supernatural plot details, though they will return when Wallace begins to introduce the occult elements of the narrative (Drinion's levitation, Fogle's concentration) after 2005. However, the 'ghost' remains, albeit nominally, through the figure of a journalist and ghostwriter.

The non-fiction narrator of *Glitterer* goes through so many contradictory changes that it is extremely difficult to map them coherently. I would argue, however, that it is important to think about why Wallace decides to incorporate the figure of a non-fiction narrator at this stage of the process. By the late 1990s Wallace had a well-established separate public persona as a writer of non-fiction, a persona he was at pains to separate from himself ('There's a certain person created, that's a little stupider and schmuckier than I am' [Lipsky, 'Lost' 173]). While journalists appear in his work before this time (Steeply in *Infinite Jest* is the most obvious example) they never assume a significant central or narrating role. The emergence of journalist characters in 'The Suffering Channel' and 'Wickedness', both of which were written in the *Glitterer* period, indicates (as I have suggested in previous chapters) that Wallace was beginning to mine his established non-fiction persona for the purposes of his fiction, as well as considering that a putatively non-fiction narrator might be the keystone to the increasingly disparate parts of his third novel.[10] Moreover, the question of the novel as memoir, rather vaguely raised in 1997, begins to re-emerge in a slightly different and more convoluted form.

Wallace produces a chapter circa 2000 titled 'Forward' (sic) which begins: 'In this little part I'm going to talk about where this book came from and why it's being published as fiction even though it's over 99% true and accurate and is really in fact a piece of journalism' (Box 39.2). The following section, which at twelve pages is one of the longest extant pieces of unpublished material from the third novel project, is a monologue set in 2000 and narrated by an undercover journalist who identifies himself as 'Frank Brown'. Brown is a reporter for a magazine called *Money and Skin* that combines soft-core pornography and investigative business journalism (the receding traces of *Sir John Feelgood* are obviously detectable here) and has been tasked with going undercover in the IRS for three to six months. Frank Brown's style involves 'amassing a huge amount of carefully observed data', which inevitably draws comparison to Wallace's own non-fiction style. Brown has a ghostwriter (a 'friendly ghost') who is advising him on how to turn this story into fiction, allowing him '10,000–11,500 words of personal, unfictional address directly to the reader', though the publisher is allowed to 'black out' any data they see fit (Box 39.2).

This section is obviously the original of the later 'Author Here' sections in *The Pale King*, with the above statements essentially rephrased by 'David Wallace' in section 9, but the tawdry nature of the publication (tagline: 'What's Sexier than Money?') also draws comparison to *Style* in 'The Suffering Channel' and *Wicked* in 'Wickedness', which were being composed around the same time (Box 39.2). Indeed, one possible motivation for the junking of both the Frank Brown section and 'Wickedness' might well have been their similarity to 'The Suffering Channel', in which case they can be considered early variations of that story.[11] However, Brown's reminiscences of his childhood lack of concentration and Ritalin prescription and his garrulous and unfocused foreword also draw comparison to the narrator of 'The Soul is not a Smithy' and 'Irrelevant' Chris Fogle's lengthy monologue. In fact, Wallace seems to have considered publishing this foreword as a stand-alone story, as a piece titled 'Ritalin' later appears in a list of stories for possible inclusion in *Oblivion* (Box 36.5). Furthermore, a marginal note on page 11 of Brown's foreword reads 'Ghost: As you can see, this guy's totally nuts, and mostly full of shit' (Box 39.2).[12] The use of 'ghost' in this context most likely refers to Brown's ghostwriter, ascribing to that narrator a similar sentiment to 'David Wallace' as he passes judgement on Fogle's long monologue in Pietsch's 2011 assembly (*Pale* 257 n3). On the same page, yet another note indicates that 'David Wallace, 18, was a cart boy w/ Frank Brown at Peoria in 1981' (Box 39.2). If this wasn't convoluted enough, a separate structural document synopsizes Brown's foreword before continuing 'Confession – he's not journalist – he wrote copy for porn spreads. [...] Alright, a lifelong IRS employee. Not a journalist or writer at all.' This document also seems to be one of the first indications of the 'special powers' subplot that comes to the fore in later drafts, as Brown 'has amazing talent – can detect falsehood. Brutal as auditor, but great as examiner' (Box 39.5).

This level of compositional paralysis is particular to the drafts of the third novel: there is nothing approaching this level of incoherence in the manuscripts of *Infinite Jest*. The 'Tornado of Characters' document from 2005 and subsequent note to self with which I began this chapter is clearly a response to a text that is spiralling out of control and coherency. Wallace's decision to include 'The Soul is not a Smithy' in *Oblivion* seems to have been something of a turning point, as he repeatedly omits it from earlier consideration for the collection (Box 36.5; 'Letter to Michael Pietsch, Oct 7th 2003'). By relenting, he abandons a part of the novel on which he has been working for seven years. Having hived off several ideas for the third novel into a collection for the second time in five years, Wallace's concern in 2005 that 'I have too much stuff, and too little' is an understandable response to the ever more protean nature of the manuscript.[13] However, the years 2005–2007 see Wallace respond to this crisis in a remarkably focused manner.

### 3. 2005–2007: 'Author Here'

Between 2005 and 2007, several major elements of what was now called *The Pale King* fell into place. When Michael Pietsch explains that Wallace had 'written deep' (*Pale* vii) into the novel, he is likely referring to the substantial work that was done in this two-year period. What remained missing was the structure of the narrative itself. Wallace writes to Bonnie Nadell in 2007 saying that '[t]he individual parts of this book would not be all that hard to read [...] It's more the juxtaposition of them' (Max 295), and Pietsch admits that 'nowhere in all these pages was there an outline or other indication of what order David intended for these chapters' (*Pale* vi–vii). It is particularly poignant that in the two years before Wallace's illness prevented him from writing, the novel's progress was more rapid and assured than it had been at any previous stage of composition. The moment of crisis crystallized by the note to self in June 2005 seems to have galvanized Wallace, with the dating of his floppy disks suggesting that the novel's most substantial sections (Fogle's monologue, 'Author Here', Rand and Drinion's dialogue) as well as the material on both the supernatural and the filmed IRS interviews all coalesced between July 2005 and August 2007.[14,15] Crucially, this period also sees the substantial solidifying of the position of the novel's narrator and plot, elements that had previously defeated Wallace.

The emergence of the 'Author Here' section, which is notably set in 2005 (*Pale* 67), can be traced to a notebook in which Wallace writes a two-page précis titled 'Fake Memoir of Job at IRS by Fake Name' which, in its formal move from article to memoir, appears to be a developed version of the earlier Frank Brown narrative (Wallace is clearly happy with this, marking the page with smiley stickers that say 'Wow!' and 'Doing Well!' [Box 41.7a]). In another notebook, seemingly in the same pen, Wallace writes 'David Wallace, a reporter/freelance for *Money and Skin*, hired to do story' (Box 41.7b). This collapses together the Frank Brown sections with the notes written during the *Glitterer* period about incorporating a 'David Wallace' character into the novel, ultimately making Wallace the memoirist who performs an amended version of Frank Brown's curatorial role. The effect of Wallace's positioning of a fictional iteration of his persona is twofold: it affords the novel, for the first time, a pervasive structural 'spine' and dramatizes Wallace's prior curatorial role over the mass of data that he has accumulated. As Staes argues, 'Wallace is aware that the jump from information to meaning rests on classification, organization and presentation' ('Work in Process' 74), and by becoming the master narrator Wallace also implicitly dramatizes his attempted mastery of *The Pale King*'s prior baggy and disparate narrative. This entry into the narrative has the effect of creating an oppositional motif in *The Pale King* in which the narrative juxtaposes and dramatizes chaotic and controlled data: the text, effectively, begins to formally model itself around the manner of its own composition.

In this sense, 'David Wallace's' dismissal of Fogle (*Pale* 257) is in one respect self-chastisement: Fogle can stand for Wallace pre-2005, garrulously producing data, 'information without value' (340).[16] This is also dramatized in the difference between Sylvanshine and Reynolds: Sylvanshine's messy, information-filled mind is associated with a shotgun, Reynolds' with a rifle (16). In this respect, I would synthesize Burn's suggestions that firstly 'Sylvanshine's role in the incomplete phase of the drafting process may have been to dramatize the difficulties that Wallace was experiencing with his novel' (Burn, 'Paradigm' 160) and that secondly the novel has a focus on binaries (Burn, *Guide* 87) to argue that several binaries occur in *The Pale King* not only at the thematic level but also as a way of commenting on the pre- and post-2005 composition processes. Indeed, a substantial amount of material written after the novel's crisis point in 2005 makes reference to the corralling of messy data: the introduction of 'fact psychics'; Sylvanshine's flight from the traumatic mess of documents in the Rome REC to the more organized Peoria REC; Chris Fogle's transition from shambolic wastoid to organized Service worker and the doubling 'Obetrolling' process that is a component of this transition[17]; the elision of the less efficient 'David Wallace' with his more skilled namesake; Rand's rehabilitation from her earlier problem with 'cutting', which is addressed by her husband, the pointedly named 'Ed'.[18]

This process might also shed some light on why Wallace still doggedly attempts to incorporate 'Cede' into the narrative, despite its apparent incompatibility. Staes argues that this piece is 'completely disconnected from the rest of *The Pale King*' and that Wallace cannot connect the child to an adult (Staes, 'Work' 82). I concur partially with this argument, but I believe that the incompatibility only occurs at the level of plot. Wallace desperately wanted 'Cede' to fit, even including it in the 'For Advance' stack found on his desk after his death (Box 38.6). In his drafts he makes numerous and often contradictory attempts to connect the section to the world of his third novel:

> Some of the best examiners can't pay attention when observed, as in condition for test against computer. But Drinion can. He's kid from Cede. (Box 39.5)
>
> Drinion and other guy (the self-kissing kid from "Cede") will be set up against the machines in a John-Henry test. (Box 40.3)
>
> who's the self-kissing kid? (Box 39.1)

Staes has pointed out that Wallace even tried unsuccessfully to make the boy into 'David Wallace 2' as late as 2007 (Staes, 'Work' 82). I would argue that the reason that Wallace wants to retain 'Cede' is strongly connected to his problems with composition, and his subsequent dramatization of this process, and that this is in turn connected to the matter of motivation in the story. In the first version of 'Cede' in 1997, the boy's mysterious self-kissing project is inscrutable: there is 'little to say about the motive cause' (Box 40.2). In the second version, written during the *Glitterer* phase, Wallace provides a possible motivation:

> This boy had, as a fetus, produced (involuntarily) a rare and toxic type of intrauterine menconium during the final hour of his late mother's labour, and that she had some hours afterward died of septic shock, and a rather cheap and shabby analysis could perhaps be offered in which the boy somehow believed unconsciously that he had 'killed' his mother and wished now in the latency of childhood symbolically to 'resurrect' her via his own reflexive access. (Box 38.6)

By the time the most recent version of 'Cede' appears, during the post-2005 composition process, all references to motivation, and all but one indirect allusion to the boy's mother (*Pale* 405), have been removed from the story. This has the effect of foregrounding both the inscrutability of the project and the relationship between the boy and his exhausted father. This version of the story, I would suggest, contains an important binary that also functions as a dramatization of Wallace's process of composition.

The boy's project in 'Cede' strikingly mirrors the way in which Wallace's writing process between 1997 and 2007 oscillates between an apparently insurmountable large-scale goal (the third novel) and attendant discrete achievements (the two story collections), with the boy's long-term project (the kissing of his whole body) only achievable through a series of small, connected projects (the kissing of each body part). This structural approach mirrors the long-term project of sobriety practised by Wallace's recovering addicts in *Infinite Jest*: the 'one day at a time' philosophy which ultimately results in permanent sobriety. However, the crucial distinction here between *Infinite Jest* and 'Cede' is that the boy's project is literally impossible to complete: in this respect, Wallace's note to Bonnie Nadell that 'Cede' is 'not even close to complete' mirrors the boy's unachievable quest. The relationship between the boy and his father suggests a binary that rhymes with those elsewhere in *The Pale King*: the 'dutiful' (403) completion of a sprawling, large-scale task set against the 'tortured' (405) messy world of the father. However, I would suggest that the development of this binary in 'Cede' could also relate to the length of its compositional period. In this more speculative reading, it is possible to see the boy, blissfully unaware of the scale of his project, as Wallace between 1991 and 1996, composing his gargantuan second novel, possessing 'nothing that anyone could ever call doubt, inside' (407). Conversely, the father then stands for the post-1996 Wallace, looking back in amazement on a younger iteration of himself while trapped in the 'cycle of torture' (406) that attends following the completion of an apparently impossible undertaking. This model chimes with Ed Rand's opinion that 'there is a particular stage of life where you get cut off from the, like, unself-conscious happiness and magic of childhood' (498).

Tracing the complex and troubled compositional history of *The Pale King* is not only important to a mapping of the novel's evolution and the elimination of some more speculative and inexact approaches to the text's form. It also allows us to make sense of how the developmental approach to form that I have traced in Wallace's work across the preceding chapters of this book might have developed towards the end of his career. By separating out the substantial work done on *The Pale King* after 2005, at which point it was the only piece of fiction on which Wallace was working, it is also possible to trace how his motifs of vocality, spatiality and visuality were still evolving in this late period. In the second half of this chapter I will return to each of these formal motifs in turn, mapping how Wallace's post-2005 fiction represented a development or mutation of these forms.

## Ghosts, Writers and Ghostwriters: Persona and Dialogism

Among the sketches for *Sir John Feelgood*, Wallace wrote a treatment that suggested he was considering an undead narrator for his third novel:

> Porn novel narrated by FNE's soul/'ghost'. We all have ghosts inside us; to live is to be a repository for ghosts. It is in virtue of ghosts that we are alive. Ghosts are the being (Heidegger) in virtue of which we exist. But all ignore our ghosts fear them (sic). (Box 37.3)

Below this, as well as the first appearance of the phrase 'every love story is a ghost story' (here attributed, bizarrely, to 'Virginia Wolff (sic) on Carson'), Wallace has sketched how the voice of the ghost, described as 'omniscient to everyone', might sound:

> Whether or not you're incredulous does not matter to me. Your ghosts are credulous, and it is they to whom I speak. Let me speak to them. Read this line without thinking or assuming or reacting. Remove your mind from the picture [...] Your mind and capacity for thought are the enemy of your ghost. Your ghost is essentially you. It is in virtue of your ghosts that you exist. You are not your possessions, or your body, or the parts of your body, nor your neural net, nor your brain. Nor your mind. Sit in a chair without moving or distracting yourself for six hours and you will know what I mean – after the terrible antsiness passes you'll feel the tiny hum of your ghosts [...] I am soul. The mind is the enemy. It will not let go. (Box 37.3)

This sketch is a repository of a number of ideas regarding meditation and concentration that emerge more fully in Wallace's subsequent writing, particularly the Kenyon commencement address and the sections of *The Pale King* that are concerned with matters of boredom. The allusion to Heidegger's concept of being (*Dasein*) suggests that Wallace's formal concept of the ghost at the beginning of his late period might also be broadly concerned with the paradox of omniscient communication with others while remaining a discrete narrating entity (although a note at the foot of the page that reads 'Research Dasein' suggests that this was not a particularly advanced model). This paradox chimes with my suggestion in Chapter 1 that Wallace was at this stage concerned with the coterminous development of the simultaneous 'flickering' materiality and insubstantiality of the 'companion ghost' figure. While Staes accurately suggests that this narrator 'clearly descends from the same ideas that inspired the wraith in *Infinite Jest*' and rehearses ideas of author disappearance that resurface in *The Pale King* ('Work' 83), I would argue that the specifically ghostly narrator of *Sir John Feelgood* is ultimately diverted elsewhere, ending up as the basis of 'Good Old Neon'. Once that story is written (Wallace had a publishable version completed by October 2001 ['Letter to Michael Pietsch, Oct 13th 2001']), the ghost narrator disappears from the third novel, transmuted in *The Pale King* into something rather different.

*The Pale King* contains several significant references to ghosts, with the most explicit dating from after the publication of 'Good Old Neon' and the 2005 revision of the novel and retaining the associated preoccupation with dialogism that characterizes Wallace's use of the supernatural. The dialogues between Meredith and Ed Rand, who is described alternately as a 'dead man' (495), 'white as a ghost' (490) and 'a corpse' (500) first emerge in November 2005, while the material on Garrity and Blumquist, the two 'actual, non-hallucinatory ghosts haunting Post 047's wiggle room' (*Pale* 315) appears to have been written late, in April 2007 (Box 38.1). Meredith and Ed's dialogues, which are of course framed within *another* dialogue between Meredith and Drinion (a character who also has supernatural, if not exactly ghostly, powers), operate as a problematized version of the ghostly dialogism in Wallace's fiction, as both dialogues are largely fallacious, tending towards the monologic (Ed and Meredith dominate the respective conversations, using the dialogic partner as a way to talk about themselves). Central to the frustrated attempts at communication in this sequence is the fact that while Drinion and Ed are given supernatural attributes, they aren't actually ghosts. Ed is described with recourse to the incorporeal, but he never actually dies (*Pale* 509), and while Drinion has an inhuman ability to concentrate, he cannot hold a proper empathetic conversation.[19]

Garrity and Blumquist, who are both primarily identifiable through their vocality, correspond strikingly to the respective figures of the absent possessor and companion ghost in the earlier work, even occupying a historical trajectory that mirrors the development of the trope in Wallace's fiction. Garrity dates from 'an earlier historical period' and his verbosity is often confused with the sound of the IRS workers' own 'yammering mind-monkey', thus giving him characteristics of the 'absent possessor', while Blumquist 'basically sits with you [...] the wigglers find him *companionable*' (316, emphasis mine).[20] Garrity's monologic logorrhoea appears to be connected to his previous job as a mirror inspector, which visually stages an unending, tortuous process of self-engagement. Conversely, Blumquist's outwardly focused dedication to his public sector job (he works, notably, on 'partnerships' [28]), which results in his being found dead at his desk (27), corresponds to a lack of vocality (he 'didn't say anything' [28] and even as a ghost 'no one ever speaks of him' [316]) implicitly similar to the communicative limitations of language expressed by Neal's ghost in 'Good Old Neon' (*Oblivion* 178). Blumquist's silence represents perhaps the most extreme iteration of the companion ghost in Wallace's fiction, a mode of dialogism represented, in a partial amendment of Bakhtin's terms, by coexistence and interaction that is not actually vocalized.

Garrity and Blumquist's ghosts are contrasted with 'phantoms', which are non-supernatural hallucinations generated by the wigglers themselves (*Pale* 314). However, in section 49 of the novel, Wallace uses the word 'phantom' in a different context during a description of the 'éclat' that precipitated Lehrl's stratospheric rise through the ranks of the IRS. Lehrl, who has launched an internal coup to overthrow resident director DeWitt Glendenning with the help of the supernatural powers of Sylvanshine and Reynolds, is celebrated for devising a strategy whereby taxpayers are required to include social security numbers in addition to the names of dependents on tax forms. This strategy is intended to combat the 'phantom dependent' (530), the phenomenon whereby citizens would continue to enjoy tax benefits by including, for example, the names of children who had already turned 18 on their tax form. As 'the requirement would greatly increase the filer's fear of a phantom dependent being detected', Lehrl's initiative results in the disappearance of 'six-point-nine million dependents' virtually overnight (531), an éclat that prefigures his involvement in the encroaching Spackman Initiative which seeks to deregulate the federal bureaucracy of the IRS and to operate it 'as a business – a going, for-profit concern' (112) set against 'the complex social engineering of the Great Society' (109). Wallace uses 'phantom' here not in its hallucinatory sense, but to refer to an individual who continues to exist beyond their prior incarnation: this is also, of course, a description of a ghost. By committing this act of supernatural genocide, Lehrl stages an early attack on the ghostly possibilities of dialogism represented by Blumquist, whose presence actually increases productivity (542). While Wouters suggests that the presence of ghosts at the IRS 'signals the center's hostility toward coherent, intelligible selfhood' (178), I would argue the opposite: that in its neoliberal hostility to the 'Great Society', the incoming Spackman Initiative performs a 'desacralising' monologic effacement, threatening the dialogic nature of the IRS and transfiguring its workers into automata.

In this sense, the Spackman Initiative threatens a resurgence of the monologic 'absent possessor' figure. In the transcription of the agent interviews, it is explained that 'Spackman's report, the subsection of interest, was resurrected by some person or persons close to the Three-Personed God' (111). Frustratingly, the supernatural-sounding Three-Personed God is never fully explored in the most recent version of the novel. A note suggests that in an early version of the novel these '3 high end players' were Glendenning, Lehrl and a 'special HR guy Glendenning needs to find gifted examiners' (540) but, in the latest assembly of the novel it is *Lehrl* who is finding the gifted examiners, and Lehrl himself is seemingly referred to as separate from the Three-Personed God during Fogle's initiation (531). Therefore, whether any of the Three-Personed God actually make an appearance is debatable, but intriguingly Wallace's note also suggests that 'we never see them, only their aides and advance men' (540). While inevitably a speculative observation, the suggestion of a binary between the absent, all-controlling Three-Personed God and the companionable, productivity increasing ghosts would stage a dramatization of the tropes of monologism and dialogism that have developed in Wallace's fiction.[21]

Conversely, the appearance of 'David Wallace' in *The Pale King* has a more vexed relationship to the developmental tropes of dialogism and authorial presence that have characterized the earlier work. I believe that the problematizing of the 'David Wallace' persona in *The Pale King* is systematically connected to Wallace's 2005 attempt to create a frame story for his increasingly disparate narrative, and that while 'Wallace's' curatorial role does indeed stage a move towards control of the novel, it also occasions a hugely ambitious but deeply problematic textual iteration of Wallace himself, one that struggles to maintain the level of dialogism attained in previous fiction and the non-'authorial' sections of *The Pale King*. At the point of composition in 2005, Wallace has never before addressed the reader of his fiction in the guise of 'David Wallace': even in 'Octet', the voice belongs to a 'fiction writer' (123). Of course, despite his claim to be 'me as a real person', 'David Wallace' is no such thing. This falsehood is immediately evident later in the same sentence when he lists his age as 40 in Spring 2005, when Wallace would have actually been 43 (*Pale* 66–7). So what iteration of Wallace is the 'author' of *The Pale King*?

I believe that a clue can be found in the reference to 'yours truly, the living author, Mr David Wallace of Philo IL' (78). Wallace did not, in reality, come from Philo, but this is not the first time he claims it as his home town: in his 1990 essay 'Derivative Sport in Tornado Alley', Wallace refers to 'my home of Philo, Illinois' (*Supposedly* 3). I contend that this deliberate return to a false detail from a fifteen-year-old essay highlights the true identity of the 'author' of *The Pale King*: it is 'written' by Wallace's non-fiction persona, *not* by the 'fiction writer'.[22] The attribution of the authorship of *The Pale King* to Wallace's non-fiction persona makes sense for a number of reasons. In Chapter 1 I argued that the increased materiality of Wallace's 'revenant' presence witnessed across the fiction, combined with the emergence of the companion ghost, performs a kind of *apophrades* whereby the so-called anxiety of influence in Wallace's work catches up with itself in a mediation of his own prior style. In *The Pale King*, Wallace goes even further: he attempts to stage a mediation of *both* his fiction and non-fiction voice by adopting a version of his now equally established non-fiction persona to comment on his writing processes within his third novel. This is, of course, complicated even further by the fact that the reference to Philo, the identifying marker that unites Wallace's non-fiction voice in 'Derivative Sport in Tornado

Alley' with the narrator of *The Pale King*, is *itself* a fictional detail within a putatively non-fiction essay.

Mike Miley argues that in *The Pale King* 'Wallace, it seems, wanted out of being David Foster Wallace so badly that he shackles his well-known personal preoccupations with sincerity and authenticity to an illusory persona that he intends to delegitimize in an attempt to violently reclaim his private self from that persona, a reclamation that […] is unsuccessful' (202). In this argument, Miley is sympathetic to Lee Konstantinou's reading of Wallace's persona in *The Pale King* as 'an object of fun, an emblem of what Wallace came to dislike most about his own literary style' ('Unfinished Form'). I agree with this analysis up to a point. The multilayered and often paralytic conflation of narrating personae implicit in the narrative of *The Pale King* undoubtedly indicates, as I have suggested above, an anxiety over, and an attempt to mediate, prior style. However, I believe that the complexity is escalated further by the fact that Wallace introduced this strategy into the novel in 2005 as an attempt to compositionally unify a series of already discordant narrative registers. Therefore, 'David Wallace's' entrance into *The Pale King* is not just a staging of anxiety over authorial personae but also a new and extraordinarily convoluted mode of collative composition, in which Wallace's staging of anxiety over his style is framed within a real-world attempt to make *The Pale King* coherent and publishable. Accordingly, this approach carries a significant risk of collapsing inward into the kind of monologic narrative that Wallace has tried to refine out of his work. In order to analyse this risk, I want to consider the matter of Wallace's 'disappearances' from the novel.

The 'ghost redundancy' in section 38 of *The Pale King* that accidentally conflates the two David Wallaces and effaces 'the "unreal" David Wallace [i.e. the author]' (414) necessarily provokes further enquiry into the mode of narrative voice. Staes asks 'does [Wallace's] disappearance stop him from being the narrator?' ('Work' 79) before ultimately concluding that 'that ghost remains the source of the text' (81).[23] I concur with this: indeed Wallace essentially confirms it in his opening 'Author Here' section when he says that 'some of the forthcoming §s have had to be distorted, depersonalised, polyphonized' (72) but that he remains the author of the entire text. The 'Author Here' sections and 'ghost redundancy' episode represent the final traces of the ghostly approaches to narration attempted by Wallace over the best part of a decade, which have progressed from a literal ghost narrator to a ghostwritten text before finally manifesting as an ostensibly 'nonfiction' narrator who reveals that he has 'depersonalised' and 'polyphonized' the accounts of others. Indeed, as Richard Godden and Michael Szalay have suggested, the 'Author Here' iteration of Wallace retains certain echoes of 'ghostliness', having been a ghostwriter in college (1279), and subsequently being 'rendered spectral' by the conflation with the other David Wallace (1278). However, by explicitly claiming to have 'polyphonized' the sections of *The Pale King* in which he does not feature, 'David Wallace' occupies a dialogically problematic position. If the prior fiction sees a gradual separation of the emergent 'revenant author' persona from his characters (a separation that reaches its apex in 'Good Old Neon' when Wallace is dramatized as character but not as author), the admission of control of the narrative in *The Pale King* complicates matters by making 'David Wallace' the self-confessed sole voice of the text. This is, essentially, a description of monologism and seemingly a regression from the prior dialogic model.

But does it make a difference if the monologic gesture is admitted up front to the reader, as it is here? Perhaps the most obvious point of comparison here is with my earlier description of the wraith scene in *Infinite Jest*, where an artist with a tendency towards the monologic (James Incandenza) is critiqued within the narrative through dialogue with a character (Gately). In the convoluted and amalgamated accretion of narrative registers in *The Pale King*, such dialogic clarity is harder to achieve, not least because the post-2005 entry of 'David Wallace' into the text is also a compositional strategy to make the novel itself cohere. In the world of *The Pale King*, 'David Wallace' is never critiqued by other characters in this way because their voices are all implicitly his voice: an unbalancing, and potential effacement, of the 'coexistence and interaction' model advanced by Bakhtin. However, 'Wallace's' admission of monologism offers an attempt to ameliorate this situation by at least being honest about the premises of monologism. In this sense, the text might perform a dialogic relationship whereby the *reader* provides the critique of the 'revenant author': an awareness of monologism inside the text could precipitate dialogism outside of it.

Of course, this dialogue ended abruptly when Wallace abandoned the novel in 2007, and *The Pale King*'s incompleteness makes it impossible to configure a complete and totalized system. What *can* be established is that Wallace's interest in ghostliness and dialogism continued into his final work at the level of both scenario and narration but becomes paralysed by both the amalgamation of his fiction and non-fiction registers and the incoherency of the novel's materials. Conversely, it is easier to trace Wallace's approach to spatiality in his final novel, as the locations of *The Pale King* are generally more stable than its narrative register.

## What is Peoria For? Institutions and Bad Wheels

The Midwest is part of Wallace's third novel from its inception. As well as the Midwestern-set scene of masturbation that was to open *Sir John Feelgood*, a mooted alternative opening sequence which Wallace rightly describes as 'odd' begins in 'a location in one of the two four-dimensional universes proved to exist by Freeman and Donaldson in 1981'.[24] This 'wide-angle opening' then narrows its scope from 'universe to supercluster to galaxy to local group to solar system to an "external" view of earth' before the narrator reveals that some of the forthcoming narrative will be titled *What Is Peoria For?*[25] Subsequently, Wallace writes that:

> a crude, unlikely, but more conceivable possibility might be that [this narrative point of view] more resembles a powerful electron microscope than a powerful telescope, implying that what we conceive as the 'finite but unbounded' (i.e. 'curved') universe is in fact nothing but one particle of one atom of one molecule of the left thumbnail of one 'individual' on one 'world'. (Box 40.7)

This opening, which evokes the 'englobing' climax of 'Lyndon' in its slow narrowing of cosmic focus towards US territory, suggests a movement that is simultaneously centripetal, as it zooms in to the Midwest from the cosmos, and centrifugal, as it invokes a framing universe outside of our comprehension. Although Wallace abandoned this opening sequence after one draft (a trace of it can arguably be found in the 'heightening of the specificity' of Sylvanshine's aerial descent into the Midwest [*Pale* 16]), this spatial and scalar tension remains in some form in the narrative of the third novel throughout its composition. Burn argues for the importance of understanding 'the scalar shifts that characterize Wallace's fiction', from 'the "cosmic" system [to] the "parochial"' ('Paradigm' 155), which not only speaks to the matters of scale described in the alternative opening above but also the later region-based narrative of *The Pale King*. In Chapter 2, I characterize the scalar and peculiarly regional tension in Wallace's earlier fiction, particularly 'Westward the Course of Empire Takes Its Way', through Wallace's 'performative' Midwestern persona, an institutionally inflected voice that anthropologically catalogues certain qualities of the Midwest before moving, in 'The Suffering Channel', to an amended model that recognizes the damage done to the region by this stereotype. In 1997 Wallace is somewhat archly asking *What Is Peoria For?* but in the post-2005 *Pale King* material his description of the Midwest has become more attuned to economic and social problems in the region. In a development of certain radial, circular and orbital motifs from his earlier fiction, Wallace approaches matters of region and institutionality in *The Pale King* through a spatial focus on centralized and decentralized motion, whereby the novel's centripetal tendencies (often characterized by matters of institutionalization) are in permanent and unresolved conflict with centrifugal gestures towards social and political engagement. At the heart of this oscillatory model is one of the novel's central plot dilemmas: the IRS is poised on the verge of an initiative that will reconfigure it as a 'going, for-profit concern' (*Pale* 112) rather than as a bureaucracy.

It is for this reason that I diverge from Mark McGurl's reading of *The Pale King* as purely a centripetally inclined 'novel of *institutionalization*' ('Institution' 37, emphasis original). In structuring his novel around the IRS, Wallace employs an institution that synthesizes both Berger and Luckmann's objective facticity (taxes, of course, being one of Benjamin Franklin's two incontrovertible facts of American life) and Goffman's total institution. Indeed, Goffman's definition of the total institution as quoted in Chapter 2 ('a place of residence and work where a large number of like-situated individuals, cut off from the wider society for an appreciable period of time, together lead an enclosed, formally administered round of life' [Goffman 11]) acts as an effective description of the Peoria REC in *The Pale King*. While I concur with McGurl that Wallace places the institution at the heart of the novel, and indeed that *The Pale King* is often 'narrowly nationalist in focus' (51), I do not read the novel's focus on institutionality as solely centripetal in nature, focused on the importance of 'getting indoors' (30). Instead, the spatial oscillation at the heart of *The Pale King* affords as much suspicion of the institution as it does valorization.[26] While some of the novel's sections (Fogle's monologue, Lane Dean Jr's decision) do indeed dramatize the institution as a kind of restorative shelter, there are numerous other references to the problems of institutionalization: institutions are referred to as 'much less intelligent than the individuals that make them up' and given to 'stupidity' (110); Lane Dean Jr is horrified at the prospect of having to go back inside after his break (122); children are described as having 'already lost their hearts' to 'institutional tedium' (255). Moreover, the lengthy Rand-Drinion conversation provides a sustained critique of institutional thinking via Rand's account of her problems within the mental health system, which she describes as engineered to prevent escape:

> [...] part of the syndrome they call some people eventually getting *institutionalized* is that they get put in a nut ward at a young age or a fragile time when their sense of themselves is not really very fixed or resilient, and they start acting the way they think people in nut wards are expected to act, and after a while they really *are* that way, and they get caught in the system, the mental-health system, and they never really get out [...] it was all an institutional structure, and once things became institutionalized then it all became this artificial, like, organism and started trying to survive and serve its own needs just like a person, only it wasn't a person, it was the opposite of a person, because there was nothing inside it except the will to survive and grow as an institution. (477, 488, emphasis original)

This centripetal/centrifugal tension is replicated on a macro scale in the sections of the novel that spatialize the IRS's bureaucratic mutation from the 1960s to the 1980s. While 'the district office predominated' in the 1960s, the 1980s is 'to be the era of the region' (113). This is a centralizing gesture, migrating power from smaller, peripheral district control to a larger regional centre, such as the Peoria REC around which the novel revolves. However, the models of bureaucracy offered in *The Pale King* also speak to the problems of a centripetally inclined system of power, suggesting instead the importance of communication between a bureaucracy and the world outside it. The two key examples in the novel both make recourse to a model that is specifically *radial*, thus developing a spatial model from Wallace's prior fiction.[27]

The first radial model can be found in the description of a bureaucracy as a 'parallel world [...] operating under its own physics and imperatives of cause' (86):

> One might envision a large and intricately branching system of jointed rods, pulleys, gears, and levers radiating out from a central operator such that tiny movements of that operator's finger are transmitted through that system to become the gross kinetic changes in the rods at the periphery. It is at this periphery that the bureaucracy's world acts upon this one. (86)

This model of a world 'both connected to and independent of this one' illustrates the importance of overlap and communication between the bureaucracy and the world outside it. Importantly, this system's operator is 'not uncaused', because this bureaucracy 'is not a closed system' (86). In this respect, the model resembles the transfiguring circular structures that underpin *Infinite Jest*'s narrative: an apparently closed system that can be reconfigured into a hermeneutic dialogue with the world outside its own. If this model represents an ideal configuration of world and bureaucracy, the second radial bureaucratic model in *The Pale King* illustrates the point at which this model breaks down. In section 38, 'David Wallace' explains how the confusion over his identity was exacerbated by a model of network integration known as the 'Bad Wheel':

> Technical Branch's networking setup through the mid-1980s resembled a wheel with a hub but no rim. In terms of computer interface, everything had to go through Martinsburg's NCC. A transfer of data from Peoria's Midwest Regional Exam Center to Midwest Region HQ up in Joliet, for example, actually entailed two separate data transfers, the first from Peoria to Martinsburg and the second from Martinsburg to Joliet [...] the whole rimless-wheel model was at odds with the much-touted decentralization of the Service. (413–14 n5)

This dysfunctional centripetal model, where everything must move to the centre in order to move out of it, recalls a less effective model of the 'hubless wheel' at the end of 'Westward'. In order to centrifugally and communicatively 'spin against the spin', the wheel in 'Westward' has to be able to move. The 'bad wheel' has a hub (thus hiding the process from view, unlike the 'disclosed' system at the end of 'Westward') but no rim, meaning that it must remain immobile and unable to produce the counter spin. In Wallace's spatial terminology, this failure is indicative of a lack of communication between bureaucracy and world, borne out by the torment of the two David Wallaces who are trying to enter the system from outside.[28]

Elsewhere in *The Pale King*, Wallace maps these more abstract circular models on to specific Midwestern territory, and it is at this level of narrative construction that it is possible to see a transfiguring of the 'performative Midwestern' persona I refer to in Chapter 2. Burn offers a useful cartography of the concentrically circular nature of the novel's 'underlying geometry' and how this is projected on to the Illinois landscape:

> At the largest scale, Peoria itself is 'an exurban ring' [...] the center can only be approached via a 'circular shape[d]' road (276). Tightening our focus further, we discover that the lower level of the building is shaped as a 'wheel' (295) with halls that 'seemed curved' (289). Near the center of the pattern of ever-decreasing circles are the accountants themselves who all work within a 'circle of light' (290). Finally, at the smallest scale, there is David Wallace who describes himself as resembling a 'racquetball' (296). ('Paradigm' 155–6)

While Burn persuasively reads this pattern as connected to the 'tornadic' composition of the novel itself, I want to suggest that the imposition of these circular structures on Midwestern geography can also elucidate Wallace's evolving response to the relationship between the region and the institution, as well as his own performative regional persona.

In keeping with Adam Kelly, who reads *The Pale King* as a strong development in Wallace's 'engaging with the discourse of political ideals' ('Novel' 17) in post-1960s America, I believe that Wallace's approach to the Midwest in the post-2005 material indicates a refocusing of the region from abstract representation of postmodern ideas in 'Westward' and towards an understanding of the region's topography as economically configured. In this sense, the stories in *Oblivion* constitute something of a stepping stone, with the corporate toxification of the environment that I describe in Chapter 2 prefiguring the transformation of aspects of the Illinois landscape into an economic wasteland in *The Pale King*. Wallace does this by making recourse, once again, to circular geography and geometry and the problem of 'centres'. Following on from Burn's identification of the suburb as a key element of *The Pale King*'s geometry ('Paradigm' 155), I would suggest that the spatial dialectic between Midwestern suburban and urban geography in the novel is representative of the centring/decentring tension that characterizes the narrative. For example, in the descriptions of Lake James, Peoria Heights, Bartonville, Sicklied Ore and Eunice, which are all characterized as 'something between a suburb and an independent township of metropolitan Peoria' (*Pale* 256 n2), 'David Wallace' notes that

> The whole separate-but-attached-district thing had to do with the city's inexorable expansion and encroachment into the rich agricultural land around it, which over time brought certain small, formerly isolated farming communities into Peoria's orbit. I know that these little satellite towns each had their own property-tax structure and zoning authority, but in many other respects (e.g., police protection) they functioned as outlying districts of Peoria proper. (*Pale* 256 n2)

While this might look like a centrifugal motion (the urban metro area expands rapidly outward) it is also a centripetal one (the towns are drawn into Peoria's 'orbit'). However, because of this process Peoria, described as one of the 'grimmest, most blighted and depressed old factory cities in Illinois' (259 n5) essentially *loses* its centre and thus its base of industrial production:

> Peoria had come in the 1980s to assume the same basic doughnut shape as so many other formerly industrial cities: The downtown center was empty and denuded, all but dead, while at the same time a robust collection of malls, plazas, franchises, business and light-industrial parks, town house developments, and apartment complexes had pulled most of the city's life

out into an exurban ring [...] the same basic thing played out in cities all over the Midwest. (272)[29]

This is not the abstract cartography of the performative Midwestern narrative of 'Westward' or the sneering register afforded to 'Kmart people' in the state fair essay. Instead, this is a development of the concern over the economic denuding of environment and its inhabitants found in *Oblivion*.[30] While this development might not lead to the effacement of Wallace's performative Midwestern persona – he is essentially performing a reconfigured version of his description of corn production in 'Westward', and in narrating this chapter he is still pretending to be the Midwesterner 'David Wallace' of Philo IL – it is significant for its refocusing on the damaging effect of economically determined geography on Midwestern communities, which are afforded more sympathetic description here than the grotesquely caricatured farmers of 'Westward'. A later attempt at recentring the economy via the gentrification of the old downtown is disastrous, as it results in the appearance of riverboat casinos 'that were not locally owned and whose base revenues Peoria never even got a plausible cut of'. The result: a 'steeply declining revenue curve that within just a few years caused most of the "New Downtown" renaissance to sputter' (272) and the second economic loss of the centre of Peoria.[31] I would argue that this problematizes McGurl's suggestion that in *The Pale King* 'the landscape of the Midwest is not embracing after all, but only, given time, an occasion for terrifying exposure' ('Institution' 30).[32] While I think that a persuasive case could be made for this statement to apply to the Midwestern landscapes of *Broom* and 'Westward', the Midwest in *The Pale King* (and in *Oblivion*, for that matter) offers more complexity in its description.

This complexity is connected to a profound ambivalence in *The Pale King* over the values of the corporate institution. The novel's valorization of the pre-Spackman Service implicitly praises the institution of federal bureaucracy, and the central section of the novel (Fogle's monologue) is an extended conversion narrative that affords the Service an air of religious epiphany. However, the concern expressed over the spatial power of the corporation in *Oblivion*, and its attendant toxification of surrounding areas, constitutes a significant element of *The Pale King*'s narrative. This is most clearly articulated in the extended conversation in the broken elevator in section 19: the federal government, described as being concordant with 'the people', is contrasted with the fallacy of ascribing 'civic obligations or moral responsibilities to corporations' (135–6). While this conversation rehashes some of Wallace's perennial concerns over individual responsibility (the Marathe-Steeply conversation in *Infinite Jest* provides another iteration of this conversation, albeit one less directly historicized and more philosophically inflected, namely by Isaiah Berlin's *Two Concepts of Liberty*) it sharpens the distinction between the federal and corporate institution. Despite the attempted dialogism of this sequence, it is pretty clear where Wallace's sympathies ultimately lie: the grotesque drugging and capture of director and federal advocate DeWitt Glendenning by Lehrl's aides in section 48 stages a disturbing usurpation of the old guard by the free market-inspired acolytes of the Spackman Initiative. The implication for the novel's conclusion, which appears, as in *Infinite Jest*, to lie outside of the narrative's frame, is that the market has won by foul means. This is compounded by the debriefing of Fogle by Reynolds and Sylvanshine in section 49, a brilliant piece of juxtaposition by Pietsch, which comes to stand for the final desacralizing of those 'called to account' by the Service. The subjugation of Fogle in the presence of Lehrl's mysterious, unreadable child, most likely the 'fierce infant' depicted in section 35, reverses the child-to-man *bildungsroman* structure of Fogle's conversion to the Service and points to a new, sinister 'birth' of the IRS. By these examples I hope to illustrate the potential problems that arise from ascribing an essentialized model of 'the institution' to *The Pale King*. While the novel does indeed frequently dramatize the transition from the world outside into the Service, it does so within an oscillatory spatial model, a development of Wallace's earlier performative Midwestern persona, which begins to resist the attribution of essential qualities to the spaces within and without.

In Chapter 2 I argue that the toxic institution in *Oblivion* performs an accretive process of constriction whereby transparent surfaces become reconfigured into reflections of the trapped subject. This process is also perceptible in *The Pale King*, but I read the post-2005 material as an attempt by Wallace to qualify these isolating, reflective institutional environments within refractive frameworks. In this sense, the late material from *The Pale King* performs a development of the evolving model of refraction and *mise-en-abyme* that I outline in Chapter 3. However, the unfinished structure of the text proves particularly problematic here in moving towards a full understanding of the reciprocal, refractive relationship between author and reader.

## Looking at But Not Into: *The Pale King*'s Surfaces

The amalgamation of much of the material from *Oblivion* and the early drafts of *The Pale King* result in the appearance of the former's claustrophobic models of isolation in the latter text. Motifs of eyes and mirrors can be found throughout *The Pale King* and are frequently associated with either narcissism or despair. Not being able to 'see' is generally configured as a failure to perceive or empathize with others and most often dramatized as a character looking *at* but not *into* something: Britton seems to Sylvanshine to be 'more like looking *at* his right eye than *into* it' (51, emphasis original); Toni Ware stares '*at* your eyes rather than *into* them' (441, emphasis original); Garrity, who has spent his working life staring at himself in a mirror, has a 'bad eye, the frozen eye' and an attendant lack of empathy with the recipients of his lengthy monologues (384); the unreadable eyes of the 'fierce infant' are almost pupil-less (392); Meredith Rand laments the failure of colleagues to see past her attractive face (499).[33] By extension, Sylvanshine's approach to information involves a perception of data but not an understanding of its application, a supernatural iteration of the failure of perception accorded to Britton and Ware. The almost direct replication in the novel of the descriptions of Ware and Britton may speak of some of the stylistic infelicities that inevitably characterize the unfinished text (such as the multiple uses of 'squeezing shoes'), but these references nevertheless reveal that Wallace was preoccupied in *The Pale King* with matters of seeing. As I argue in the previous chapter, the claustrophobic reflections in work environments in *Oblivion* are not so much a straight revival of the narcissistic mirror gazing of the earlier fiction but more obviously connected to the loss of the coherent self within an institutional environment, most clearly illustrated via Schmidt's failure to recognize himself in a mirror in 'Mister Squishy' and the narrator's absorption in the window's mesh in 'The Soul is not a Smithy'. This develops in *The Pale King* to incorporate the condition of 'being in a stare' described by an IRS employee:

> Being in a stare referred to staring fixedly and without expression at something for extensive periods of time [...] in a stare, you are not really looking at this thing you are seeming to stare at, you are not even really noticing it – however, neither are you thinking of something else. You in truth are not doing anything, mentally, but you are doing it fixedly, with what appears to be intent concentration. It is as if one's concentration becomes stuck the way an auto's wheels can be stuck in the snow, turning rapidly without going forward, although it looks like intent concentration. And now I too do this. I find myself doing it. It's not unpleasant, but it is strange. Something goes out of you [...] As if your face, like your attention, belongs to someone else. Sometimes now in the mirror, in the bathroom, I'll come to myself and catch myself in a stare, without any recognition. The man has been dead for twelve years now. (116–17)

This is worth quoting at length because it is an extraordinarily fecund passage in terms of Wallace's formal models in *The Pale King*. It contains the tropes of absent possession and ghostliness (the lack of ownership over one's face; the 'dead' man in the mirror) and combines a loss of the communicative self with the image of a 'bad wheel'. However, the 'stare' is a new iteration of the gaze in Wallace's fiction and is associated not with the vacant, self-regarding gaze of the mirror-bound narcissist but with the lost, absent workplace self: something 'goes out of you' during the process. The 'stare' comes across here as an amended version of Cavell's theory of cinematic 'screening' discussed in the previous chapter ('it screens me from the world it holds – that is, it makes me invisible' [24]) except that rather than being generated by the cinema screen, the screening of the self from the world is created by the work environment. Wallace's anxiety over seeing therefore develops in *Oblivion* and *The Pale King* into a vexed continuum: while the narcissistic near-sighted processes of image viewing in *Infinite Jest* result in the caged, trapped self, giving oneself away to the world of work might engender the opposite: a far-sighted, empty gaze and concomitant loss of the self.[34] In this sense, the kind of redemptive refraction practised in the earlier fiction must be qualified: while it is important to look *through* rather than *at*, without a corresponding dialogic object on the other side of the refractive surface, the gaze becomes a thousand-yard stare.³⁵

In 2005, after the publication of *Oblivion*, Wallace writes two long sections of *The Pale King* (Fogle's monologue and the Rand-Drinion conversation) which attempt to address the matter of this loss of the self by dramatizing extended scenarios that work around this problem, both based around motifs of mirroring, narcissism and refraction. In this period Wallace also writes the 'Author Here' material to corral the structure of the book, and I want to argue that in this latter section Wallace enacts a model of *mise-en-abyme*, and specifically an aporetic duplication, to attempt a refractive model similar to that used in 'Octet' that stands at once inside and outside of the work environment. Any success attributed to this model can only be partial, for its effectiveness relies on an understanding of the novel's final structure which, of course, we can never see.

Fogle's lengthy monologue dramatizes this oscillation between narcissism and loss of the self in the workplace. The conversion from 'wastoid' to productive Service employee, which might initially be glossed as a redemptive narrative of the loss of the narcissistic self to the world of work, is problematized by 'David Wallace's' dismissive comment about Fogle's logorrhoea. Indeed, Fogle's lengthy monologue, which according to 'Wallace' is apparently 'heavily edited and excerpted' (257) despite running to nearly 100 pages, is partly responsible for the failure of 'the abortive 1984 Personnel Division motivational/recruitment faux documentary debacle' because it took up so much tape. Considering that the debacle began as an attempt to 'humanise' the IRS by demystifying the Service, Fogle's garrulity actually prevents this humanizing gesture from taking place (257). I would venture another reason for the project's failure: the attempt to connect with the general public is framed as a series of monologues. By inviting someone to talk at length about themselves (Fogle being the *ne plus ultra*) the interviews enact an inherently non-dialogic position and fail as communication with the public. Indeed, Fogle's lengthy self-description provokes the documentary crew to 'stare into space', uninterested, while he talks (257).

Fogle's conversion is a qualified giving away of the self to the workplace. While his monologue affords his subjugation to the Service a religiously inflected aura, his repetitive reflections on his own thought processes ironically enact a form of the 'doubling' self-consciousness that he has purportedly escaped. This oscillation is evident in the multivalent uses of mirrors and reflections in this section. It might be tempting to see Fogle's conversion as an escape from the narcissistic 'hall of mirrors' (188) that he associates with the most extreme examples of his Obetrol use (also referring to as 'doubling' [181]), particularly as the traumatizing event that precipitates his conversion, his father's death, is witnessed *refractively* by Fogle through a glass train door (200). However, the circumstances of Fogle's conversion are characterized by images of *reflection* rather than refraction, of looking *at* rather than *through*: the students in the lecture theatre where Fogle experiences his conversion reflect the light (220), while the IRS recruiter subsequently sought out by Fogle is inexplicably wearing sunglasses indoors (243). The conversion itself takes place within a room mistakenly entered by Fogle because it is 'an identical mirror image of the adjoining building's correct room' (190), the buildings being 'literally almost mirror images of one another' (189). While this mistake, and the subsequent conversion, might be described as a dramatization of Hutcheon's theory that the mirror can be made 'productive', the scenario just as easily evokes the 'two planar mirrors' of James Incandenza's self-referential 'Cage'. The spatial circumstances of Fogle's monologue, and indeed all the filmed interviews, are also characterized by looking at, rather than into:

> It's an IRS examiner in a chair, in a room. There is little else to see. Facing the tripod's camera, addressing the camera, one examiner after another [...] The room could be anywhere, nowhere [...] Eyes are a problem. If the examiner looks at the documentarian instead of the camera, it can appear evasive or co-erced [...] the pre-briefer's advice is to *look into the camera as one would a trusted friend's eyes, or a mirror, depending*. (100–3, emphasis mine)

The success of the enterprise hinges on that 'depending'. Fogle can only see the camera reflectively, narcissistically, as a mirror, and this is compounded by the advice to look not into the eyes of the interlocutor but the unblinking, un-reciprocal eye of the camera, a dramatization and torquing of the Jesuit's 'welcome to the world of reality – there is no audience' (229). Here, the lack of audience is configured as a lack of a dialogic partner, and Fogle's 'giving away' of the self to the Service is therefore partially fallacious.

Wallace makes a note during composition attributing Fogle with the power of 'total concentration', contingent on the memorization of a string of numbers (*Pale* 539). In the post-2005 material he gives this power to Drinion, where it is accompanied with the ability to levitate. The lengthy conversation between Rand and Drinion in section 46 affords a different perspective on the matters of narcissism, reflection and refraction that characterize Fogle's monologue by providing a dialogic partner for a narcissistically inclined character. Drinion occupies a similar position to the camera in this scene, 'there but in an unusual way; he becomes part of the table's environment, like the air or ambient light' (448). He provides a present counterpart for Rand's self-analysis, but he can only process the data and, like an automaton, provide logical and un-empathetic responses to her questions. In his most substantial revelation during the conversation, Drinion reveals to Rand that his apparent lack of self-consciousness and absence of proclivity to narcissism is due to the fact that 'no-one paid enough attention to me [in childhood] to even wonder what was going on inside me [...] I don't think I'm really anything' (462). In this sense, and in stark contrast to Vance Vigorous in *The Broom of the System*, whose childhood is obsessively perceived by his father Rick, Drinion has only semi-transitioned into the Lacanian Symbolic: by not being 'seen' by his family, he has no real perception of himself as an object in the world, and thus no propensity for self-consciousness.[36] Godden and Szalay read Drinion as needing 'no mirror or double; his capacity to become the object of his attention makes him the equivalent of Obetrol' (1298). I partially agree with this reading, but I would amend this last sentence to 'the object of *others*' attention'. Godden and Szalay's observation is useful in providing a link between the Fogle and Rand-Drinion sections and helps us to understand how the latter is a putatively dialogic version of the former. While Rand believes that she is engaging in a dialogue, Drinion is simply fulfilling the same role as the doubled Fogle during his 'Obetrolling'.[37]

However, Rand and Drinion's conversation, in a gesture of Simple Duplication by Wallace, frames a secondary iteration of itself. The prevailing subject of the conversation is the reproduction of the dialogues that took place between Meredith and Ed Rand during the former's institutionalization. Ed analyses Meredith's problems, but as she subsequently says to Drinion 'he was talking about himself, which I knew, even though he didn't spell it out' (500). This is despite Ed's protestations that 'we weren't in here talking about him, it didn't matter about him because all he really was was a kind of mirror for me' (490), elsewhere referring to himself as 'more just like a mirror' (480). The monologically inflected second-order conversation between Meredith and Ed, characterized by reflection rather than refraction, thus problematizes the dialogic quality of the conversation between Meredith and Drinion that frames it, with Meredith essentially repeating large parts of the conversation verbatim to Drinion. Meredith's final line to Drinion ('Anyway, that's how I met him' [509]) pointedly cycles back to the beginning of her story: no dialogic change has been effected.

These scenarios of failed communication are subsequently framed within the 'Author Here' sections of *The Pale King* in a gesture of *mise-en-abyme*, specifically an aporetic duplication which encloses the work that encloses it. 'David Wallace's' address to the reader, which explains and stands outside the narrative he is now collating, is also enclosed deeply *within* the framework of that narrative. I would argue that this is the reason that Wallace indicated the 'Author Here' sections should not appear until several sections into the book (*Pale* vii). Spatially, this instance of *mise-en-abyme* most strongly recalls the placement of 'Octet' in *Brief Interviews with Hideous Men*, as the rest of the text must necessarily be viewed 'through' the voice of the author persona, who is directly addressing the reader. These sections thus attempt to frame the monologic, reflective sections with a refractive 'author'-reader dialogue. In fact the 'Author Here' sequence offers at least one instance of Simple Duplication to dramatize its difference from the Fogle monologue: Fogle's mistaken entry of the 'mirror' building prior to his epiphany is itself mirrored in 'David Wallace's' confused entry into the mirrored frontage of the REC, a building that used to be a mirror factory, during his induction (282). 'David Wallace' reports that a picture plate of the mirrored frontage of the REC cannot be reproduced in the 'Author Here' section, which makes sense when one considers that the objective of *these* sections is to refract, *not* to reflect (283).

The placement of the 'Author Here' sections *within* the body of the text, rather than paratextually outside it, also speaks of the refractive quality ascribed by Wallace in *The Pale King* to sustained and close reading. This is enacted through the suggestion that the reading surface itself can, when studied closely, reveal hidden information, and that one can look 'through' and not just 'at' text itself. One example of this can be found in the section which appears at first to simply describe multiple characters as they 'turn a page' (310–13) but which contains hidden information referring to the transfiguration of one thing into another ('Devils are actually angels […] Every love story is a ghost story' [312]).[38] Notably, among the secreted information is a reference to 'one square acre of hidden mirror' (312). This hidden mirror, a reflective surface, is itself hidden in the text, and the reader must perform an act of 'looking through' the text to ascertain its existence: to paraphrase Hutcheon, the (hidden) mirror thus becomes productive. Relatedly, 'Wallace' asserts the importance of close reading to his understanding of the changes undergone by the IRS in the 1980s, through his full reading of the related (and extensive) documentation, claiming that he is 'the only living American who's actually read these archives all the way through' (84 n25) despite their being 'in full public view' (84).[39]

However, this also means that the refractive structure of the 'Author Here' sections can once again become dialogically problematic. As I have indicated above, by framing himself as a kind of supreme reader 'David Wallace' asserts an interpretive power that risks monologism: the author figure as 'correct' reader and writer of everything, framing a narrative that is filled with 'bad' readers (Sylvanshine can receive data but not make sense of it, while Drinion can make sense of the data but not emphasize) and where being able to 'read' others, as Lehrl does, is configured as a source of power. In this context, the instruction to 'read these' (4) in section 1 of the novel can be read as didactic command. It is possible to speculate that 'Wallace's' monologic control of the whole document may have had its readerly counterpart in the transfiguration of the narrative of *The Pale King* when read in its entirety, but the novel remains unfinished. Indeed, it is possible to read some degree of desperation into the appeal to textual coherency in the 'Author Here' sections, knowing that, as I have argued above, they were at least partially created in an attempt to bind the narrative together into a totalized document. Again, the novel betrays a dramatization of its own composition: perhaps if one reads all these sections together, and closely enough, they will cohere. Ultimately *The Pale King* will never completely cohere, however much we read it, but as its lengthy and often convoluted composition reveals, it attempts to substantially address and advance the formal configurations of vocality, spatiality and visuality that characterize Wallace's fiction.

At time of writing, little of Wallace's fiction remains unpublished. Fragments of stories and juvenilia can be found among his papers but there can be little argument that his canon is essentially complete. However, through examining the archival materials of the fiction in tandem with the extraordinary structural complexity of the published work, we are afforded a valuable opportunity to engage with a compositional process that frames those dialogic formal strategies that underpin so much of the completed fiction. By tracing Wallace's conversations with himself over form and structure, we can construct that secondary compositional conversation that informs those oscillations between character, author and reader that form an essential element of the fiction. Another dialogue can begin.

# Notes

## Introduction

1. The pre-2008 monographs are Stephen J. Burn's *Infinite Jest: A Reader's Guide* (2003), Marshall Boswell's *Understanding David Foster Wallace* (2003) and Greg Carlisle's *Elegant Complexity* (2007). In addition to these monographs, Tom LeClair's article 'The Prodigious Fiction of Richard Powers, William Vollmann, and David Foster Wallace' (1996), N. Katherine Hayles' 'The Illusion of Autonomy and the Fact of Recursivity: Virtual Ecologies, Entertainment, and *Infinite Jest*' (1999), Mary K. Holland's '"The Art's Heart's Purpose": Braving the Narcissistic Loop of David Foster Wallace's *Infinite Jest*' (2006) and Timothy Jacobs' 'The Brothers Incandenza: Translating Ideology in Fyodor Dostoevsky's *The Brothers Karamazov* and David Foster Wallace's *Infinite Jest*' (2007) have been extensively cited.

2. See Timmer, *Do You Feel It Too? The Post-Postmodern Syndrome in American Fiction at the Turn of the Millennium* (2010), Ryan, *The Novel After Theory* (2012) and Holland, *Succeeding Postmodernism* (2013). Wallace also appears in Jeremy Green's *Late Postmodernism* (2005) and regularly in Burn's *Jonathan Franzen at the End of Postmodernism* (2009). Paul Giles' 'All Swallowed Up: David Foster Wallace and American Literature' locates Wallace's fiction in response to pre-twentieth-century American literature.

3. Nick Maniatis' *The Howling Fantods* and Ryan Niman's *The Know(e)* were two key early online repositories of Wallace-related information: *The Know(e)* is now defunct but Maniatis' excellent site remains the major online database of Wallace materials. Wallace-l, a still-active listserv currently administrated by Matt Bucher, was also an early gathering point for Wallace readers and scholars. Accordingly, a characteristic element of Wallace studies is the intermingling of scholarly and non-scholarly responses to the work within environments usually occupied only by academics. The two (thus far) annual David Foster Wallace conferences held in Normal, Illinois, were striking for their hybrid of academically and non-academically affiliated responses. I participated in a related roundtable discussion at the second annual conference in 2015 titled

'Wallace Scholarship in and out of the Academy' with a number of affiliated and unaffiliated scholars (Matt Bucher, Mary K. Holland, Mike Miley, Josh Roiland).

4   To pick two of a number of examples, see Burn's illustration of Wallace's intertextual response to Joyce in 'Order and Flux in Northampton' and *Infinite Jest* (*Guide* 24–5) and Boswell's location of Wallace in 'Modernism's Third Wave' (*Understanding* 1).

5   Kelly published 'The Death of the Author and the Birth of a Discipline' in 2010, which provides an important summation of the situation of Wallace criticism up to that point, and begins to discuss the implications of a Wallace 'industry' alongside the centrality of the 'essay-interview nexus' to Wallace criticism (referring to 'E Unibus Pluram' and the 1993 interview with Larry McCaffery, respectively).

6   Allard Den Dulk's *Existentialist Engagement in Wallace, Eggers and Foer* (2014) performs a broader survey of a shared philosophical dimension in the work of Wallace and two other contemporary American authors, Dave Eggers and Jonathan Safran Foer.

7   Burn examines the cultural context of these appearances in his analysis of the 'post-Wallace novel' in the revised edition of his guide to *Infinite Jest* (*Guide* 5). On the 'post-Wallace novel', see also Hoberek, 'The Novel After David Foster Wallace'.

8   See Santel, 'On David Foster Wallace's Conservatism' and McGurl, 'The Institution of Nothing'. Wallace also offers a notably conservative response to the AIDS crisis in his 1996 essay 'Back in New Fire', which received a wider audience when republished in the essay collection *Both Flesh and Not* in 2012. A number of recent essays have stressed the importance of political context, or lack of it, in Wallace's fiction and non-fiction: see Hogg, 'Subjective Politics in *The Pale King*', Kelly, 'David Foster Wallace and the Novel of Ideas' and Konstantinou, 'The World of David Foster Wallace'. Perhaps the most excoriating critical response thus far is Amy Hungerford's 'On Not Reading DFW' in *Making Literature Now*, which performs a damning reading of Wallace's politics of gender both inside and outside his writing.

9   I first argued for the value of critiquing Wallace via Bakhtin in my 2011 article 'Theorising David Foster Wallace's Toxic Postmodern Spaces' in *US Studies Online* 18.

10  Stephen Burn and Marshall Boswell make brief reference to the 'combination of centripetal and centrifugal energies' that characterize Wallace's writing in their preface to *A Companion to David Foster Wallace Studies* (xi).

11  Alongside this formal mapping of the fiction, I make sustained references to the now-substantial body of Wallace criticism. Through this process I want to create a secondary dialogic framework: a map of Wallace scholarship that is in continuous conversation with my own.
12  For the most substantial articles of this wave so far, see Burn, 'Paradigm', Groenland, 'King of Shreds and Patches', Staes, 'Work in Progress' and Miley, 'And Starring…'.
13  This is not Bowman's neologism: in his article 'Genetic Criticism' he attempts to collate in English a series of terms from French genetic criticism for Anglophone usage. 'Foretext' is Bowman's approximation of the French 'avant-texte' (627).
14  This problem occurs when Sullivan attempts a genetic reading of 'Cede' using only two documents: a reading from 2000 and the version published in *The New Yorker* in 2011 (260–5). The reading is incomplete because the first version of 'Cede' dates from 1997 and there is another iteration of the story c.2001 before its final form. The material in the other versions renders the argument that Wallace never made 'a bold excision' and 'never adds substantial material within a sentence or even within a paragraph' incorrect (263). In mitigation, Sullivan admits to not having seen the drafts of the novel. For my reading of 'Cede', see Chapter 4.

# Chapter 1

1  For a contextualizing of the intersection between modernist culture and spirit mediumship, see Sword, *Ghostwriting Modernism*.
2  I refer implicitly here to Brian McHale's famous argument about the development from modernist epistemology into postmodern ontology (McHale, *Postmodernist* 10).
3  In his negative review of Edwin Williamson's biography of Borges Wallace disparages the 'simplistic, dishonest kind of psychological criticism' (287) which presumes the work as simply 'correlative of the author's emotional state' ('Borges on the Couch' 290). Wallace later uses Frank Bidart's poem 'Borges and I', which shares its name with Borges' own rumination on the split between self and authorial persona, as an epigraph for *The Pale King* (see Chapter 4).
4  Widiss comes closest to analysing the kind of 'revenant' authorial presence I will describe in Wallace's later work when discussing Dave Eggers' *A*

*Heartbreaking Work of Staggering Genius*, during which the author/narrator construct importunes the reader to take physical part in his death (Eggers 437), conflating the codex with the authorial body 'held in the reader's hand like a communion wafer' (Widiss 128). However, as I will suggest below, while corporeality is at the heart of Wallace's strategy, he enacts authorial materiality in a more explicitly dialogic manner.

5   Wallace tells David Lipsky in 1996 that 'I believe in Harold Bloom's theory of *misprision*' (Lipsky *Although* 127, emphasis original). For an extensive analysis of Bloomian misprision in Wallace's fiction, see Harris. A.O Scott argues that for Wallace 'anxiety may not be a strong enough word; panic is more like it' ('The Panic of Influence').

6   For further discussion of Wallace's response to Wittgenstein, see Boswell (*Understanding* 23–6), Hayes-Brady ('The Book, the Broom and the Ladder'; *Unspeakable Failures*), Ramal, Baskin and Horn.

7   The structure of 'Lyndon' also draws heavily from Donald Barthelme's story 'Robert Kennedy Saved from Drowning' from *Unspeakable Practices, Unnatural Acts*. For an analysis of Wallace's debts to these writers, see Boswell's chapter on the collection (*Understanding* 65–116). Wallace revealed in an interview in 2005 that in his twenties 'there was very little difference between my admiring some writer's particular ability and my wishing to appropriate that ability for myself' ('Interview with Didier Jacob' 156).

8   When I use materials from Wallace's archive of papers, I refer to the box number and folder in which it can be found within the collection of his papers at the Harry Ransom Centre: this reference is to Box 15, folder 1. When I refer to different or deleted drafts of the fiction, the full citation can be found in the bibliography under the name of the novel/collection from which the material comes. When I refer to correspondence, I cite in-text as 'Letter to …', and the full citation can be found in the bibliography in the subsection 'Letter to …' within Wallace's bibliography. Correspondents are referred to alphabetically by first name within this subsection.

9   Charles Harris argues that the inclusion of a 'Novelist Aspirant' character in Barth's 2001 novel *Coming Soon!!!* indicates that 'Barth himself suffered a kind of reverse anxiety of influence, with Wallace becoming the Bloomian *apophrades* who actually influences his precursor' (121).

10  It is also, of course, an intertextual reference to *Hamlet*, from which the novel takes its name.

11  An example of permeable narration would be the intrusion of the titular siblings into the unwitting voice of the narrator at the end of Nabokov's 'The Vane Sisters', where the final sentences of the narrator's account unknowingly contain acrostic messages transmitted by the deceased sisters (Nabokov 238).
12  See also Burn, 'Webs of Nerves Pulsing and Firing'.
13  Boswell reads the wraith 'as Wallace' (*Understanding* 170). I suggest presently that the wraith is instead a 'flickering' amalgamation of author figures.
14  Burn associates Wallace's use of ghosts with generational dialogue ('the dead speak to us' [Burn, *Guide* 1]) and also reads the presence of 'a tall, sometime alcoholic ghost named James' as an invocation of another ancestor figure, James Joyce (25).
15  Toon Staes has suggested that the interaction between the wraith and Gately is part of a larger system of permeable narrative uncertainty that characterizes the entire narrative ('Wallace and Empathy' 33). Andrew Warren, who terms this mode the 'free indirect wraith' model, highlights the wraith's suggestion that before his death he was trying to 'contrive a medium' (838) to converse with his son, noting that 'medium' here linguistically conflates the invention of a form with communication with the dead (Warren 78).
16  Wallace originally titled an early partial draft of the novel 'It was a great marvel that they were in the father without knowing him' (Box 15.6), which is named after the prologue of *The Anxiety of Influence* (Bloom 3).
17  The brief appearance of the Lyle-wraith is one of the novel's prevailing mysteries, as it seems to suggest that it is possible for the living to move to a more insubstantial state. Wallace's notes for the novel describe a deleted sequence where the second wraith appears in Gately's memory of his mother's kitchen (Box 15.5), which seems to indicate that wraiths may also be able to invade memories. More speculatively, it could prefigure Lyle's death in the imminent terrorist attack on ETA.
18  In 'No Bull: David Foster Wallace and Postironic Belief' Lee Konstantinou associates the author figure in 'Octet' and later 'Good Old Neon' directly with Wallace himself (94, 98). I read the author figure here differently, as an *accretion* of authorly characteristics rather than Wallace's direct presence, which is dramatized in the work but is never unmediated. In this sense I am closer to the position taken by Mike Miley, who reads all iterations of 'Wallace' in the work as being problematized by Wallace's public persona. Miley orientates

much of this criticism around the difference between 'David Wallace' and 'David Foster Wallace' (195).

19  The wraith explains that his experience of the 'dramatic pathos of a figurant [...] *trapped* and *encaged* [...] in his mute peripheral status' in the show led to his development of 'radical realism', whereby 'you could bloody well hear every single performer's voice' (835, emphasis original), while Neal's realization that 'I'd managed to con myself' into thinking of a 'truer or more promising way to conceive of the problem of fraudulence', leaving him in the position of 'one of those stock comic characters who is always both the butt of the joke and the only person not to get the joke', is triggered by a gag shared by the show's two analysts Frasier and Lilith (*Oblivion* 168–9). While Neal suggests that this moment of realization was a contributing factor to his decision to commit suicide, it is ironically implied that he has misguidedly placed his faith in artificial representations of analysts rather than his real-life analyst Dr Gustafson, and his fear that his sense of fraudulence would be 'laughed off *the stage*' is merely another iteration of his anxiety over his 'performance' in the eyes of others (169, emphasis mine).

20  Neal's compulsion when alive about 'how to appear in a certain way' (148) is recontextualized in his post-corporeal appearance in the car.

21  The school attended by Neal and David Wallace and named in the climactic convergence of narratives is named 'Aurora West' (180), a word that homophonically implies a collective self ('our aura') while perhaps nodding to the direction ('Westward') associated with the appearance of a metafictional alter ego in Wallace's work (the 'Dave' of Mark's story).

22  Staes makes the related point that the wraith 'acts out what most third-person narrators covertly do in *Infinite Jest* by taking over another character's brain voice' ('Wallace and Empathy' 34).

23  This could also be described as an iteration of Bakhtin's concept of 'double-voiced discourse' which 'serves two speakers at the same time and expresses simultaneously two different intentions: the direct intention of the character who is speaking, and the refracted intention of the author' (Bakhtin, *Dialogic* 324). This model will develop substantially in 'Good Old Neon'. Such a 'double-voicing' can also on occasion be perceived in Wallace use of footnotes and endnotes as a counterpoint voice to the main narrative. This is perhaps most obviously enacted in 'Death is not the End' where the final footnote ('That is not wholly true' [*Brief* 3]) appears to directly contradict the narrative that precedes

it. In 'Good Old Neon' the process of 'double voicing' undergoes a categorical change from ironic to communicative, as the living Neal's ironically inflected voice is subsumed into a heteroglossic discourse after death.

24 Paddy Dignam's revenant in *Ulysses* tells of the 'summit possibilities of atmic development' afforded to the dead (289). In theosophy 'the Atmic plane is the plane of pure existence, where the soul's divine powers are in their fullest manifestation. Those who achieve this plane have completed the cycle of human evolution through a succession of lives and are perfect in wisdom, bliss and power' (Gifford and Seidman 330). As Stephen J. Burn has illustrated, Wallace establishes an intertextual relationship between *Ulysses* and *Infinite Jest* (*Guide* 25).

# Chapter 2

1 This is reminiscent of the human incursion indicated by 'your shoes' brand incised in the dew' during the opening description of the Midwestern landscape in *The Pale King* (4).
2 Marx's book is one of a series of influential studies of the problematic symbolism of American landscape and the frontier and its relationship to urbanity. See also Kolodny, *The Lay of the Land*; Lewis, *The American Adam*; Limerick, *The Legacy of Conquest*; and Nash Smith, *Virgin Land*.
3 Connie Luther draws comparison between Jameson's description and the landscape of Wallace's short story 'Westward the Course of Empire Takes Its Way' (Luther 53).
4 In *Touring Cultures* Rojek and Urry suggest that the total institution model could also be applied, if only temporarily, to the cruise ship. The luxury cruise is, of course, the subject of one of Wallace's most famous essays, 'A Supposedly Fun Thing I'll Never Do Again' (Rojek and Urry 106).
5 Both tendencies appear markedly in Wallace's essay 'The View from Mrs Thompson's' (which concerns the experience of 9/11 from within the Midwest), where they are often almost indistinguishable ('What these Bloomington ladies are, or start to seem to me, is innocent' [*Lobster* 139]). Josh Roiland persuasively argues that Wallace's three Midwestern essays ('Derivative Sport in Tornado Alley'; 'Getting Away from Already Being Pretty Much Away from It All'; and 'The View From Mrs Thompson's') trace a move from a sarcastic register towards

a more 'accepting and comfortable' perspective on the Midwest (Roiland, 'Spiritually'). I agree that Wallace's register does indeed soften across these essays, though I believe that the valorization of the 'innocence' of the Midwestern women and the collapsing of the culture of the Midwest into a single 'view' still betrays the perspective of an outsider, one who cannot synthesize both 'views' of the terrorist attack.

6   Wallace does not pretend that this image carries the transcendent quality associated with its Emersonian near-namesake. While Emerson's 'transparent eye-ball' is explicitly associated with the eradication of the ego ('all mean egotism vanishes [...] I am nothing' [Emerson 39]), Wallace takes pains to emphasize the subjective provisionality of his account ('welcome to *my* mind for twenty pages, see through *my* eyes' [Lipsky, *Although* 173, emphasis mine]).

7   I am indebted to Quinn here for his subtle invocation of the idea of subsumption in Wallace's topographies (90) although, as I suggest, I think that this is only one element of Wallace's spatial anxiety.

8   See Boswell, *Understanding* 53–62 for the most sustained critical model of systems theory and solipsism in Wallace's earlier fiction. Outside of direct Wallace criticism, Stephen Burn offers an analysis of the function of systems theory as it relates to 'post-postmodern' fiction (with which he associates Wallace) in his study *Jonathan Franzen at the End of Postmodernism* (75–81).

9   See Boswell, *Understanding*, O' Donnell, 'Almost a Novel' and Hayes-Brady, 'The Book, the Broom and the Ladder'.

10  This comparative lack of autonomy is compounded by the fact that inhabitants of East Corinth are 'required by zoning code to paint their facilities in the most realistic colours possible' to reflect that their community has been designed, according to the whim of its 'fanatical' founder (Lenore's grandfather) in the shape of the profile of Jayne Mansfield. Lenore traverses the claustrophobic 'Inner Belt Section' in her car while driving to work (45).

11  This architectural structure bears traces of the Benthamite panopticon famously described by Foucault in *Discipline and Punish*. However, unlike that model, which 'induce[s] in the inmate a state of conscious and permanent visibility' (201), the nursing home has the opposite effect of enclosing individuals in discrete monadic environments. Gramma's escape is, conversely, proof of her *invisibility* to the authorities.

12  LeClair's book is published after *Broom* so cannot have directly influenced the structure of that novel. I use the example here to illustrate a general confluence of thought over narrative design. For further structural comparison between

*Ratner's Star* and Wallace, see Burn, 'Webs'. For discussion of Wallace and the recursive 'loop', see Burn, 'Paradigm' and Hayles.

13 For an extended comparison of *Broom* to Baudrillard, see Foster.

14 Wallace was influenced enough by the novel to write apologetically to DeLillo in July 1992, disclosing certain manuscript pages of *Infinite Jest* that 'seem to me to exploit the flavour and rhythms' of *End Zone* ('Letter to Don DeLillo, July 15th 1992').

15 Harkness nevertheless feels 'threatened' by the silence of the desert in *End Zone* (30). Conversely, see Douglas Coupland's formulation of the desert in *Generation X* as a place where those who 'wanted silence' from an 'endless stress of pointless jobs' can 'have that silence now' (14), an environment that bears kinship with Wallace's later use of AA meeting places and recovery facilities in *Infinite Jest*.

16 In contrast to the monadic focus of the first half of *Broom*, Julie, the protagonist of 'Little Expressionless Animals' is immediately described as 'sort of permeable' (13) while her lover Faye lives in a glass apartment (28).

17 '[Lenore's] brother was at Amherst, her father had gone to Amherst, her sister had gone to Mount Holyoke, a few miles away […] her grandfather had gone to Amherst, her great-grandfather had gone to Amherst, her grandmother and great-grandmother to Mount Holyoke, her great-grandmother on to Cambridge in the twenties' (*Broom* 63).

18 Wallace's suggestion in the essay that 'the contemporary artist can simply no longer afford to regard the work of critics or theorists or philosophers […] as divorced from his own concerns' (63) is arguably as 'pre- and proscriptive' as the tenets of the MFA itself, and the association with 'poststructuralist literary theory' has been identified by Mark McGurl as part of Wallace's 'technomodernism', a literary formulation bound up with the development of the program era (McGurl, 'Institution' 33).

19 As 'Westward' makes such substantial use of the image of a target, it is tempting to think of the englobing motif in Lyndon as one of the target's outer concentric rings, and 'Westward' as the bullseye.

20 See also the self-fertilization of the insular town of Minogue 'under dirt's curve' in 'John Billy' (*Girl* 144).

21 See Boswell (*Understanding* 102–15), Luther, Coleman and Foster for examples of this critical position, as well as Wallace's own stated aim ('the Armageddon-explosion, the goal metafiction's always been about' ['Interview with Larry McCaffery' 41]).

22  Conversely, McGurl suggests that 'the aristocratic Southern planter [...] lives happily within the bounds of his organic traditional society' (151).

23  In this context, Gass' 'heart of the heart of the country' conversely takes on the form of an imprisoning structure, of a location bound within another location, rather than the more multivalent englobement of Wallace's story.

24  In a copy of Michael Martone's edited collection *A Place of Sense: Essays in Search of the Midwest* from his personal library, Wallace tellingly underlined the following passage in Martone's essay 'The Flatness' which encapsulates the tension between the idea of the Midwest landscape as region and as incorporeal abstraction: 'I dislike the metaphor of the Heartland [...] The Midwest is too big to be seen like that. I think of it more as a web of tissue, a membrane, a skin [...] The Midwest transmits in fields and waves' (32–3).

25  An early draft has the handwritten heading 'Pt. II open?' (Box 16.5). There are also two sequences involving Mario and Hal talking at night that are both titled 'Nocturne' ('Nocturne 1' [Box 16.3] and 'Nocturne 2' [Box 16.7]) which might indicate an early desire to have mirroring sequences on either side of a two-part division.

26  The form of the narrative is 'lopsided' because a substantial amount of material was cut from *Infinite Jest* before publication. Wallace stated that 'the manuscript that I delivered was 1700 manuscript pages, of which close to 500 were cut' (Interview, Salon.com), but this is not borne out by the extant archive material, or indeed a letter from Wallace to Don DeLillo in which he states the following: 'Little Brown made nice noises but said it was too long. I, largely unaided, cut 310 pages from the fucker over the winter (it is, still, pretty long), and now even as it's at the copyeditor they say they'd like another 100 or so cut' ('Letter to Don DeLillo, May 1995'). Based on the material currently in the archive, the amount removed seems to be in the region of 150 pages. There may, of course, be more deleted material held outside the archive.

27  Slansker is an early name for Hugh Steeply's female persona.

28  For more extensive discussion of the circular motif in *Infinite Jest* and its association with physical constraint, see Hering, '*Infinite Jest*: Triangles, Cycles, Choices and Chases'. For additional discussion of the Sierpinski Gasket model, see Carlisle (20), McGurl, 'Institution' (40) and Wallace's 1996 *Bookworm* interview with Michael Silverblatt.

29  In another cut sequence that recalls the climax of 'Westward', Orin uses a picture of his mother's face as the bullseye on a dartboard (Box 16.3).

30  In an associated observation, Stephen Burn highlights the pedagogical inescapability at E.T.A. of Edwin Abbot's novel *Flatland*, which has reduced Orin and Hal's perceptions from three to two dimensions (Burn, *Guide* 48).

31  An antecedent to this formal model can be found in 'Derivative Sport in Tornado Alley', where Wallace describes how in his youth he was able to 'Play The Whole Court [...] I knew my limitations and the limitations of what I stood inside, and adjusted thusly' (*Supposedly* 4).

32  See also Wallace's qualified explanation that 'the guy who essentially runs the academy now is a fascist, and, whether it comes out or not, he's really the only one there who to me is saying anything that's even remotely non-horrifying, except it *is* horrifying because he's a fascist' (Interview, *Bookworm* 1996).

33  Despite my divergence from her conclusion, I find Holland's alignment of Wallace and Christopher Lasch's positions persuasive.

34  The escape suggested in the novel's final scene, where Don Gately comes to lying outside on a beach, is tempered by the reader's understanding that this is a memory and not a chronological event. The final chronological event in *Infinite Jest*'s narrative instead involves Hal Incandenza's paralysing involution within another educational institution, the University of Arizona.

35  Wallace cut two stories from the collection, 'Crash of '62' and 'Yet Another Example of the Porousness of Certain Borders VIII', just before publication. 'Crash of '62', a story set in the world of financial trading that has the same structural voice format as 'Say Never', shares the institutional setting of the rest of the collection, while the other story would later be retitled 'Philosophy and the Mirror of Nature' for inclusion in *Oblivion*. Another mooted title for this latter story was 'Everything that Rises Must Converge', which indicates a debt to Flannery O' Connor's story with which it broadly shares a setting and protagonists (Box 3.3).

36  The footnotes in 'The Depressed Person' are, alongside the endnotes in *Infinite Jest*, Wallace's strongest spatial use of paratext to dramatize psychological process. In the case of 'The Depressed Person' the effect is of encroaching psychological paralysis, which is mirrored in the reader's difficulty in following the main narrative. *Infinite Jest*'s endnotes tend to perform a dramatization of what Marlon Bain describes as 'marijuana thinking', the reference to which is tellingly buried in a footnote to a footnote (*Jest* 1048 n269a). For criticism of the foot/endnote in Wallace, see Goerlandt, Letzler and Nadel.

37  In her analysis of the story, Zadie Smith literally identifies the poet's shrubbery with money (Smith 292).

38  Burn argues that this 'twin tower' motif is representative of the collection's response to 9/11 (*Guide* 81).
39  The counter-narrative featuring the climbing figure was inserted into the story at a fairly late stage (Box 24.5).
40  This image is a regression from the 'mess of green' observed by the narrator of *Girl with Curious Hair*'s 'Everything is Green', although in that story the discrepancy between the age of the narrator and his younger partner indicates that even this 'mess' of green is progressively receding (she believes that 'everything is green', while he observes that 'every thing is not green' [230]). In this context, the 'green vivid and inescapable' fauna of 'Death is not the End' (3) acts as both progressive and *regressive* environmental motif, an artificially constructed 'natural' environment that has the constraining properties later afforded to the institutional facilities that characterize the stories in *Oblivion*.
41  In the toxic institutional environments of 'Mr Squishy', 'The Soul is not a Smithy' and 'Philosophy and the Mirror of Nature', even the physical accessories of the white collar worker take on an uncanny or threatening air, with briefcases playing an implicit role in, respectively, Schmidt's plan to poison the snack cakes (51), the risk posed by Mr Johnson (99) and the release of lethal venomous spiders (189).
42  Burn correspondingly suggests that '$\Delta y$ has become a kind of recursive structure, forever bending back in on itself, never embracing anything outside' (*Guide* 82).
43  Manderley's name is a semi-homophonic echo of another tower-dwelling intern, Candy Mandible, in *The Broom of the System*.
44  The figure of the compromised journalist reappears in a late, unfinished story, 'Wickedness', which will be discussed in detail in the next chapter. This story has an unclear provenance, but was likely a nascent or alternative version of 'The Suffering Channel' (Box 39.5).
45  It is significant that 'Soul' contains a reference to the indirect pollution of the natural area around the Scioto River after 'the University unduly influenced the city fathers into building the Maryville commuter road' (82).

# Chapter 3

1  Wallace would certainly have encountered this reference, if not in Borges then in John Barth's essay 'The Literature of Exhaustion' ('an instance of the story-within-the-story turned back upon itself' [73]).

2   For an expounding of this position, see Abrams' seminal *The Mirror and the Lamp*, from which this quotation is taken.
3   For a fuller analysis of Wallace's response to Rorty, see Tracey, 'The Formative Years' and Hayes-Brady, *Unspeakable Failures*.
4   Rick's later conversation with Andrew 'Wang Dang' Lang at a bar in Amherst pointedly begins and ends by being conducted through 'the huge mirror we were all looking into' behind the counter (223).
5   The reference to the 'wobbled' infantile mirror will return in *Infinite Jest*: the lens used by James Incandenza to make the lethal film 'Infinite Jest' has an 'auto-wobble' to reflect the 'wobbled and weird' POV of newborn infants (*Jest* 939).
6   Rick's description of Vance as 'the absent who cannot return' (78) is pure Lacan. It is also notable that the 'subjective impasses' resultant from existentialism in Lacan's essay on the mirror stage ('a freedom that is never so authentically affirmed as when it is within the walls of a prison; a demand for commitment that expresses the inability of pure consciousness to overcome any situation; a voyeuristic-sadistic idealization of sexual relationships; a personality that achieves self-realization only in suicide; and a consciousness of the other that can only be satisfied by Hegelian murder' [80]) can all be found, often in multiple iterations, as scenarios across the body of Wallace's fiction, particularly in *Brief Interviews with Hideous Men*.
7   This period is bordered by the composition of 'Little Expressionless Animals' at the University of Arizona in 1986 (Max 75) and the publication in 1993 in *Review of Contemporary Fiction* of 'E Unibus Pluram'.
8   Wallace's quoting in 'E Unibus Pluram' of Lewis Hyde's maxim that irony 'is the voice of the trapped who have come to enjoy their cage' (67) further unites the motifs of metafiction and narcissism.
9   When citing another example of contemporary writing in 'E Unibus Pluram', Stephen Dobyns' 1980 poem 'Arrested Saturday Night', Wallace quotes a sequence that makes explicit use of Infinite Duplication and television, with a couple watching themselves watching themselves on TV ad infinitum (*Supposedly* 46).
10  Boswell makes substantial reference to Orin's narcissism in his extended analysis of the Lacanian imagery in *Infinite Jest* (*Understanding* 128–32, 151–6, 159–60).
11  Wallace briefly attended Cavell's philosophy seminars as a graduate student in 1989 (Max 132) and had a copy of Cavell's *Pursuits of Happiness* in his personal library.
12  The word 'despair' is underlined and circled in Wallace's copy. Relatedly, Burn has argued for the influence of Percy's work on the subject matter of *The Pale King* ('Paradigm' 157).

13  This has always struck me as a rather reductive, US-centric analysis of the medium, whereby television is characterized only as being dumb because of its responsibilities to its advertisers. Given that Wallace was an avowed viewer of *The Wire* (Lipsky, 'Lost' 180) it would have been interesting to see if his position on television had changed in the so-called 'Golden Age' of subscription channels like HBO.

14  Wallace's fascination with the work of David Lynch is evidently bound up with his interest in the art/entertainment continuum, as Lynch has managed to implement a specifically auteur-led aesthetic across both avant-garde cinema (*Eraserhead*) and commercial network television (*Twin Peaks*) as well as extending an influence 'into mainstream Hollywood movies' (*Supposedly* 165). The dream-inflected narrative of 'Oblivion', with its role-reversal-upon-waking plot twist, is strikingly similar to Lynch's *Lost Highway*, the subject of Wallace's essay 'David Lynch Keeps His Head' from *A Supposedly Fun Thing I'll Never Do Again*.

15  A source for much of the film-related detail in *Infinite Jest* is *The Cinema Book*, a battered copy of which is one of the most heavily marked-up books in Wallace's personal library. Wallace did not have any formal film education of which I am aware (though he may have briefly encountered some film-related material in Cavell's Harvard class), so I must presume that he draws much of his technical/historical information from this book. The front page of Wallace's copy bears the date '92', which suggests that he bought the book to assist with research for *Infinite Jest*. There are sustained underlinings made in the sections relating to Andre Bazin (Cook 39, 59), the role of genre in cinema (60, 63), Fritz Lang (123) and auteur theory (137, 165): all of these have a significant role in the plot of *Infinite Jest*. Elsewhere, the marginal note 'Film – art/commodity/entertainment [...] Art cinema vs. popular cinema' displays Wallace's preoccupation with the art-entertainment continuum described in this chapter. Wallace also notes passages that relate to obsessive watching and film as instrument of death. He heavily underlines a section on Michael Powell's *Peeping Tom* (105), which concerns a murderous filmmaker who records his victims at the point of death, their own faces reflected in a concave mirror atop his camera. Wallace displays a related interest here in some of the concepts explored by Laura Mulvey in *Visual and Other Pleasures*, notably 'scopophilic instinct' (Cook 70): in *Infinite Jest* Joelle Van Dyne describes the titular film as 'the allegedly fatally entertaining and scopophiliac thing' (sic) (*Jest* 230). There is even a suggestion that *The Cinema*

*Book* might have influenced some of the fiction subsequent to *Infinite Jest*. Next to a reference to Godard's *Une Femme Mariée* (Cook 134–5), Wallace has written 'use'. No details are present that suggest how Wallace might 'use' it, but Godard's film features an extended interview sequence in which an interviewee responds to unheard questions: this is, of course, how the interviews in *Brief Interviews with Hideous Men* are structured.

16 Iimura's 1963 short *Onan* shares a name with the new configuration of the American continent in *Infinite Jest*.

17 While the filmography does not draw a direct connection between Incandenza's 'Cage' and Sidney Peterson's 1947 film *The Cage*, the latter's central motif of a man walking down a street with a cage around his head recalls Joelle's invocation of solipsism ('What looks like the cage's exit is actually the bars of the cage' [222]). Peterson's film can also be seen playing in the background of Incandenza's film *Good-Looking Men in Small Clever Rooms That Utilize Every Centimeter of Available Space with Mind-Boggling Efficiency* (911), while Joelle is a fan of the director (185) and one of Molly Notkin's director-shaped chairs is moulded in the form of Peterson (788). Peterson's film, like *Infinite Jest*, also ends on a beach.

18 Speculatively, it is possible that, in a moment of Aporetic Duplication, the sequence on pages 157–69 actually *is* 'As of Yore', with the chapter heading ('Winter B.S. 1960 – Tucson AZ' [157]) a title card within the film itself.

19 On instruction from Michael Pietsch ('Letter to David Foster Wallace, Feb 19th 1995') Wallace cut a scene in which James Incandenza's father immolates black widows in the family garage (Box 16.1). This scene is dramatized by Incandenza in the film 'Widower' (*Jest* 987), which oddly remains in the novel without its counterpart scene.

20 The breaking of a mirror to suggest escape from a pathological cycle of behaviour is implicitly referenced in a number of references to Maya Deren's *Meshes of the Afternoon* (185, 222). Deren's film ends when a repetitive narrative loop is terminated by the breaking of a mirrored veil, which reveals a body on a beach. *Infinite Jest* concludes with Gately at his lowest point and surrounded by mirrors, before breaking through to his memory of lying prone on a beach (*Jest* 981).

21 Around the same time as he is drafting *Sir John Feelgood*, Wallace is exploring similar territory in his non-fiction. He uses the term 'F/X Porn' in his article 'The (As It Were) Seminal Importance of Terminator 2' to characterize certain

Hollywood blockbusters: 'if you substitute F/X for intercourse, the parallels between the two genres become so obvious they're eerie' (*Flesh* 177).

22  In the outline to the novel, Wallace expands on this point: 'A perpetual problem is the male actors: you want, in the fantasy, to substitute yourself for the male actors [...] Porn watching is not voyeurism: you're not getting off watching some <u>other</u> man have sex' (Box 37.4, underlining original).

23  The only archival evidence of what the early pornography project may have looked like can be found in what may be a structural outline in Wallace's copy of George N. Gordon's book *Erotic Communications*:
    1. The library and Step on it. 2. Legal Insert. 3. The Legal Bed. 4. Kindergarten Love Object (Tami Monroe). 5. Hints to Pilgrims. 6. Adultery in a Narrow Bunk. 7. Poultry in Motion. 8. Eric Shawn's Cranio-Facial Pain. 9. Blue Valley.
    This outline is intriguing, not to say perplexing, because it combines lines from *Infinite Jest* ('The library and Step on it') with the names of porn actors (Tami Monroe) and, latterly, news journalists (Eric Shawn) who covered traumatic and violent cultural events. This latter subject matter looks forward to the plot of 'The Suffering Channel'.

24  Compare, for example, Rick's assertion that 'Vance was for me a reflection' (*Broom* 75) with 'the child appeared in a sense to be the mother's own reflection in a diminishing and deeply flawed mirror' in 'Suicide as a Sort of Present' (*Brief* 243).

25  The ever-encroaching footnotes in 'The Depressed Person' constitute a literalizing of a mirror-narrative that metastatically grows on the page in tandem with, and in response to, the patient's self-absorption. Notably, the depressed person's therapist's technique of 'mirroring' (33) only seems to aggravate her condition.

26  Boswell suggests that 'Octet' is the 'descriptive core' of the collection (*Understanding* 187).

27  In this sense, the communicative positioning of 'Octet' also invokes the radial structures found within 'Westward' and *Infinite Jest* and discussed in the previous chapter.

28  The pointed use of 'belletristic' in 'Octet' incorporates the dual definition of something that is both aesthetically attractive and ungovernable.

29  For discussion of Wallace's journalism in relation to the Nietzschean concept of oblivion, see Roiland, 'Getting Away'.

30  While Boswell positions 'Good Old Neon' as the central node of a three-narrative chain including 'The Depressed Person' and the Chris Fogle chapter of *The Pale*

King ('Constant' 157) I believe that, while the plot of 'Good Old Neon' could undoubtedly be called an advancement of the solipsistic position set out in 'The Depressed Person', it could not exist without the structural formula established by Wallace in 'Octet'.

31  The draft of 'Wickedness' is extremely messy and unstable. There is a single handwritten copy with multiple (often illegible) amendments and no 'final' version. In this quote from the story, I have therefore had to make some clarifications in parentheses to ensure the sentences are legible.

# Chapter 4

1  Wallace wrote to Jonathan Franzen around the same time with a similar sentiment: 'What's missing is some … thing […] the whole thing is a tornado that won't hold still long enough for me to see what's useful and what isn't, which tends to lead to the idea that I'll have to write a 5,000 page manuscript and then winnow it by 90%' (Max 289). Wallace also prepared an early 'stack' of 150pp of the novel in 2005, according to Max, which emphasizes the importance of this year to the novel's composition (296).
2  This is the title of Herman and Staes' introduction to their co-edited issue of *English Studies* 95.1.
3  On 8 August 1992 Wallace wrote a semi-serious half-page piece on the question 'Why do unattractive people tend to end up with unattractive people?' and saved it with the file name 'SJF16' (Box 37.3). While this is the first record of anything related to the name 'Sir John Feelgood', there is no evidence to suggest that it has any concrete connection to the later novel project.
4  Notes on this synopsis make reference to Douglas Trumbull's film *Brainstorm*, in which scientists experimenting with technology that allows the wearer to feel the emotions of another suffer from a series of personal breakdowns, including catatonia. The influence of Trumbull's film on the plot of both *Infinite Jest* and *Sir John Feelgood* is evident. Wallace also makes reference in a note to Brett Leonard's virtual reality-based film of Stephen King's *The Lawnmower Man* as well as Philip Kaufman's adaptation of Michael Crichton's *Rising Sun*, which features digital manipulation as a principal plot point.
5  In a disturbing development, the porn films are shot in the bedroom of Drinion's incapacitated mother, who is moved out before the room is turned into a 'blinding white set' (Box 37.4).

6   It appears that Wallace may have been influenced during the construction of these arcs by the work of the Harvard psychopathologist Elton Mayo. Among Wallace's notes for *The Pale King* can be found a printout of a document about Mayo and 'The Hawthorne Effect', an increase in output by workers who believe they are being perceived or studied, which is of course a key plot element of the novel (Box 26.7). This information originates in Mayo's *The Human Problems of an Industrial Civilization*, but that book is not to be found in Wallace's materials in the archive.

7   A later amendment juxtaposes this sequence with the opening section of *The Pale King* that begins 'Past the flannel plains …' (Box 40.3).

8   At one stage, Drinion had a sister named Fern, which is, of course, the name of Neal's sister in 'Good Old Neon' (Box 36.1).

9   Wallace made a very brief attempt at a journalist monologue when trying to start *Sir John Feelgood*, writing a three-page handwritten sketch about Drinion's porn career from the perspective of a journalist (Box 40.7). However there is no more material pertaining to this approach and the journalistic narrative appears to have been dropped before being revived in different form during the *Glitterer* period.

10  In contrast to the difficulties he was having with his novel, 1998–2005 was a particularly fecund time for Wallace's non-fiction, with several major essays (including 'Consider the Lobster', 'Up, Simba', 'Authority and American Usage' and 'Big Red Son') being written and published in this period.

11  Numerous references to Reagan in Frank Brown's monologue further connect it to the Reagan-centric plot of 'Wickedness'.

12  This 'ghost' is referred to in this note as 'FNE', a term which is also ascribed to the suggested ghost narrator in *Sir John Feelgood*. Despite numerous attempts to do so, I could not locate the meaning of this term. If pushed, I would speculate that FN might stand for 'First Narrator'. Wallace first uses the term in 1990 (Box 37.5).

13  Wallace's progress on the novel during this second period is also interrupted by the troubled composition of *Everything and More*, his non-fiction book on mathematician Georg Cantor. Wallace was commissioned in June 2000 but was still working on the 'wretched math book' over two years later, in September 2002, to his evident frustration (Max 275).

14  Elements of Fogle's monologue had been floating around since as early as 2001, when Fogle was called 'Robbie Van Note' (Box 39.6) but the 2005–2007 period saw the piece rewritten and expanded to its full length.

15 A marginal note suggests that the supernatural elements of *The Pale King*, specifically the agents with special powers, were influenced by both Kurt Vonnegut's 'Report on the Barnhouse Effect' from *Welcome to the Monkey House* (Box 41.5) and Borges' 'Funes the Memorious' from *Labyrinths* (Box 41.7a).

16 Staes suggests something similar, arguing that 'Wallace's' position is influenced by Tor Nørretranders' concept of 'exformation', defined as 'the "discarded information" that is inherent to all attempts to communicate or interpret meaning' (Staes, 'Work' 72). Of course, despite his disabusing of Fogle's uncontrolled flow of information 'Wallace' has still incorporated the entire unedited monologue into his memoir.

17 Fogle's initials ('CF') are also typographic shorthand to indicate a comparison.

18 In this respect I diverge from Boswell's assertion that 'David Wallace' 'enters the novel and disappears amid its welter of data' (Boswell, 'Author Here' 34) and Miley's argument that the 'David Wallace' sections are 'the bleakest and most despairing' parts of the novel (197), as I believe that the post-2005 appearance is actually a reassertion of authorial presence in an attempt to corral and control data.

19 Latterly, Ed gives Meredith 'a quiz about the overall topics we'd covered', which could be an indirect allusion to Wallace's concern over the potential redundancy inherent in his process in 'Octet'. Meredith's comment that 'It was both a joke and not' seems to reinforce this uncertainty (506).

20 The sinister Toni Ware, who may be involved in the IRS coup, has the power to mimic 'twenty different voices' (510).

21 A number of references to *The Exorcist* (*Pale* 137, 139, 374, 381), which is also referred to in the associated 'The Soul is not a Smithy' [94]) compound the theme of malevolent possession.

22 I agree with Mike Miley's proposal that Wallace referred to himself in marginal notes as 'DFW' when referring to his authorial persona and 'DW' when referring to his 'real' self, and that Wallace encountered attendant difficulty in separating his two personae (195). However, I do not think that this formula is mappable on to the narrative of *The Pale King*, where 'David Wallace'/DW indicates a different persona altogether.

23 One must be careful when referring to the two notes in the drafts of *The Pale King* that 'David Wallace disappears – becomes creature of the system' and 'David Wallace disappears 100pp in' (*Pale* 546), as these are written some years before the 'Author Here' sections and should not be considered as coterminous

with Wallace's post-2005 adaptation of the frame narrative. To consider them as such risks an inexact analysis, collapsing together two distinct temporal periods of composition.

24 Wallace is referring to the mathematician Michael H. Freeman, whose article 'There Is No Room to Spare in Four-Dimensional Space' can be found directly beside this handwritten alternate opening in Wallace's papers. A marginal note suggests that Wallace came across Freeman in a book of McArthur Fellows, which would presumably date this opening to around the time Wallace received the award in 1997 (Box 40.7).

25 The title of this draft identifies it as *Sir John Feelgood*, but the work seems to be referred to in the chapter as *What Is Peoria For?*, a title that Wallace toyed with around the late 1990s. It is difficult to tell if *What Is Peoria For?* was intended to be a subsection of *Sir John Feelgood* or whether this is simply a messy draft.

26 I concur with McGurl's general ascription of centrifugal/centripetal spatial tension to the novel ('what makes the IRS interesting as a center of thematic gravity is the way its binding disciplinary energies move both inward, toward its employees, and outward to the nation from which it collects money' ['Institution' 47]). However, as I will explain presently, I believe that this oscillatory tension is not solely attributable to the IRS and is not always an assimilatory gesture.

27 Burn notes that the characters travel in 'radial streams' towards the Peoria REC (376). The 'tingle table', the specially constructed desk of the IRS examiner, is also a radial shape.

28 The other major centrifugal model that shadows *The Pale King* – the tornado – is constantly in spinning motion but has no centre. The references to the figure of the tornado in the novel's construction (*Pale* 545) suggest that Wallace, who considered tornadoes 'a transfiguration' (*Supposedly* 17), considered this model as important. Paul Quinn, who offers a reading of the importance of the tornado to Wallace's construction of narrative, suggests a correspondence between 'the regional-meteorological phenomenon and the narrative technique of Wallace's long novels' (102). However, while Quinn's reading of *Infinite Jest* usefully describes how the tornadic model underpins that novel's 'data swirl' (102), I find the references to tornadoes in the materials for *The Pale King* to be more redolent of a failure of coherence: Wallace's 'tornado of characters', of course, engenders the crisis point of the novel in 2005.

29 Wallace drew a sketch of Peoria and the surrounding developments in his notes for the novel. In the sketch, Peoria itself is completely circular and surrounded by

a ring of developments in a manner that chimes with his 'doughnut' description (Box 39.4).

30 The Cormac McCarthy-esque tone of the Toni Ware sections, which is more problematic in its gothic-inflected aestheticizing of poor Midwestern communities, was written nearly a decade before the sections in question here.

31 The takeover of the 'regional Mister Squishy Company' by corporate owners results in expansion into other snacks including, pointedly, 'doughnuts' (*Oblivion* 4–5).

32 McGurl's suggestion that 'the institution in Wallace is not a place of gothic entrapment and abuse' (37) is problematized by the nightmarishly inescapable layers of interiority that characterize the corporate environments of 'Mister Squishy' and 'The Suffering Channel'.

33 In 'Toward a General Theory of Vision in Wallace's Fiction' Stephen Burn argues that 'only by examining the mediating eye, rather than treating it as a transparent window, do we understand the variable nature of perception' (90). I read the motifs of visual perception in *The Pale King* differently from Burn, who connects the focus on eyes in the novel to a neuroscientifically inflected model. As will be evident from the previous chapter, I believe that transparency remains central to Wallace's models of seeing.

34 The reference to the stare occurs as part of a series of interviews conducted by the IRS with the putative objective of humanizing the Service in a film (100), the irony being that the stare is a description of how the Service *de*humanizes its workers. The IRS film, like 'Infinite Jest VI', is never released, but in this case it is because it isn't entertaining *enough*: it becomes bogged down by 'maundering grandstanders' such as Chris Fogle and ends up as a 'debacle' (257). It is impossible to place on the art/entertainment continuum because it ultimately embodies neither quality.

35 In a note on a draft of Cusk's story, Wallace proposes that he has '20/10' vision, which is the ability to see objects far away, making him ideally suited to an environment that induces 'the stare' (Box 39.5).

36 This is reflected in the physical position of Rand and Drinion's bodies as the conversation progresses. As Rand becomes more self-conscious, she is more aware of the materiality of her clothes and body (494) while as Drinion becomes more absorbed in Rand's story he forgets his body and begins to levitate (485).

37 Speculatively, I would also argue that the relationship between Fogle's monologue and this scene might have had a later counterpoint in the sketched scene where Drinion was to engage in an efficiency test with a computer as part of the implementation of the Spackman Initiative (Box 40.3), the scenes forming a three-part chain: self in dialogue with self; self in dialogue with unselfconscious other; and unselfconscious other in dialogue with machine.

38 In an early draft, and in another gesture of Simple Duplication, 'The Pale King, by David Foster Wallace' and 'All Rights Reserved' also appear hidden within this section (Box 36.1).

39 Speculatively, 'David Wallace' might constitute here the next stage of the kind of suffering subject embodied by Atwater in 'The Suffering Channel' or Skyles in 'Wickedness', with the subject moving from covert to overt authorial presence.

# Works Cited

Abbott, Edwin. *Flatland: A Romance of Many Dimensions*. London: Dover Publishing, 1992. Print.

Abrams, M.H. *The Mirror and the Lamp: Romantic Theory and the Critical Tradition*. New York: Oxford University Press, 1953. Print.

Ashbery, John. *Collected Poems 1956-1987*. Ed. Mark Ford. London: Carcanet, 2010. Print.

Bachelard, Gaston. *The Poetics of Space*. Boston: Beacon Press, 1994. Print.

Bakhtin, Mikhail. *The Dialogic Imagination*. Texas: University of Texas Press, 1981. Print.

Bakhtin, Mikhail. *Problems of Dostoevsky's Poetics*. Manchester: Minnesota University Press, 1984. Print.

Barth, John. *The Friday Book*. New York: Putnam, 1984. Print.

Barthelme, Donald. *Unspeakable Practices, Unnatural Acts*. New York: Pocket Books, 1978. Print.

Barthes, Roland. *Image Music Text*. London: Fontana, 1993. Print.

Baskin, John. 'Untrendy Problems: The Pale King's Philosophical Inspirations'. *Gesturing Toward Reality: David Foster Wallace and Philosophy*. Ed. Robert K. Bolger and Scott Korb. New York: Bloomsbury, 2014: 141–157. Print.

Baudrillard, Jean. *Simulacra and Simulation*. Trans. Sheila Faria Glaser. Ann Arbor: Michigan University Press, 1994. Print.

Bazin, André. *What Is Cinema?* Berkeley and Los Angeles: California University Press, 1967. Print.

Berger, Peter L. and Thomas Luckmann. *The Social Construction of Reality: A Treatise in the Sociology of Knowledge*. London: Penguin, 1991. Print.

Berlin, Isaiah. *Two Concepts of Liberty*. Oxford: Clarendon Press, 1962. Print.

Bidart, Frank. 'Borges and I'. *Great American Prose Poems: From Poe to the Present*. Ed. David Lehman. New York: Scribner, 2003: 132–134. Print.

Bloom, Harold. *The Anxiety of Influence: A Theory of Poetry*. Second Edition. Oxford: Oxford University Press, 1997. Print.

Boddy, Kasia. 'A Fiction of Response: Girl with Curious Hair in Context'. *A Companion to David Foster Wallace Studies*. Ed. Marshall Boswell and Stephen J. Burn. New York: Palgrave Macmillan, 2013: 23–43. Print.

Bolger, Robert K. and Scott Korb. *Gesturing Toward Reality: David Foster Wallace and Philosophy*. New York: Bloomsbury, 2014. Print.

Borges, Jorge Luis. *Labyrinths*. London: Penguin, 2000: 282–284. Print.

Boswell, Marshall. 'Author Here: The Legal Fiction of David Foster Wallace's The Pale King'. *English Studies* 95:1 (2014), 25–39. Print.

Boswell, Marshall. 'The Constant Monologue Inside Your Head: *Oblivion* and the Nightmare of Consciousness'. *A Companion to David Foster Wallace Studies*. Ed. Marshall Boswell and Stephen J. Burn. New York: Palgrave Macmillan, 2013: 151–171. Print.

Boswell, Marshall, ed. *David Foster Wallace and the 'Long Thing': New Essays on the Novels*. New York: Bloomsbury, 2014. Print.

Boswell, Marshall. *Understanding David Foster Wallace*. South Carolina: South Carolina University Press, 2003. Print.

Boswell, Marshall and Stephen J. Burn, eds. *A Companion to David Foster Wallace Studies*. New York: Palgrave Macmillan, 2013. Print.

Bowman, Frank Paul. 'Genetic Criticism'. *Poetics Today* 11:3 (Autumn 1990), 627–646. Print.

Bryant, William Cullen. 'The Prairies'. *The Norton Anthology of American Literature*. Fifth Edition, Vol. 1. Ed. Nina Baym. New York: Norton, 1998: 1042–1045. Print.

Burn, Stephen J. *Conversations with David Foster Wallace*. Mississippi: Mississippi University Press, 2012. Print.

Burn, Stephen J. *David Foster Wallace's Infinite Jest: A Reader's Guide*. Second Edition. New York: Continuum, 2012. Print.

Burn, Stephen J. *Jonathan Franzen at the End of Postmodernism*. London: Continuum, 2008. Print.

Burn, Stephen J. 'The Machine Language of the Muscles: Reading, Sport and the Self in *Infinite Jest*'. *Upon Further Review: Sports in American Literature*. Ed. Michael Cocchiarale and Scott D. Emmert. Connecticut: Praeger, 2004: 41–52. Print.

Burn, Stephen J. 'A Paradigm for the Life of Consciousness: *The Pale King*'. *David Foster Wallace and the 'Long Thing': New Essays on the Novels*. Ed. Marshall Boswell. New York: Bloomsbury, 2014: 149–169. Print.

Burn, Stephen J. 'Toward a General Theory of Vision in Wallace's Fiction'. *English Studies* 95:1 (2014), 85–93. Print.

Burn, Stephen J. 'Webs of Nerves Pulsing and Firing: *Infinite Jest* and the Science of Mind'. *A Companion to David Foster Wallace Studies*. Ed. Marshall Boswell and Stephen J. Burn. New York: Palgrave Macmillan, 2013: 59–87. Print.

Burn, Stephen and Mary Holland, eds. *Approaches to Teaching the Works of David Foster Wallace*. MLA. Forthcoming.

Cahn, Stephen M. and Maureen Eckert, eds. *Freedom and the Self: Essays on the Philosophy of David Foster Wallace*. New York: Columbia University Press, 2015. Print.
Carlisle, Greg. *Elegant Complexity: A Study of David Foster Wallace's Infinite Jest*. Los Angeles/Austin: SSMG, 2007. Print.
Castle, Terry. 'Phantasmagoria: Spectral Technology and the Metaphorics of Modern Reverie'. *Critical Enquiry* 15 (1988), 26–61. Print.
Cavell, Stanley. *Pursuits of Happiness: The Hollywood Comedy of Remarriage*. Cambridge: Harvard University Press, 1984. Print.
Cavell, Stanley. *The World Viewed: Reflections on the Ontology of Film*. Cambridge: Harvard University Press, 1980. Print.
Cohen, Sam and Lee Konstantinou, eds. *The Legacy of David Foster Wallace*. Iowa: Iowa University Press, 2012. Print.
Coleman, Philip, ed. *Critical Insights: David Foster Wallace*. Ipswich: Salem Press, 2015. Print.
Cook, Pam, ed. *The Cinema Book*. London: British Film Institute, 1985. Print.
Coupland, Douglas. *Generation X: Tales for an Accelerated Culture*. London: Abacus, 1991. Print.
Dällenbach, Lucien. *The Mirror in the Text*. Oxford: Polity Press, 1989. Print.
DeLillo, Don. *Americana*. London: Penguin, 2006. Print.
DeLillo, Don. *End Zone*. London: Picador, 2011. Print.
DeLillo, Don. *Running Dog*. London: Picador, 2011. Print.
DeLillo, Don. *White Noise*. London: Picador, 2011. Print.
Den Dulk, Allard. *Existentialist Engagement in Wallace, Eggers and Foer: A Philosophical Analysis of Contemporary American Literature*. New York: Bloomsbury, 2014. Print.
Deren, Maya, dir. *Meshes of the Afternoon*. Mystic Fire Video, 1943. DVD.
Dickstein, Morris. *A Mirror in the Roadway: Literature and the Real World*. Princeton: Princeton University Press, 2005. Print.
Eggers, Dave. *A Heartbreaking Work of Staggering Genius*. London: Picador, 2007. Print.
Emerson, Ralph Waldo. *Nature and Selected Essays*. London: Penguin, 2003. Print.
Eugenides, Jeffrey. *The Marriage Plot*. London: Fourth Estate, 2012. Print.
Fitzpatrick, Kathleen. *The Anxiety of Obsolescence: The American Novel in the Age of Television*. Nashville: Vanderbilt University Press, 2006. Print.
Foster, Graham. 'A Blasted Region: David Foster Wallace's Man-Made Landscapes'. *Consider David Foster Wallace: Critical Essays*. Ed. David Hering. Austin/Los Angeles: Sideshow Media, 2010: 37–49. Print.

Foucault, Michel. *Discipline and Punish: The Birth of the Prison*. Trans. Alan Sheridan. London: Penguin, 1991. Print.

Foucault, Michel. *The Order of Things: An Archaeology of the Human Sciences*. New York: Vintage, 1994. Print.

Franzen, Jonathan. *Freedom*. London: Fourth Estate, 2010. Print.

Freeman, Michael H. 'There Is No Room to Spare in Four-Dimensional Space'. *Notices of the American Mathematical Society* 31:1 (1984), 3–6. Print.

Friedkin, William, dir. *The Exorcist*. Warner Bros, 1973. DVD.

Gass, William. *In the Heart of the Heart of the Country*. New York: New York Review Books, 2015. Print.

Gide, André. *The Counterfeiters*. London: Penguin, 1990. Print.

Gifford, Don and Robert J. Seidman. *Ulysses Annotated: Notes for James Joyce's Ulysses*. Revised and Expanded edition. London: University of California Press, 1988. Print.

Giles, Paul. 'All Swallowed Up: David Foster Wallace and American Literature'. *The Legacy of David Foster Wallace*. Ed. Sam Cohen and Lee Konstantinou. Iowa: Iowa University Press, 2012: 3–23. Print.

Giles, Paul. *The Global Remapping of American Literature*. Princeton: Princeton University Press, 2011. Print.

Godard, Jean-Luc, dir. *Une Femme Mariée*. Eureka Masters of Cinema, 1964. DVD.

Godden, Richard and Michael Szalay. 'The Bodies in the Bubble: David Foster Wallace's *The Pale King*'. *Textual Practice* 28:7 (2014), 1273–1322. Print.

Goerlandt, Iannis. 'That Is Not Wholly True: Notes on Annotation in David Foster Wallace's Shorter Fiction (and Non-Fiction)'. *Consider David Foster Wallace: Critical Essays*. Ed. David Hering. Austin/Los Angeles: SSMG, 2010: 156–171. Print.

Goffman, Erving. *Asylums: Essays on the Social Situation of Mental Patients and Other Inmates*. London: Penguin, 1991. Print.

Gordon, George N. *Erotic Communications: Studies in Sex, Sin and Censorship*. New York: Hastings House, 1980. Print.

Green, Jeremy. *Late Postmodernism: American Fiction at the Millennium*. London: Palgrave, 2005. Print.

Greenberg, Clement. 'Modernist Painting'. *The Collected Essays and Criticism, Volume 4: Modernism with a Vengeance, 1957–1969*. Ed. John O'Brian. Chicago: Chicago University Press, 1995: 85–94. Print.

Groenland, Tim. 'A King of Shreds and Patches: Assembling Wallace's Final Novel'. *Critical Insights: David Foster Wallace*. Ed. Philip Coleman. Ipswich: Salem Press, 2015: 221–238. Print.

Harbach, Chad. *MFA vs NYC: The Two Cultures of American Fiction*. New York: n+1/Faber and Faber, 2014. Print.

Harris, Charles B. 'The Anxiety of Influence: The John Barth/David Foster Wallace Connection'. *Critique: Studies in Contemporary Fiction* 55:2 (2014), 103–126. Print.

Hayes-Brady, Clare. 'The Book, the Broom and the Ladder: Philosophical Groundings in the Work of David Foster Wallace'. *Consider David Foster Wallace: Critical Essays*. Ed. David Hering. Austin/Los Angeles: Sideshow Media, 2010: 24–36. Print.

Hayes-Brady, Clare. *The Unspeakable Failures of David Foster Wallace: Language, Identity and Resistance*. New York: Bloomsbury, 2016. Print.

Hayles, N. Katherine. 'The Illusion of Autonomy and the Fact of Recursivity: Virtual Ecologies, Entertainment, and *Infinite Jest*'. *New Literary History* 30:3 (1999), 675–697. Print.

Hering, David. *Consider David Foster Wallace: Critical Essays*. Austin/Los Angeles: Sideshow Media, 2010. Print.

Hering, David. '*Infinite Jest*: Triangles, Cycles, Choices and Chases'. *Consider David Foster Wallace: Critical Essays*. Ed. David Hering. Austin/Los Angeles: Sideshow Media, 2010: 89–101. Print.

Hering, David. 'Theorising David Foster Wallace's Toxic Postmodern Spaces'. *US Studies Online* 18 (Spring 2011). Web. 15 August 2015.

Herman, Luc and Toon Staes. 'Can the Pale King Please Be a Novel?' *English Studies* 95:1 (2014), 1–6. Print.

Hix, H.L. *Morte d'Author: An Autopsy*. Philadelphia: Temple University Press, 1990. Print.

Hoberek, Andrew. 'The Novel After David Foster Wallace'. *A Companion to David Foster Wallace Studies*. Ed. Marshall Boswell and Stephen J. Burn. New York: Palgrave Macmillan, 2013: 211–229. Print.

Hogg, Emily J. 'Subjective Politics in *The Pale King*'. *English Studies* 95:1 (2014), 59–69. Print.

Holland, Mary K. ' "The Art's Heart's Purpose": Braving the Narcissistic Loop of David Foster Wallace's *Infinite Jest*'. *Critique: Studies in Contemporary Fiction* 47:3 (2006), 218–242. Print.

Holland, Mary K. 'Mediated Immediacy in Brief Interviews with Hideous Men'. *A Companion to David Foster Wallace Studies*. Ed. Marshall Boswell and Stephen J. Burn. New York: Palgrave Macmillan, 2013: 107–131. Print.

Holland, Mary K. *Succeeding Postmodernism*. New York: Bloomsbury, 2013. Print.

Horkheimer, Max and Theodor W. Adorno. *Dialectic of Enlightenment: Philosophical Fragments*. Trans. Edmund Jephcott. Stanford: Stanford University Press, 2002. Print.

Horn, Patrick. 'Does Language Fail Us? Wallace's Struggle with Solipsism'. *Gesturing Toward Reality: David Foster Wallace and Philosophy*. Ed. Robert K. Bolger and Scott Korb. New York: Bloomsbury, 2014: 245–271. Print.

Houser, Heather. '*Infinite Jest*'s Environmental Case for Disgust'. *The Legacy of David Foster Wallace*. Ed. Sam Cohen and Lee Konstantinou. Iowa: Iowa University Press, 2012: 118–143. Print.

Hungerford, Amy. *Making Literature Now*. Stanford: Stanford University Press, 2016. Print.

Hutcheon, Linda. *Narcissistic Narrative: The Metafictional Paradox*. Waterloo: Wilfrid Laurier University Press, 1980. Print.

Iimura, Takahiko. *Onan*. Film-makers Co-operative, 1963. Film.

Iimura, Takahiko. *Self-Introduction*. Distributor unknown, 1982. Film.

Iimura, Takahiko. *TV Confrontation*. Distributor unknown, 1986. Film.

Irr, Caren. *Toward the Geopolitical Novel: U.S. Fiction in the Twenty-First Century*. New York: Columbia University Press, 2014. Print.

Jacobs, Timothy. 'The Brothers Incandenza: Translating Ideology in Fyodor Dostoevsky's *The Brothers Karamazov* and David Foster Wallace's *Infinite Jest*'. *Texas Studies in Literature and Language* 49:3 (Fall 2007), 265–292. Print.

Jacobs, Timothy. 'The Eschatological Imagination: Mediating David Foster Wallace's *Infinite Jest*'. Diss. McMaster University, 2003. Web. 14 August 2014.

Jameson, Fredric. *Postmodernism, or the Cultural Logic of Late Capitalism*. London: Verso, 1991. Print.

Joyce, James. *Ulysses*. New York: Dover, 2009. Print.

Kaufman, Philip, dir. *Rising Sun*. Twentieth Century Fox, 1993. DVD.

Kelly, Adam. 'David Foster Wallace and the Novel of Ideas'. *David Foster Wallace and the 'Long Thing': New Essays on the Novels*. Ed. Marshall Boswell. New York: Bloomsbury, 2014: 3–22. Print.

Kelly, Adam. 'David Foster Wallace: The Death of the Author and the Birth of a Discipline'. *Irish Journal of American Studies Online* 2 (Summer 2010). Web. 15 July 2011.

Kelly, Adam. 'Dialectic of Sincerity: Lionel Trilling and David Foster Wallace'. *Post45 Peer-Reviewed* (2014). Web. 15 August 2015.

Kermode, Frank. *The Sense of an Ending: Studies in the Theory of Fiction*. New York: Oxford University Press, 2000. Print.

Kolodny, Annette. *The Lay of the Land: Metaphor as Experience and History in American Life and Letters*. Chapel Hill: North Carolina University Press, 1984. Print.

Konstantinou, Lee. 'No Bull: David Foster Wallace and Postironic Belief'. *The Legacy of David Foster Wallace*. Ed. Sam Cohen and Lee Konstantinou. Iowa: Iowa University Press, 2012: 83–113. Print.

Konstantinou, Lee. 'Unfinished Form'. *Los Angeles Review of Books*. 6 July 2011. Web. 15 August 2015.

Konstantinou, Lee. 'The World of David Foster Wallace'. *Boundary 2* 40:3 (2013), 59–86. Print.

Lacan, Jacques. *Écrits*. Trans. Bruce Fink. New York: W.W. Norton, 2006. Print.

Lasch, Christopher. *The Culture of Narcissism: American Life in an Age of Diminishing Expectations*. New York: Norton, 1991. Print.

LeClair, Tom. *In the Loop: Don DeLillo and the Systems Novel*. Illinois: Illinois University Press, 1988. Print.

LeClair, Tom. 'The Prodigious Fiction of Richard Powers, William T. Vollmann, and David Foster Wallace'. *Critique: Studies in Contemporary Fiction* 38:1 (1996), 12–37. Print.

Leonard, Brett, dir. *The Lawnmower Man*. Prism, 1993. DVD.

Lethem, Jonathan. *Chronic City*. London: Faber, 2011. Print.

Letzler, David. 'Encyclopedic Novels and the Cruft of Fiction'. *David Foster Wallace and the 'Long Thing': New Essays on the Novels*. Ed. Marshall Boswell. New York: Bloomsbury, 2014: 127–149. Print.

Lewis, R.W.B. *The American Adam: Innocence, Tragedy and Tradition in the Nineteenth Century*. Chicago: Chicago University Press, 1959. Print.

Limerick, Patricia Nelson. *The Legacy of Conquest: The Unbroken Past of the American West*. New York: W.W. Norton, 1988. Print.

Lipsky, David. *Although of Course You End Up Becoming Yourself: A Road Trip with David Foster Wallace*. New York: Broadway Books, 2010. Print.

Lipsky, David. 'The Lost Years and Last Days of David Foster Wallace'. *Conversations with David Foster Wallace*. Ed. Stephen Burn. Mississippi: Mississippi University Press, 2012: 161–183. Print.

Luther, Connie. 'David Foster Wallace: Westward with Fredric Jameson'. *Consider David Foster Wallace: Critical Essays*. Ed. David Hering. Austin/Los Angeles: Sideshow Media, 2010: 49–61. Print.

Lutz, Tom. *Cosmopolitan Vistas: American Regionalism and Literary Value*. Ithaca: Cornell University Press, 2004. Print.

Lynch, David, dir. *Eraserhead*. Criterion Collection, 1977. DVD.

Lynch, David, dir *Lost Highway*. October Films, 1997. DVD.

Lynch, David. *Twin Peaks*. Universal, 1989. DVD.

Lynch, Kevin. *The Image of the City*. Boston: MIT Press, 1960. Print.
Maas, Willard. *Geography of the Body*. Kino International, 1943. DVD.
Martone, Michael. 'The Flatness'. *A Place of Sense: Essays in Search of the Midwest*. Ed. Michael Martone. Iowa: Iowa University Press, 1988. Print.
Marx, Leo. *The Machine in the Garden: Technology and the Pastoral Ideal in America*. Oxford: Oxford University Press, 2000. Print.
Max, D.T. *Every Love Story Is a Ghost Story: A Life of David Foster Wallace*. London: Granta, 2012. Print.
Mayo, Elton. *The Human Problems of an Industrial Civilisation*. London: Routledge, 2010. Print.
McElroy, Joseph. *Lookout Cartridge*. New York: Overlook Press, 2003. Print.
McGurl, Mark. 'The Institution of Nothing: David Foster Wallace in the Program'. *Boundary 2* 41:3 (2014), 55–91. Print.
McGurl, Mark. *The Program Era: Postwar Fiction and the Rise of Creative Writing*. Cambridge: Harvard University Press, 2009. Print.
McHale, Brian. '*The Pale King*, or, The White Visitation'. *A Companion to David Foster Wallace Studies*. Ed. Marshall Boswell and Stephen J. Burn. New York: Palgrave Macmillan, 2013: 191–211. Print.
McHale, Brian. *Postmodernist Fiction*. London: Routledge, 1987. Print.
McLuhan, Marshall. *Understanding Media: The Extensions of Man*. Cambridge: MIT Press, 1994. Print.
Metz, Christian. *The Imaginary Signifier: Psychoanalysis and the Cinema*. Bloomington/Indianapolis: Indiana University Press, 1982. Print.
Miley, Mike. 'And Starring David Foster Wallace as Himself'. *Critique: Studies in Contemporary Fiction* 57:2 (2016), 191–207. Print.
Miller, Adam S. *The Gospel According to David Foster Wallace: Boredom and Addiction in the Age of Distraction*. New York: Bloomsbury, 2016. Print.
Mulvey, Laura. *Visual and Other Pleasures*. London: Macmillan, 1989. Print.
Nabokov, Vladimir. 'The Vane Sisters'. *Tyrants Destroyed and Other Stories*. London: Weidenfeld & Nicholson, 1975: 217–238. Print.
Nadel, Ira. 'Consider the Footnote'. *The Legacy of David Foster Wallace*. Ed. Sam Cohen and Lee Konstantinou. Iowa: Iowa University Press, 2012: 218–241. Print.
Nash Smith, Henry. *Virgin Land: American West as Symbol and Myth*. Cambridge: Harvard University Press, 1974. Print.
Norris, Frank. *McTeague: A Story of San Francisco*. London: Penguin, 1994. Print.
O' Donnell, Patrick. 'Almost a Novel: *The Broom of the System*'. *A Companion to David Foster Wallace Studies*. Ed. Marshall Boswell and Stephen J. Burn. New York: Palgrave Macmillan, 2013: 1–23. Print.

Percy, Walker. *The Moviegoer*. New York: Vintage, 1998. Print.
Peterson, Sidney, dir. *The Cage*. Kino International, 1947. DVD.
Pietsch, Michael. 'Letter to David Foster Wallace, Feb 19th 1995'. Little Brown and Company Collection of David Foster Wallace. Harry Ransom Humanities Research Center, University of Texas at Austin. Box 3.2. Print.
Powell, Michael, dir. *Peeping Tom*. Warner Bros, 1960. DVD.
Powers, Richard. *Generosity*. London: Atlantic, 2011. Print.
Pynchon, Thomas. *Vineland*. London: Vintage, 1992. Print.
Quinn, Paul. 'Location's Location: Placing David Foster Wallace'. *A Companion to David Foster Wallace Studies*. Ed. Marshall Boswell and Stephen J. Burn. New York: Palgrave Macmillan, 2013: 87–107. Print.
Ramal, Randy. 'Beyond Philosophy: David Foster Wallace on Literature, Wittgenstein and the Dangers of Theorizing'. *Gesturing Toward Reality: David Foster Wallace and Philosophy*. Ed. Robert K. Bolger and Scott Korb. New York: Bloomsbury, 2014: 177–199. Print.
Ribbat, Christoph. 'Seething Static: Notes on Wallace and Journalism'. *Consider David Foster Wallace: Critical Essays*. Ed. David Hering. Austin/Los Angeles: Sideshow Media, 2010: 187–199. Print.
Richardson, Brian. *Unnatural Voices: Extreme Narration in Modern and Contemporary Fiction*. Ohio: Ohio State University Press, 2006. Print.
Roiland, Josh. 'Getting Away from It All: The Literary Journalism of David Foster Wallace and Nietzsche's Concept of Oblivion'. *The Legacy of David Foster Wallace*. Ed. Sam Cohen and Lee Konstantinou. Iowa: Iowa University Press, 2012: 25–53. Print.
Roiland, Josh. 'Spiritually Midwestern: What Middle America Meant to David Foster Wallace'. *Medium*. 7 August 2015. Web. 15 August 2015.
Rojek, Chris and John Urry. *Touring Cultures: Transformations of Travel and Theory*. London: Routledge, 1997. Print.
Ryan, Judith. *The Novel After Theory*. New York: Columbia University Press, 2012. Print.
Santel, James. 'On David Foster Wallace's Conservatism'. *Hudson Review*. (Winter 2014). Web. 15 August 2015.
Sayers, Andrew. 'Representing Entertainment in *Infinite Jest*'. *David Foster Wallace and the 'Long Thing': New Essays on the Novels*. Ed. Marshall Boswell. New York: Bloomsbury, 2014: 107–127. Print.
Schwartzburg, Molly. 'Observations on the Archive at the Harry Ransom Center'. *The Legacy of David Foster Wallace*. Ed. Sam Cohen and Lee Konstantinou. Iowa: Iowa University Press, 2012: 24–261. Print.

Scott, A.O. 'The Panic of Influence'. *The New York Review of Books*. 10 February 2000. Web. 15 August 2015.

Shakespeare, William. *Hamlet*. Oxford: Oxford World's Classics, 2008. Print.

Smith, Zadie. *Changing My Mind: Occasional Essays*. London: Penguin, 2011. Print.

Staes, Toon. 'Wallace and Empathy: A Narrative Approach'. *David Foster Wallace and the 'Long Thing': New Essays on the Novels*. Ed. Marshall Boswell. New York: Bloomsbury, 2014: 23–43. Print.

Staes, Toon. 'Work in Process: A Genesis for *The Pale King*'. *English Studies* 95:1 (2014), 70–84. Print.

Stendhal, Henri Beyle. *The Red and the Black: A Chronicle of the Nineteenth Century*. Oxford: Oxford World's Classics, 2009. Print.

Sullivan, Hannah. *The Work of Revision*. Cambridge: Harvard University Press, 2013. Print.

Sword, Helen. *Ghostwriting Modernism*. Ithaca: Cornell University Press, 2002. Print.

Timmer, Nicoline. *Do You Feel It Too? The Post-Postmodern Syndrome in American Fiction at the Turn of the Millennium*. Amsterdam: Rodopi, 2010. Print.

Tomaiulo, Saverio. *Victorian Unfinished Novels: The Imperfect Page*. London: Palgrave Macmillan, 2012. Print.

Tracey, Tom. 'The Formative Years: David Foster Wallace's Philosophical Influences and the Broom of the System'. *Gesturing Toward Reality: David Foster Wallace and Philosophy*. Ed. Robert K. Bolger and Scott Korb. New York: Bloomsbury, 2014: 157–177. Print.

Trumbull, Douglas, dir. *Brainstorm*. Warner Bros, 1983. Blu-ray.

Vonnegut, Kurt. *Welcome to the Monkey House*. New York: Dial Press, 2014. Print.

Wallace, David Foster. *Both Flesh and Not: Essays*. London: Hamish Hamilton, 2012. Print.

Wallace, David Foster. *Brief Interviews with Hideous Men*. London: Abacus, 1999. Print.

Wallace, David Foster. *Brief Interviews with Hideous Men*. Draft Materials. David Foster Wallace Papers. Harry Ransom Humanities Research Center, University of Texas at Austin. Boxes 2.4–3.3 and 26.13. Print.

Wallace, David Foster. *The Broom of the System*. New York: Penguin, 1987. Print.

Wallace, David Foster. *The Broom of the System*. Draft Materials. David Foster Wallace Papers. Harry Ransom Humanities Research Center, University of Texas at Austin. Boxes 3.4–4.4. Print.

Wallace, David Foster. *Consider the Lobster and Other Essays*. London: Abacus, 2005. Print.

Wallace, David Foster. *Everything and More: A Compact History of* ∞. London: Phoenix, 2005. Print.
Wallace, David Foster. *Fate, Time and Language: An Essay on Free Will*. New York: Columbia University Press, 2010. Print.
Wallace, David Foster. *Girl with Curious Hair*. London: Abacus, 1997. Print.
Wallace, David Foster. *Girl with Curious Hair*. Draft Materials. David Foster Wallace Papers. Harry Ransom Humanities Research Center, University of Texas at Austin. Boxes 14.6–15.3. Print.
Wallace, David Foster. *Infinite Jest*. London: Abacus, 1997. Print.
Wallace, David Foster. *Infinite Jest*. Draft Materials. David Foster Wallace Papers. Harry Ransom Humanities Research Center, University of Texas at Austin. Boxes 15.4–24.7. Print.
Wallace, David Foster. 'Interview with Didier Jacob'. *Conversations with David Foster Wallace*. Ed. Stephen Burn. Mississippi: Mississippi University Press, 2012: 152–158. Print.
Wallace, David Foster. 'Interview with Larry McCaffery'. *Conversations with David Foster Wallace*. Ed. Stephen Burn. Mississippi: Mississippi University Press, 2012: 21–53. Print.
Wallace, David Foster. 'Interview with Laura Miller'. *Conversations with David Foster Wallace*. Ed. Stephen Burn. Mississippi: Mississippi University Press, 2012: 58–66. Print.
Wallace, David Foster. 'Interview with Michael Goldfarb'. *Conversations with David Foster Wallace*. Ed. Stephen Burn. Mississippi: Mississippi University Press, 2012: 136–152. Print.
Wallace, David Foster. 'Interview with Michael Silverblatt'. *Bookworm*. KCRW, California. 11 April 1996. Web. 15 August 2015.
Wallace, David Foster. 'Interview with Ostap Karmodi'. *The New York Review of Books*. 13 June 2011. Web. 15 August 2015.
Wallace, David Foster. 'Interview with Patrick Arden'. *Conversations with David Foster Wallace*. Ed. Stephen Burn. Mississippi: Mississippi University Press, 2012: 94–101. Print.
Wallace, David Foster. 'Interview with Stacy Schmeidel'. *Amherst Magazine*. Spring 1999. Web. 15 August 2015.
Wallace, David Foster. 'Interview with Steve Paulson'. *Conversations with David Foster Wallace*. Ed. Stephen Burn. Mississippi: Mississippi University Press, 2012: 127–136. Print.
Wallace, David Foster. 'Letter to Bonnie Nadell, Oct 31st 1985'. Bonnie Nadell Collection of David Foster Wallace. Harry Ransom Humanities Research Center, University of Texas at Austin. Box 1.1. Print.

Wallace, David Foster. 'Letter to Bonnie Nadell, Dec 31st 1988'. Bonnie Nadell Collection of David Foster Wallace. Harry Ransom Humanities Research Center, University of Texas at Austin. Box 1.2. Print.

Wallace, David Foster. 'Letter to Bonnie Nadell, May 11th 1989'. Bonnie Nadell Collection of David Foster Wallace. Harry Ransom Humanities Research Center, University of Texas at Austin. Box 1.2. Print.

Wallace, David Foster. 'Letter to Bonnie Nadell, Aug 29th 1998'. Bonnie Nadell Collection of David Foster Wallace. Harry Ransom Humanities Research Center, University of Texas at Austin. Box 1.2. Print.

Wallace, David Foster. 'Letter to Don DeLillo, July 15th 1992'. Don DeLillo Papers. Harry Ransom Humanities Research Center, University of Texas at Austin. Box 101.10. Print.

Wallace, David Foster. 'Letter to Don DeLillo, May 1995'. Don DeLillo Papers. Harry Ransom Humanities Research Center, University of Texas at Austin. Box 101.10. Print.

Wallace, David Foster. 'Letter to Gerald Howard, April 25th 1988'. Bonnie Nadell Collection of David Foster Wallace. Harry Ransom Humanities Research Center, University of Texas at Austin. Box 1.8. Print.

Wallace, David Foster. 'Letter to Michael Pietsch, Aug 17th 1998'. Little Brown and Company Collection of David Foster Wallace. Harry Ransom Humanities Research Center, University of Texas at Austin. Box 1.6. Print.

Wallace, David Foster. 'Letter to Michael Pietsch, Oct 13th 2001'. Little Brown and Company Collection of David Foster Wallace. Harry Ransom Humanities Research Center, University of Texas at Austin. Box 3.5. Print.

Wallace, David Foster. 'Letter to Michael Pietsch, Oct 3rd 2003'. Little Brown and Company Collection of David Foster Wallace. Harry Ransom Humanities Research Center, University of Texas at Austin. Box 3.5. Print.

Wallace, David Foster. 'Midwesternisms notebook, undated'. David Foster Wallace Papers. Harry Ransom Humanities Research Center, University of Texas at Austin. Box 31.12. Print.

Wallace, David Foster. *Oblivion: Stories*. London: Abacus, 2004. Print.

Wallace, David Foster. *Oblivion: Stories*. Draft Materials. David Foster Wallace Papers. Harry Ransom Humanities Research Center, University of Texas at Austin. Boxes 24.1–25.7. Print.

Wallace, David Foster. 'Order and Flux in Northampton'. *Conjunctions* 17. Ed. Bradford Morrow. New York: Bard, 1991: 91–119. Print.

Wallace, David Foster. *The Pale King*. New York: Little, Brown, 2011. Print.

Wallace, David Foster. *The Pale King*. Draft Materials. David Foster Wallace Papers. Harry Ransom Humanities Research Center, University of Texas at Austin. Boxes 26.1–26.8 and 36.1–41.9. Print.

Wallace, David Foster. 'The Planet Trillaphon as It Stands in Relation to the Bad Thing'. *The David Foster Wallace Reader*. Eds. Bonnie Nadell, Karen Green and Michael Pietsch. London: Hamish Hamilton, 2014. Print.

Wallace, David Foster. *A Supposedly Fun Thing I'll Never Do Again*. London: Abacus, 2006. Print.

Warren, Andrew. 'Modelling Community and Narrative in *Infinite Jest* and *The Pale King*'. *David Foster Wallace and the 'Long Thing': New Essays on the Novels*. Ed. Marshall Boswell. New York: Bloomsbury, 2014: 61–82. Print.

Widiss, Benjamin. *Obscure Invitations: The Persistence of the Author in Twentieth Century American Literature*. Stanford: Stanford University Press, 2011. Print.

Wouters, Conley. 'What Am I, a Machine? Humans and Information in *The Pale King*'. *David Foster Wallace and the 'Long Thing': New Essays on the Novels*. Ed. Marshall Boswell. New York: Bloomsbury, 2014: 169–187. Print.

Yeats, William Butler. 'Swedenborg, Mediums, and the Desolate Places'. *If I Were Four-and-Twenty*. Dublin: Cuala, 1940: 21–68. Print.

# Index

Abrams, M.H. 86, 175 n.2
Adorno, Theodor 101
Ashbery, John 57, 94, 108

Bachelard, Gaston 62
Bakhtin, Mikhail 7–8, 18–19, 33–7, 39, 42, 142, 146, 164 n.9, 168 n.23
Barth, John 11, 16, 20, 24, 38, 85, 96–7, 98, 166 n.9, 174 n.1
Barthelme, Donald 85, 166 n.7
Barthes, Roland 5, 16–18, 38, 81, 85, 101–2, 105, 111
  'The Death of the Author' 16, 18
  'Upon Leaving the Movie Theater' 101
Baskin, John 166 n.6
Baudrillard, Jean 53, 171 n.13
Bazin, André 106, 176 n.15
Berger, Peter 44–5, 64, 148
Berlin, Isaiah 154
Bidart, Frank 165 n.3
Bloom, Harold 5, 18, 21, 26, 166 n.5, 166 n.9, 167 n.16
Boddy, Kasia 56
Borges, Jorge Luis 84, 165 n.3, 174 n.1, 181 n.15
Boswell, Marshall 1, 18, 24, 36, 57, 67, 70, 89, 93, 104, 108, 114, 118, 163 n.1, 164 n.4, 164 n.10, 166 n.6, 166 n.7, 167 n.13, 170 n.8, 170 n.9, 171 n.21, 175 n.10, 178 n.26, 178 n.30, 181 n.18
Bowman, Frank Paul 10, 12, 165 n.13
Bryant, William Cullen 42–3, 74–5, 78
Bucher, Matt 163 n.3
Burn, Stephen J. 1, 2, 25, 65, 126, 137, 148, 151, 152, 163 n.1, 163 n.2, 164 n.4, 164 n.7, 164 n.10, 165 n.12, 167 n.12, 167 n.14, 169 n.24, 170 n.8, 171 n.12, 173 n.30, 174 n.38, 174 n.42, 175 n.12, 182 n.27, 183 n.33

*Cahiers Du Cinema* 106
Carlisle, Greg 163 n.1, 172 n.28
Castle, Terry 16
Cavell, Stanley 100–1, 102, 156, 175 n.11, 176 n.15
  *Pursuits of Happiness* 175 n.11
  *The World Viewed* 100
*The Cinema Book* 176 n.15
Coleman, Philip 2, 171 n.21
Cook, Pam 176 n.15
Coupland, Douglas 171 n.15
Crichton, Michael 179 n.4

Dällenbach, Lucien 80–1, 82, 83–4, 88
DeLillo, Don 50, 53, 54, 85, 98, 171 n.14, 172 n.26
  *Americana* 85
  *End Zone* 54, 171 n.14, 171 n.15
  *Ratner's Star* 53, 171 n.12
  *Running Dog* 85
  *White Noise* 85, 98
Deren, Maya 177 n.20
dialogism 5, 7–8, 10, 18–19, 33–5, 37–8, 39, 42, 83, 86, 140, 141–4, 146, 147, 154
  use in Dostoevsky 19, 33–4, 36–7
  relation to heteroglossia 7, 8, 169 n.23
Dickstein, Morris 86
Dostoevsky, Fyodor 19, 33–4, 36–7, 118, 163 n.1

Eggers, Dave 164 n.6, 165 n.4
Emerson, Ralph Waldo 94, 170 n.6
Eugenides, Jeffrey 2

Fitzpatrick, Kathleen 98
Foster, Graham 171 n.13
Foucault, Michel 80–1, 82–3, 84, 93, 99, 101, 111, 120, 170 n.11
Franzen, Jonathan 2, 163 n.2, 170 n.8, 179 n.1
Freeman, Michael H. 147, 182 n.24

Gaddis, William 50
Gass, William 20, 47–8, 172 n.23
Gide, Andre 83, 84
Giles, Paul 42, 46, 47, 163 n.2
Godard, Jean-Luc 177 n.15
Godden, Richard 146, 159
Goffman, Erving 45, 46, 51, 69, 148
Gordon, George N. 178 n.23
Green, Jeremy 163 n.2
Greenberg, Clement 80, 81, 96, 106
Groenland, Tim 165 n.12

*Hamlet* 83, 84, 88, 166 n.10
Harbach, Chad 49–50
Harry Ransom Centre 3, 8, 166 n.8
Hayes-Brady, Clare 3, 166 n.6, 170 n.9, 175 n.3
Hayles, N. Katherine 163 n.1, 171 n.12
Hering, David 172 n.28
Herman, Luc 124, 179 n.2
Hix, H.L. 16, 18
Hoberek, Andrew 164 n.7
Hogg, Emily 164 n.8
Holland, Mary 2, 66, 112, 163 n.1, 163 n.2, 164 n.3, 173 n.33
Horkheimer, Max 101
Horn, Patrick 166 n.6
Houser, Heather 64
Howard, Gerald 38
Hungerford, Amy 164 n.8
Hutcheon, Linda 85, 98, 99, 158, 161
Hyde, Lewis 175 n.8

Iimura, Takahiko 104, 117 n.16
Iowa Writers' Workshop 49–50, 60
Irr, Caren 60

Jacobs, Timothy 34–5, 163 n.1
Jameson, Fredric 43, 81, 84, 169 n.3
Joyce, James 164 n.4, 167 n.14
  *Ulysses* 169 n.24

Kelly, Adam 1–2, 7, 33–4, 62, 66, 151, 164 n.5, 164 n.8
Kermode, Frank 124
Kolodny, Annette 169 n.2
Konstantinou, Lee 73–4, 145, 164 n.8, 167 n.18

Lacan, Jacques 81, 85, 89, 96, 101–2, 112, 116, 159, 175 n.6, 175 n.10
Lasch, Christopher 96, 173 n.33
*Lawnmower Man, The* 179 n.4
LeClair, Tom 1, 27, 28, 35–6, 53, 108, 163 n.1, 170 n.12
Lethem, Jonathan 2
Letzler, David 173 n.36
Lewis, R.W.B. 169 n.2
Limerick, Patricia Nelson 169 n.2
Lipsky, David 2, 102, 103, 111, 133, 166 n.5, 170 n.6, 176 n.13
Luckmann, Thomas 44–5, 64, 148
Luther, Connie 169 n.3, 171 n.21
Lutz, Tom 42, 49
Lynch, David 176 n.14
Lynch, Kevin 71

Maas, Willard 104
Maniatis, Nick 163 n.3
Martone, Michael 172 n.24
Marx, Leo 43, 169 n.2
Max, D.T. 2, 8, 38, 47, 51, 56, 60, 67, 86, 92, 111, 126, 132, 136, 175 n.7, 175 n.11, 179 n.1, 180 n.13
Mayo, Elton 180 n.6
McCaffery, Larry 15, 17, 20, 24, 29, 35, 37, 38, 39, 51, 58, 67, 68, 102, 108, 164 n.5, 171 n.21
McElroy, Joseph 85
McGurl, Mark 5, 11, 49, 50, 60, 66, 76–7, 78, 148, 149, 153, 164 n.8, 171 n.18, 172 n.22, 172 n.28, 182 n.26, 183 n.32
McHale, Brian 44, 165 n.2
McLuhan, Marshall 115–16
metafiction 11, 20, 21, 23–4, 30–3, 37, 59, 85, 89, 96–8, 99, 108, 113, 168 n.21, 171 n.21, 175 n.8
Metz, Christian 81, 101–2, 105, 106, 111
Miley, Mike 118, 145, 164 n.3, 165 n.12, 167 n.18, 181 n.18, 181 n.22
Miller, Adam S. 3
*mise-en-abyme* 6, 81, 83–4, 86, 88, 90, 92, 98–9, 104, 106, 108, 111, 112, 114, 117, 157, 160
Mulvey, Laura 176 n.15

Nabokov, Vladimir 50, 167 n.11
Nadel, Ira 173 n.36
Nadell, Bonnie 21, 38, 79, 110, 129, 136, 139
Nash Smith, Henry 169 n.2
Norris, Frank 54

O' Donnell, Patrick 170 n.9

Percy, Walker 101, 102, 175 n.12
Peterson, Sidney 177 n.17
Pietsch, Michael 67, 113, 123, 125, 129, 131, 132, 135, 136, 141, 154, 177 n.19
Powell, Michael 176 n.15
Powers, Richard 2, 163 n.1
Pynchon, Thomas 27, 28, 50, 85

Quinn, Paul 46, 76, 170 n.7, 182 n.28

Ramal, Randy 166 n.6
Reagan, Ronald 2, 119, 180 n.11
Ribbat, Christoph 76
Richardson, Brian 25, 28
Roiland, Josh 164 n.3, 169 n.5, 178 n.29
Rorty, Richard 86, 175 n.3
Ryan, Judith 17, 85, 163 n.2

Santel, James 164 n.8
Sayers, Andrew 101–2, 103
Schwartzburg, Molly 9, 10
Scott, A.O. 166 n.5
Sierpinski Gasket 63, 172 n.28
Silverblatt, Michael 63, 172 n.28
Smith, Zadie 173 n.37
Staes, Toon 124, 136, 137, 138, 141, 145, 165 n.12, 167 n.15, 168 n.22, 179 n.2, 181 n.16
Stendhal 86, 93, 109
Sullivan, Hannah 11, 165 n.14
Sword, Helen 165 n.1
Szalay, Michael 146, 159

Timmer, Nicoline 163 n.2
Tomaiulo, Saverio 125
Tracey, Thomas 175 n.3
Trumbull, Douglas 179 n.4

Velázquez, Diego 79–83, 84, 101
 *Las Meninas* 79–83, 84, 93, 99, 111
virtual reality 110, 111, 127, 131, 179 n.4
Vonnegut, Kurt 181 n.15

Wallace, David Foster
 'Authority and American Usage' 180 n.10
 'Big Red Son' 111, 119, 180 n.10
 'Borges on the Couch' 165 n.3
 *Both Flesh and Not* 164 n.8
 'Brief Interview #20' 86
 'Brief Interview #28' 30, 62
 'Brief Interview #59' 62, 69, 70, 74
 'Brief Interview #79' (unreleased) 128
 *Brief Interviews with Hideous Men* 12, 30, 62, 63, 67, 70, 77, 112, 113, 114, 127, 128, 129, 130, 160, 175 n.6, 177 n.15
 *The Broom of the System* 15, 19–20, 21, 22, 24, 26, 33–4, 38, 39, 40, 51–5, 56, 59, 61, 62, 63, 64, 67, 71, 88–91, 92, 93, 96, 97, 100, 105, 108, 112, 153, 159, 170 n.12, 171 n.13, 171 n.16, 171 n.17, 174 n.43, 178 n.24
 'Consider the Lobster' 180 n.10
 Crash of '62' 173 n.35
 'David Lynch Keeps his Head' 176 n.14
 'The Depressed Person' 68, 113, 173 n.36, 178 n.25, 178 n.30
 'E Unibus Pluram: Television and U.S. Fiction' 28, 60, 86, 92, 93, 94, 96, 98, 99, 115, 164 n.5, 175 n.7, 175 n.8, 175 n.9
 *Everything and More* 180 n.13
 *Fate, Time and Language: An Essay on Free Will* 2
 'Fictional Futures and the Conspicuously Young' 16, 18, 56, 92
 *Girl with Curious Hair* 20–4, 25, 26, 38, 39, 48, 54, 55–62, 63, 64, 70, 83, 85, 91, 92, 93–9, 100, 171 n.20, 174 n.40
 *Glitterer* 130, 131–3, 136, 138, 180 n.9
 'Good Old Neon' 31–3, 34, 36, 37, 39, 115, 116, 132, 141, 142, 146, 167 n.18, 168 n.23, 178 n.30, 180 n.8

'Greatly Exaggerated' 16–17, 18
'Incarnations of Burned Children' 129, 132, 133
*Infinite Jest* 1, 15, 24–30, 31, 32, 34–6, 38–9, 51, 54, 62–7, 77, 79, 83, 84, 86, 89, 92, 99–110, 111, 112, 113, 116, 117, 120, 123, 126, 127, 133, 135, 139, 141, 146, 150, 154, 156, 163 n.1, 164 n.4, 164 n.7, 168 n.22, 169 n.24, 171 n.14, 171 n.15, 172 n.26, 171–2 n.28, 173 n.34, 173 n.36, 175 n.5, 175 n.10, 176 n.15, 177 n.16, 177 n.17, 177 n.19, 177 n.20, 178 n.23, 178 n.27, 179 n.4, 182 n.28
Interview with Didier Jacob 118, 166 n.7
Interview with Larry McCaffery 15, 17, 20, 24, 29, 35, 37, 38, 39, 51, 58, 67, 68, 102, 108, 164 n.5, 171 n.21
Interview with Laura Miller 172 n.26
Interview with Michael Goldfarb 132
Interview with Michael Silverblatt 63, 172 n.28
Interview with Ostap Karmodi 2
Interview with Patrick Arden 67
Interview with Stacy Schmeidel 10, 11
Interview with Steve Paulson 116, 117
'Joseph Frank's Dostoevsky' 33, 34, 118
'Las Meninas' 79, 83, 86, 92, 126
Letter to Gerald Howard 38
Letters to Bonnie Nadell 38, 79, 110, 129, 136, 139
Letters to Don DeLillo 171 n.14, 172 n.26
Letters to Michael Pietsch 67, 113, 132, 135, 141
'Midwesternisms' notebook 41
'Mister Squishy' 71, 72, 115, 116, 117, 132, 156, 183 n.31, 183 n.32
'My Appearance' 22–3, 92
'Oblivion' 115, 176 n.14
*Oblivion: Stories* 12, 30, 31, 70–6, 77–8, 79, 86, 112, 114–18, 119, 120, 124, 126, 128, 129, 130, 132–3, 134, 135, 142, 152, 153, 154, 155, 156, 157, 168 n.19, 173 n.35, 174 n.40, 176 n.14, 183 n.31
'Octet' 30–1, 32, 33, 34, 36, 37, 39, 112, 113–14, 116, 144, 157, 160, 167 n.18, 178 n.26, 178 n.27, 178 n.28, 179 n.30, 181 n.19
'Order and Flux in Northampton' 164 n.4
*The Pale King* 2, 4, 6, 8, 10, 12, 15, 41, 44, 45, 70, 77, 87, 110, 115, 117, 119, 121, 123–62, 164 n.8, 165 n.3, 169 n.1, 175 n.12, 180 n.6, 180 n.7, 181 n.15, 181 n.22, 181 n.23, 182 n.28, 183 n.33, 184 n.38
'The Planet Trillaphon as it Stands in Relation to the Bad Thing' 87–8
*Sir John Feelgood* 110–12, 119, 127–30, 131, 133, 134, 140, 141, 147, 177 n.21, 179 n.3, 179 n.4, 180 n.9, 180 n.12, 182 n.25
'A Supposedly Fun Thing I'll Never Do Again' 169 n.4
*A Supposedly Fun Thing I'll Never Do Again* 176 n.14
'Up Simba' 180 n.10
'The View from Mrs Thompson's' 169 n.5
'Westward the Course of Empire Takes its Way' 11, 15, 20, 23–4, 25, 27, 28, 30, 31, 38, 48, 55, 56, 57, 58, 59–61, 63, 64, 65, 71, 73, 74, 77, 92, 93, 94–9, 100, 102, 103, 104, 105, 106, 108, 113, 114, 116, 148, 151, 152, 153, 168 n.21, 169 n.3, 171 n.19, 172 n.29, 178 n.27
*What is Peoria For?* 128, 147–8, 182 n.25
'Wickedness' 117, 118–20, 133, 134, 174 n.44, 179 n.31, 180 n.11, 184 n.39
Warren, Andrew 167 n.15
Widiss, Benjamin 17, 165 n.4
Wouters, Conley 125, 143

Yeats, W.B. 16

www.ingramcontent.com/pod-product-compliance
Ingram Content Group UK Ltd.
Pitfield, Milton Keynes, MK11 3LW, UK
UKHW021902220326
469204UK00008B/140